# Breaking The Silence: The Truth Behind Domestic Violence

**Copyright Page for Breaking the Silence: The Truth Behind Domestic Violence. Author: Josiah Cornell**

**ISBN:** 9798899659874


This book is a work of non-fiction. While every effort has been made to ensure accuracy, the information provided is not a substitute for professional legal, psychological, or medical advice. Readers are encouraged to seek appropriate support services where necessary.
Published in the United Kingdom Cover design by Josiah Cornell
First Edition - 2025

**Content Warning: Please Read Before Continuing**

This book contains material that discusses domestic abuse in detail, including emotional, psychological, sexual, financial, and physical violence. It explores the behaviours of perpetrators, the experiences of survivors, and the long-term impacts of abuse on individuals and families.

Certain sections may be distressing or triggering for readers who have lived through trauma. You may encounter references to suicide threats, coercion, threats to children, and manipulative tactics that reflect real-life experiences.

Please take care of your emotional safety as you read. It's okay to pause, skip sections, or return later if needed. If you find yourself overwhelmed, consider reaching out to a support organisation, therapist, or someone you trust.

This book is written with deep respect for survivors. You are not alone. You are believed. You deserve safety, freedom, and healing.

For immediate support, a list of domestic abuse helplines and resources is provided at the back of the book.

# Introduction

Domestic violence is not merely an individual concern; it has evolved into a pervasive epidemic veiled by a cloak of silence. Often, it is simplified to a black eye or a raised voice echoing through a hallway, conjuring images of visible bruises and shattered furniture. However, this perception fails to capture the profound complexity and hidden nature of the issue at hand. Domestic violence can manifest in ways that are not always conspicuous. It can appear as a suffocating silence, debilitating isolation, and insidious control masquerading as love. Instead of roaring loudly, it may whisper incessantly, leading victims to question their own perceptions and sanity.

This book emerges from that pervasive silence. It is crafted to illuminate the harsh truths that seldom make headlines, shedding light on the invisible wounds that many endure in isolation. Its purpose is to give voice to the millions who feel unheard and unseen within the confines of their own homes.

What Is Domestic Violence? is not your typical clinical manual or dry academic text. It is a compassionate, trauma-informed examination of the realities of enduring abuse, as well as the arduous journey toward liberation. This exploration is a rich tapestry woven from survivor testimonies, psychological insights, legislative frameworks, and deeply personal lived experiences. Above all, this work stands as a testament to the indomitable spirit of those who have survived unspeakable horrors, while also serving as a beacon for those currently seeking a path to freedom.

Domestic violence transcends mere expressions of anger; it is fundamentally about power and control. It represents a calculated system of behaviours designed to isolate, dominate, and undermine another individual's sense of autonomy. This form of abuse wears multiple masks: coercive control, emotional manipulation, financial entrapment, technological surveillance, sexual coercion, gas lighting, and threats cloaked in a guise of concern for others. Though the physical scars may be invisible, the psychological damage is profound and often reshapes the survivor's body, mind, and self-identity in ways that frequently go unacknowledged, invalidated, and untreated.

This book thoughtfully guides readers through the complex layers of abuse, extending far beyond just the physical realm. We delve into how domestic violence rewires the nervous system, how traumatic experiences lead survivors to doubt their own realities, and why escaping such a situation is rarely as simple as just packing a bag. We examine the cyclical nature of abuse, the psychological grip of trauma bonding, and the significant grief that can accompany even the act of achieving freedom. Each chapter is founded on concrete research, frontline experiences, and the insights of survivors who have walked this difficult path.

Moreover, we pull back the veil on societal perceptions that frequently overlook the intricacies of abuse. We explore how domestic violence intersects with race, disability, gender identity, immigration status, and sexuality. Marginalized survivors often face systematic failures from the very institutions that are intended to offer them protection. Additionally, we address how advancements in smart home technology and the pervasive nature of social media can be weaponized, extending the reach of abuse beyond the physical front door. Despite these challenges, we also showcase the resilience of survivors who find ways to heal, to find their voice, and to reconstruct their lives.

Throughout this book, you will encounter real individuals such as Banaz Mahmod, Heshu Yones, and Shafilea Ahmed, whose lives were tragically cut short under the guise of honour. You will learn about Nimco Ali's brave campaign against female genital mutilation and Georgia Harrison's landmark legal battle to combat image-based abuse. These narratives are included not for the sake of sensationalism, but because they reflect the undeniable reality of human lives, each with dreams, aspirations, families, and futures once vibrant and full of potential.

Whether you are a survivor, a concerned friend, a dedicated professional, a curious student, or someone grappling with feelings of "is this really abuse?", this book is designed for you. It does not preach or invoke pity. Instead, it offers empowerment through knowledge, practical tools, and stark truths. Above all, it extends a message of hope.

For while abuse may attempt to steal your voice, the journey of healing provides an opportunity to reclaim it.
While abuse seeks to isolate you, the truth has the power to forge communities.
And while abuse aims to instil fear, this book reassures you that a life of fear was never your destiny. You were meant to experience freedom.

Let this journey be the beginning of reclaiming that freedom, page by page and truth by truth.

While this book often refers to women as victims and men as perpetrators, reflecting the statistical majority and legal discourse around domestic violence it is vital to acknowledge that abuse knows no gender, sexuality, or identity.

Domestic abuse affects people of all genders, sexual orientations, and backgrounds. Men, transgender individuals, non-binary people, and those within the LGBTQ+ community also experience intimate partner violence, often with added layers of stigma, underreporting, and systemic invisibility.

Where examples in this book reflect heterosexual or gendered dynamics, they are not intended to exclude or diminish other experiences. Abuse thrives in silence, and everyone's story deserves to be heard, respected, and believed regardless of identity.

If you are a survivor and you don't see yourself fully reflected in this book, please know:

**You still matter. Your pain is valid. And you are not alone.**

# History of Domestic Abuse – A Long Road to Recognition and Reform

Domestic abuse is far from a modern phenomenon; it is deeply woven into the fabric of human history. For centuries, violence within the home was not just tolerated but often codified within legal and social frameworks. To understand the roots of domestic abuse, it is essential to examine the historical, legal, social, and psychological structures that allowed this issue to remain largely obscured or accepted for such an extended period.

*Ancient Roots and Patriarchal Structures*

In many early civilizations, including Ancient Mesopotamia, Greece, and Rome, patriarchal norms defined societal roles and rights for men and women. Women were often viewed as the property of their fathers or husbands, and their value was primarily defined by their reproductive capabilities and obedience. The Code of Hammurabi (circa 1754 BC), one of the earliest known legal codes, explicitly included laws that permitted husbands to beat their wives and slaves as a form of discipline. In Ancient Rome, the doctrine of "patria potestas" granted the male head of the household immense power, including the legal right to punish, confine, or even kill his wife and children.

*The Middle Ages: Religious Justification and Silence*

During the medieval period, the Church played a significant role in reinforcing patriarchal authority. Marriage was deemed a sacred institution, and women were instructed to submit to their husbands' authority without question. While ecclesiastical courts occasionally addressed marital disputes, domestic violence was frequently treated as a private affair, not warranting legal intervention or societal outrage. Legal doctrines across Europe continued to embed male dominance, further marginalizing women's rights.

The phrase "rule of thumb," often mistakenly attributed to English common law, is believed to refer to a supposed legal standard allowing men to beat their wives with a stick no thicker than their thumb. Although no explicit law with this wording has been found in official records, the phrase encapsulates the long-standing trivialization of spousal abuse in societal discourse.

### *Case Study: Margaret Evans (1664, England)*

In a poignant illustration of the era's norms, Margaret Evans was beaten repeatedly by her husband, John. After enduring years of abuse culminating in a particularly brutal attack that resulted in a miscarriage, she sought help from local magistrates. Tragically, her pleas were dismissed as a "private domestic affair," underscoring the societal belief that domestic abuse did not warrant legal scrutiny or intervention.

### *17th–19th Century: Institutionalized Control and Early Rebellion*

Throughout the 17th and 18th centuries, domestic abuse remained largely hidden from the public eye. Laws in both Europe and colonial America permitted husbands physical discipline of their wives as long as it did not lead to death or permanent injury. The legal doctrine of "coverture" in British and American law stripped married women of their separate legal identity, rendering them unable to own property, sign contracts, or seek legal recourse for abuse.

Yet, during the Enlightenment, the seeds of resistance began to germinate as philosophers and activists questioned established authority, advocating for freedom and equality. Prominent feminist thinkers, such as Mary Wollstonecraft, in her 1792 work ‘A Vindication of the Rights of Woman’, passionately argued for women's autonomy, moral worth, and the right to live free from oppression.

*Case Study: The Trial of James M'Naghten (1843, UK)*

While not a direct case of domestic violence, the trial of James M'Naghten introduced key legal concepts, such as criminal responsibility and the insanity defence, which would later influence the prosecution of domestic abuse cases. This trial spurred discussions around how courts interpret the actions and psychological states of perpetrators, as well as responses from victims, including the evolving understanding of concepts like 'battered woman syndrome.'

*The 19th Century: Social Reform and First Legal Recognition*

By the mid-1800s, the women's rights movement began gaining momentum, with early feminists like Elizabeth Cady Stanton and Susan B. Anthony advocating for suffrage, property rights, and protections against spousal abuse. Movements like the Temperance Movement highlighted the link between substance abuse and domestic violence, bringing further attention to the issue.

In 1857, England passed the Matrimonial Causes Act, allowing women limited access to divorce, but even this legislation imposed significant obstacles, requiring proof of aggravated cruelty and adultery, which made escape from abusive marriages nearly impossible for many women.

*20th Century: Shelter Movements and Legal Reform*

The 1960s and 70s marked a pivotal turning point for domestic abuse awareness. The feminist movement brought the issue into public discourse, fostering a newfound recognition of the complexities of domestic violence. Women's shelters, such as the one founded by Erin Pizzey in Chiswick, London, in 1971, provided refuge for victims and raised awareness about the pervasive issue of domestic abuse.

In the United States, significant legal milestones were established, such as the Violence Against Women Act (1994), which created comprehensive frameworks for supporting victims and enhancing legal protections. In the UK, the Domestic Violence and Matrimonial Proceedings Act 1976 afforded courts the authority to issue injunctions against abusive partners, while the Family Law Act 1996 expanded protective measures for victims. Notably, it wasn't until the 21st century that coercive control—a non-physical but equally damaging form of abuse was criminalized, reflecting a broader understanding of the nature of intimate partner violence.

### *Case Study: Kiranjit Ahluwalia (UK, 1989)*

One of the most notable cases of the late 20th century involved Kiranjit Ahluwalia, a British-Indian woman who endured years of extreme abuse at the hands of her husband. After a particularly harrowing episode of violence, she killed him in what she believed was a desperate act of self-defence. Her case brought attention to the complexities surrounding victimhood and the need for the legal system to accommodate the realities of life for those trapped in cycles of abuse.

Through the exploration of these historical trajectories, it becomes evident that the recognition and understanding of domestic abuse have evolved over time, shaped by cultural, legal, and social changes. While significant progress has been made, the journey toward comprehensive recognition and reform continues as society wrestles with these enduring issues.

### *The Present Day: From Silence to Voice*

In contemporary society, domestic abuse has transitioned from a hidden issue to being acknowledged as a grave public health crisis and a serious criminal offense. Modern legal frameworks now encompass a broad spectrum of abuse, recognizing that domestic violence extends beyond mere physical harm to include emotional, financial, sexual, and psychological abuse. In England and Wales, the implementation of the Domestic Abuse Act 2021 marks a significant step forward; this legislation not only offers a formal definition of domestic abuse but also enhances support mechanisms for victims. Key provisions include improved access to justice in family courts, reforms aimed at policing and victim support, and measures to protect vulnerable individuals during legal proceedings.

Despite these legal advancements, there remains a persistent gap between policy and practice, as enforcement of these laws is often inconsistent. Societal attitudes toward domestic abuse continues to evolve slowly, and survivors frequently confront stigma, disbelief, and systemic failures that undermine their experiences. The enduring legacy of silence and normalisation surrounding domestic abuse reveals deep-rooted cultural challenges. Many victims still struggle to find their voices in a society that has historically marginalized their suffering.

**Conclusion**

The history of domestic abuse represents a complex tapestry woven with threads of control, invisibility, and resistance. Spanning from ancient patriarchal codes that placed women in positions of subservience to modern legislation addressing coercive control, the journey toward justice and empowerment has been long and fraught with obstacles. Throughout various historical eras, survivors have bravely pushed back, using their narratives to raise awareness, advocating for legal reforms, and reclaiming their agency in a world that often seeks to silence them. Understanding this legacy is essential; it ensures that domestic abuse is recognized not merely as a "private matter" but as a profound violation of human rights that demands collective attention and action from all sectors of society. In recognizing and addressing this issue, we affirm our commitment to a future where every individual's right to safety and dignity is protected.

# What is Domestic Violence?

Domestic violence extends far beyond visible injuries and raised voices that might echo through thin walls. It resides in the silent corners of our minds and manifests through the subtle, often unrecognized language of self-blame, as well as the insidious patterns of control that infiltrate everyday life. This form of violence doesn't just occur during shocking incidents or sensational scandals; rather, it thrives in the mundane, quietly eroding dignity with a smile, a soft word, or a dismissive gesture. At its core, domestic violence is a systematic pattern of coercive behaviours, a deliberate strategy aimed at establishing dominance. It is defined not by fleeting moments of anger but by an ongoing effort to reshape another person's sense of reality, identity, and autonomy.

This process often begins with seemingly insignificant fractures: questions that undermine memory, constant doubt cast on decisions, isolation from friends and family, denial of financial independence, invasive monitoring of communications, or ridicule directed at personal aspirations. Such patterns fall under the definition of "coercive control," recognized by both the UK legal system and mental health experts as a significant form of abuse. This coercion creates a psychological prison, often without physical bars, that severely limits an individual's freedom and sense of self.

Extensive research from institutions like the NHS highlights how this gradual erosion of autonomy does more than just damage confidence, it rewires the brain itself. In response to the constant volatility of an abuser, the brain adapts by enhancing the activity of the amygdala, which triggers fear, while suppressing the prefrontal cortex responsible for reasoning and self-regulation. Consequently, even when the abuser is absent, the victim's body remains on high alert, perpetually tense in areas meant for relaxation and suspicious of stillness in places where safety should reside. This state reflects a trauma physically encoded in muscle and nerve pathways; it is not merely a figment of the imagination but a manifestation of survival instinct.

The prevalence of domestic violence is staggering: one in four women and one in six men in the UK will experience domestic abuse by the end of their lives. This equates to over 2.4 million adults annually, each number representing an individual whose sense of self, safety, and fundamental freedom has been forcibly extracted, often by someone they once trusted completely. The narrative around these experiences rarely concludes with a single act of violence. Women, in particular, face a disproportionate burden, not only from physical assaults but also from ongoing patterns of suppression, control, and pervasive fear. The consequences of such abuse are dire, leading to injuries, homelessness, mental health issues, and tragically, even death.

The ramifications of domestic violence extend beyond the immediate victims, silently infiltrating homes and spreading across generations. Children who are exposed to domestic abuse often bear the brunt of its effects. According to Barnardo's, a child protection charity in the UK, simply witnessing domestic violence constitutes a form of child abuse. As a result, these children frequently grapple with issues such as anxiety, depression, learning difficulties, attachment disorders, and aggressive behaviours that persist into adulthood. Their developmental trajectories are altered, as their brains learn to normalize fear, intertwining trauma deeply into their upbringing.

Survivors of domestic violence often carry lasting mental and physical health challenges long after the abuse has ceased. A study from the University of Glasgow published in BMJ Mental Health found that women who experienced domestic abuse nearly 30 years ago remain significantly more susceptible to conditions such as PTSD, depression, anxiety, sleep disturbances, and even traumatic brain injuries. This type of trauma does not simply fade with time; instead, it often deepens and embeds itself more deeply within the individual.

Compounding the struggle, many survivors internalise feelings of blame, believing that they somehow provoked the abuse or deserved it. These harmful beliefs are frequently – though unintentionally, reinforced by systems designed to provide assistance. For instance, when medical professionals pose the question, “Why didn’t you leave?” or when legal systems require survivors to repeatedly justify their experiences, it results in what is known as secondary victimisation, an additional layer of trauma inflicted by institutions that should be offering support rather than scrutiny.

Yet, healing is achievable. Understanding coercive control as a distinct form of trauma rather than merely a relationship conflict can change the entire discourse. Rather than asking, "Why didn’t they leave?" we begin with, "How were they kept there?" This shift from judgment to empathy is crucial. By adopting a “trauma-informed” approach, reframing questions from "What’s wrong?" to "What happened?". We can transform hospitals, courts, and community services into environments that validate survivors' experiences rather than question their legitimacy.

Recent legal progress reflects this evolution in understanding. The 2021 Domestic Abuse Act expanded the definitions of abuse to encompass emotional, economic, and coercive control, moving beyond the narrow confines of physical or sexual violence. This legislative change acknowledges what survivors have long recognized: domestic violence is not confined to isolated moments of rage; it represents a sustained method of control and oppression. The heart of this issue lies in the understanding that true domestic violence is not fuelled by anger, it is fundamentally about control. It is an ongoing, intentional act of manipulation and domination that strips individuals of their safety, distorts their sense of self, and isolates them until they can no longer recognize who they are.

While the marks of domestic violence might not always be visible, they leave profound, often hidden scars. The critical question thus becomes: What did it cost you to survive? The answer is not always apparent, yet it holds weight. This complexity demands a response that is equally grounded in reality: a commitment to listening, understanding, and creating systems that uphold survivors rather than question their experiences. Communities must step forward with messages of recognition and belief, affirming to survivors, "We see you. We believe you. You deserve better."

Engaging in discussions about domestic violence requires us to acknowledge the full spectrum of its impact, the silences, the manipulations, and the lingering shadows of shame. Only by shining a light on these aspects can we begin to dismantle the structures of abuse and foster lives grounded in autonomy, safety, and respect.

- Reflection prompt: 'What were the earliest signs that something didn't feel right in your relationship?'
- Myth-busting journal: List common myths you believed about abuse and the truths you've since learned.
- Safety signal: Choose a code word you could use if you needed urgent support from a friend.
- Resource: Link to Women's Aid abuse definition page (www.womensaid.org.uk/information-support/what-is-domestic-abuse/)

# Domestic Abuse Around the World – A Global Crisis in the Shadows

Domestic abuse is a pervasive issue that transcends national borders, cultures, and socioeconomic standings. It lurks in every corner of the globe, concealed behind closed doors, veiled in silence, supported by long-standing traditions, and in many instances, sanctioned by legal frameworks. For millions of individuals, the home, which should offer sanctuary, turns into the most perilous environment. The World Health Organization reports that approximately one in three women worldwide will face physical or sexual violence from an intimate partner during their lifetime. However, these statistics fail to encapsulate the full dimension of the crisis, as countless victims remain voiceless. silent, unreported, and overlooked, particularly in regions where cultural stigmas, entrenched patriarchal norms, and ineffective legal systems discourage victims from coming forward.

In several cultures, domestic violence is trivialized, normalized, or even legalized. For instance, in Russia, a controversial law passed in 2017 effectively decriminalized certain instances of domestic violence. This law redefined first-time offenses that do not result in severe physical injuries, specifically, broken bones, as administrative rather than criminal offenses, provided that such incidents occur no more than once a year. This legislative change conveyed a chilling message to survivors: the state would only intervene once the injuries escalated. Similarly, in parts of the Middle East and North Africa, domestic violence statutes are either non-existent, poorly enforced, or overridden by social expectations that prioritize female obedience over the safety of women. In countries such as Iran and Afghanistan, women fleeing violent households can face imprisonment under 'moral crimes', including leaving their families or partaking in extramarital relationships even if they were forced into such actions.

The notion of women as second-class citizens is not merely symbolic in many regions; it is ingrained in the very fabric of legal and societal structures. For example, in Saudi Arabia, historical laws required women to obtain permission from a male guardian to travel or receive essential medical care. In Yemen, it remains lawful for a husband to rape his wife, as marital rape is not recognized as a legitimate crime. In certain rural communities in India and Pakistan, "honour" killings are perpetrated with minimal consequence when women are perceived to have brought disgrace upon their families, whether through seeking divorce, refusing arranged marriages, or speaking out against their abuse. Cultural narratives often disguise these acts of control, framing a woman's silence as virtue and her suffering as duty.

Violence, however, does not always manifest in explicitly physical forms; it can be embedded in subtler, systemic mechanisms. Economic dependence, limited access to safe housing, religious coercion, and legal barriers serve as tools of entrapment for many women. In sub-Saharan Africa, restricted access to education and job opportunities reinforces a woman's reliance on her abuser. In parts of Southeast Asia, dowry-related violence surfaces when a bride's family fails to meet financial expectations set by the groom's family. In nations with high rates of child marriage, such as Niger, Chad, Bangladesh, and Ethiopia girls as young as nine are trafficked into early unions with older men in arrangements that basically amount to sanctioned abuse. These children are frequently pulled out of school, stripped of independence, and subjected to sexual violence disguised as tradition.

Even in countries that have established domestic violence laws, enforcement is often inconsistent and inadequate. In Japan, social pressure dissuades survivors from reporting abuse, and law enforcement frequently regards it as a private concern rather than a criminal issue. In South Korea, the criminalization of marital rape only occurred in 2013, highlighting the slow progression of legal reforms. In Hong Kong, despite possessing a sophisticated legal framework, statistics reveal a troubling rise in intimate partner violence cases, particularly affecting migrant domestic workers who face additional vulnerabilities due to their dependence on employers for housing and work visas. In Europe and North America, domestic abuse persists as a pressing public health crisis, exemplified by climbing femicide rates, despite decades of advocacy and awareness efforts. The United Nations Office on Drugs and Crime (UNODC) reports that over half of all female homicide victims are killed by intimate partners or family members, disproportionately in the very settings where they should feel safest.

The roots of this widespread crisis are deeply entrenched in gender inequality, cultural narratives, and historical legacies. The phrase "rule of thumb," often cited as a principle of English common law, allowed men to beat their wives with sticks no thicker than their thumbs, exemplifying a legal system that historically sanctioned domestic violence. Although modern legal systems in countries like the UK, Canada, and Australia have made significant progress, vestiges of such oppressive traditions still remain, often prioritizing the preservation of family units over the protection of individual safety. Even in seemingly progressive nations, ensuring the safety of survivor's post-separation proves challenging, as abusers utilize the legal system through child custody disputes and financial entanglements as tools to maintain their power and control.

Religion plays a complex and multifaceted role in this issue as well. In ultra-conservative communities regardless of whether they are Christian, Muslim, Hindu, or part of other faiths, some women are encouraged by religious authorities to endure abuse under the guise of obedience and family unity. Spiritual abuse is also manifested in the manipulation of sacred texts to isolate, shame, or coerce partners, thereby transforming places of worship into spaces of confinement rather than safety.

It is crucial to recognize that domestic abuse is not merely an issue of individual acts of violence but a global crisis that demands our collective attention and action. Recognizing the systemic roots and broad-ranging consequences of domestic abuse is essential in creating a world where all individuals can find safety and support within their homes.

It is crucial to recognize that domestic abuse is an issue that affects not only women but also men, challenging the misconception that it is solely a women-specific concern. In countries such as the UK, Australia, and the United States, there is a growing movement to bring attention to male survivors of domestic violence, particularly within LGBTQ+ relationships. In these contexts, stigma and underreporting remain significant barriers, making it difficult for male victims to seek help and find support. However, it's important to understand that domestic abuse is fundamentally a gendered crime, with a substantial majority of severe and fatal incidents committed by men against women. This disparity highlights the pervasive nature of gender-based violence as an epidemic with global ramifications, deeply embedded in social structures that intersect with issues such as poverty, migration, conflict, and the enduring impacts of colonization.

Efforts to address domestic abuse and support survivors vary significantly across different countries. Some nations have pioneered innovative responses that could serve as models for others. For instance, Spain established specialized domestic violence courts to streamline legal proceedings and focus on victim protection. Norway mandates comprehensive batterer intervention programs that aim to rehabilitate offenders, while Rwanda has implemented promising community-based initiatives led by local women who empower survivors and foster resilience. On an international level, the Istanbul Convention, a vital legal framework ratified by many European nations sets binding obligations for governments to prevent violence, protect victims, and prosecute perpetrators. Despite its significance, not all member states fully uphold these commitments, with some withdrawing from the convention under political pressure and resistance.

Nevertheless, signs of gradual change are emerging. Grassroots movements, survivor-led campaigns, and international frameworks are transforming the conversation around domestic violence. In recent years, movements like #MeToo and #NiUnaMenos have amplified the voices of survivors worldwide, challenging the longstanding culture of impunity that has allowed violence to persist unchecked. The fight against domestic abuse must be global in scope, intersectional in approach, and relentless in its pursuit of justice. It is imperative to assert that safety is a fundamental human right, not merely a cultural privilege reserved for some.

The stark reality is that in many parts of the world, being born female equates to inheriting a heightened risk of harm, particularly within the confines of one's own home. Each statistic relating to domestic violence represents a life marked by trauma and struggle. Every survivor who bravely steps forward to share their story dismantles generations of silence and stigma. Furthermore, each nation that takes meaningful steps to enact and enforce laws designed to protect the vulnerable contributes to a broader solution. While domestic violence remains a pressing global issue, so too does the collective resistance against it. The pertinent question is no longer whether domestic violence occurs, it is about what we, as a society, are prepared to do to confront and eradicate this pervasive threat.

# The Power and Control Wheel: Mapping the Heart of Coercive Control

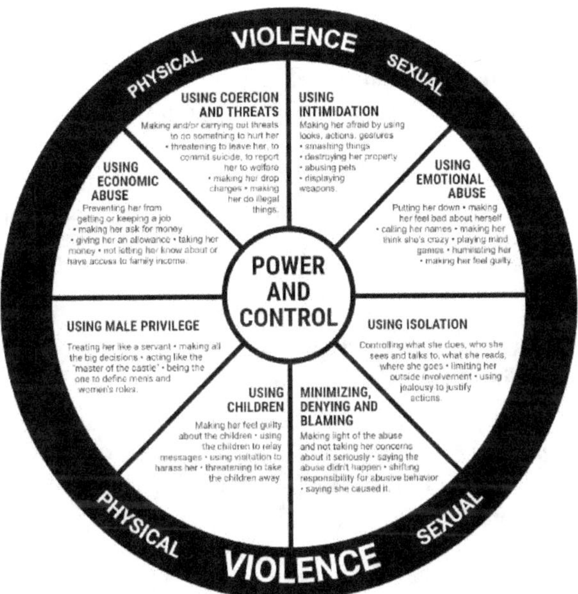


DOMESTIC ABUSE INTERVENTION PROGRAMS
202 East Superior Street
Duluth, Minnesota 55802
218-722-2781
www.TheDuluthModel.org

The Power and Control Wheel, developed by the Duluth Domestic Abuse Intervention Project, serves as a powerful framework for understanding the complex dynamics of coercive control. This tool is not just a simple diagram; it is an intricate reflection of the lived experiences of survivors, illuminating how various tactics of abuse, whether physical, sexual, emotional, or economic, are systematically employed to establish dominance and in still fear in the victim.

### *The Structure of Power*

At the centre of the Wheel is the core concept of Power & Control, surrounded by eight distinct spokes that represent interconnected abusive strategies:

1. Using Intimidation: Abusers may use threats, menacing body language, or display weapons. They might also destroy property to in still fear and compliance in their victims.

2. Emotional Abuse: This includes tactics like name-calling, shaming, ridicule, and gas lighting, which can erode a victim's self-esteem and sense of reality.

3. Isolation: Abusers often work to systematically eliminate the victim's support networks by cutting off friends and family, thus reinforcing their dependence.

4. Minimizing, Denying, & Blaming: Abusers refuse to take accountability for their actions, often twisting the narrative to shift the blame onto the victim, thereby creating confusion and self-doubt.

5. Using Children: Threatening to take children away, manipulating parental duties, or using the children as pawns in disputes can further entrap victims.

6. Economic Abuse: This involves controlling a victim's access to finances, which undermines their independence and contributes to their vulnerability.

7. Male Privilege / Gendered Control: The reinforcement of traditional gender roles serves to justify and perpetuate control, often marginalizing women's voices and choices.

8. Coercion & Threats: Abusers use threats of violence, abandonment, or self-harm as tools for manipulation, further maintaining dominance.

The outer rim of the Wheel includes Physical & Sexual Violence, which provides context for the other tactics. It highlights that intimidation alone, without any physical contact, can still wield tremendous power as a psychological weapon.

### *Psychology in Motion: Why It Works*

Each spoke of the Wheel chips away at a victim's self-identity, systematically dismantling their autonomy and resilience:

Emotional Abuse: Research indicates that emotional abuse can rewire aspects of self-belief and is linked to mental health challenges such as depression, anxiety, and PTSD-like symptoms, even in the absence of physical injury.

Isolation: By undermining social safety nets, abusers deepen a victim's reliance on them. This process heightens feelings of learned helplessness, making it increasingly difficult for victims to seek help.

Economic Control: Economic restrictions can trigger elevated cortisol levels, anxiety, and chronic stress. Financial independence is often a critical factor in recovery, making this dimension of abuse particularly insidious.

Neuroimaging Studies: Chronic exposure to abusive environments has been shown to heighten the amygdala's response—the brain's emotional centre—while suppressing prefrontal cortex functions, which regulates critical thinking and impulse control. This results in increased anxiety, hyper-vigilance, and emotional responses that manifest as fighting or freezing in stressful situations.

### *Counselling Through the Wheel*

Therapists and counsellors employ the Power and Control Wheel as a structured foundation for healing:

Psychoeducation: Practitioners utilize the Wheel to explain that abuse is not random; it is part of a systemic issue. When survivors recognize emotional abuse as a specific tactic, it helps them transition from feelings of self-blame to a clearer understanding of their situation.
Pattern Recognition: Identifying abusive tactics allows survivors to create psychological distance from their experiences. They learn that their sensitivity is not a flaw but a response to a learned pattern of control.

- Cognitive Reframing (CBT): Cognitive Behavioural Therapy encourages survivors to challenge and change internal narratives, transforming thoughts from "I deserved it" to "This was intentional abuse." This cognitive shift aids in rewiring neural pathways related to shame and self-judgment.

- Trauma-Informed Interventions: Techniques such as Eye Movement Desensitization and Reprocessing (EMDR), somatic experiencing, and grounding exercises assist survivors in moving from a state of constant threat to one of safety, effectively retraining the brain's default settings.

- Boundary Building: As survivors gain insight into control tactics, they learn to assert themselves by saying "No" to even minor violations. Therapist-led group exercises, role-playing, and real-life practice build their confidence in asserting boundaries.

- Social Reconnection & Peer Support: Group therapy provides a space for participants to witness shared narratives and experiences. This communal recognition combats feelings of isolation and shame, reinforcing the critical role of mutual support in recovery.

### *The Medical Power Wheel: A Call for Better Practice*

Healthcare professionals must be aware that they can inadvertently replicate power dynamics unintentionally. When they minimise disclosures or question the motives of victims, they reinforce the tactics represented in the Wheel.

The Medical Power Wheel enumerates detrimental responses such as pressuring a victim to justify their decision to leave, breaching confidentiality, or ignoring risk signs during assessments.

Trauma-informed communication can include phrases like:

- "No pressure, you decide what feels right for you."
- "Would you feel safer speaking in private?"
- "What strategies have helped you feel safe in the past?"

These dialogues echo the principles of empowerment found in counselling, steering clear of coercion or obligation, and fostering an environment that prioritizes safety.

### *Beyond the Wheel: Reclaiming Agency*

Complementing the Power and Control Wheel is the Equality Wheel, where healthy relationships are centred on shared decision-making, trust, and mutual respect, antithetical to coercive control. By understanding the characteristics of positive relationships, survivors can begin to envision new paths rooted in dignity and equality.

## Summary: An Empowerment Roadmap

Ultimately, the Power and Control Wheel serves as more than an educational tool; it's a vital resource for recovery. It helps identify subtle abusive tactics that may otherwise go unnoticed and validates the experiences of survivors, contributing to their journey toward reclaiming power, agency, and ultimately, their lives.

# Technology and Abuse

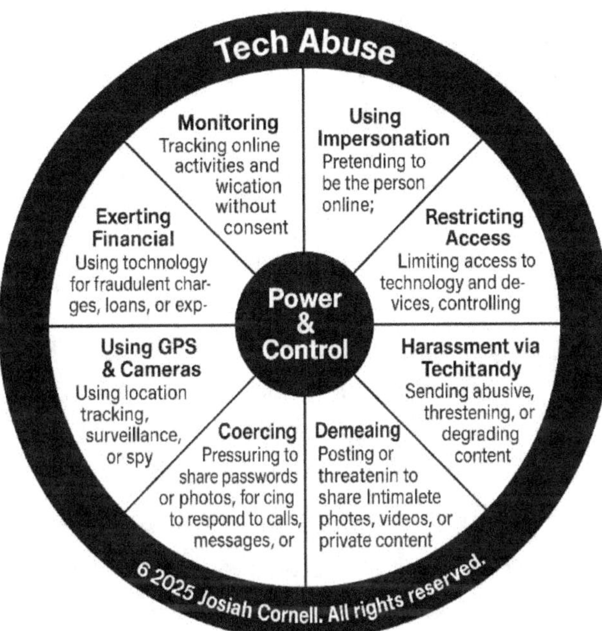
Tech Abuse
Monitoring
Tracking online activities and wication without consent
Using Impersonation
Pretending to be the person online;
Restricting Access
Limiting access to technology and devices, controlling
Harassment via Techitandy
Sending abusive, threstening, or degrading content
Demeaing
Posting or threatenin to share Intimalete photes, videos, or private content
Coercing
Pressuring to share passwords or photos, for cing to respond to calls, messages, or
Using GPS & Cameras
Using location tracking, surveillance, or spy
Exerting Financial
Using technology for fraudulent charges, loans, or exp-
Power & Control
6 2025 Josiah Cornell. All rights reserved.

**Why I Created the Tech Abuse Power & Control Wheel**

This is a quick overview on tech abuse and further discussed on page 143.

Domestic abuse doesn't always leave bruises. And in today's world, it often doesn't even leave the house.

When I began working in the domestic violence space, one of the most widely used tools was the *Duluth Power & Control Wheel*. It's a foundational resource, one that has helped practitioners, counsellors, survivors, and court systems visualise the complex patterns of abuse beyond the physical. But the world has changed. Abuse has evolved. And our tools must evolve with it.

That's why I created this: **The Tech Abuse Power & Control Wheel**, a modernised, clinically informed visual aid that captures the insidious ways abusers are using technology to harm, isolate, monitor, and control.

*Why This Wheel Matters More Than Ever*

Technology has become both a lifeline and a weapon. Survivors today are no longer only being followed home or intercepted in person, they're being watched through their phones, manipulated via messaging apps, tracked through smart devices, and impersonated on social media.

What once required physical presence now requires nothing more than access to a device.

This wheel was born out of a recognition that the ways abuse shows up are changing, but the pain, fear, and psychological damage remain just as devastating. Too often, survivors try to explain what's happening to them only to be met with confusion, minimisation, or outright disbelief. "He hasn't hit you, though." As if that's the only metric for harm.

This visual breaks down the modern methods of **technologically enabled coercive control**, and it does so in language survivors and professionals can both understand.

Each segment of the wheel reflects a specific tactic of tech-facilitated abuse:

- **Monitoring**: This isn't just about checking texts. It's a complete invasion of autonomy. Abusers track online activity, use spyware or access call logs, and surveil social media to maintain dominance. It creates a climate of fear where the survivor is never truly alone.

- **Impersonation**: This includes creating fake profiles, posing as the victim online, or intercepting messages to damage relationships, job prospects, or reputation. The aim? To erase the survivor's credibility and steal their voice.
- **Restricting Access**: Survivors are often blocked from their own phones, computers, or social media accounts. Controlling access to the internet or devices is a way of shrinking their world, isolating them from support, employment, and safety.
- **Harassment via Technology**: Constant texting, threats over email, degrading voice notes, or group humiliation in online chats, it's a barrage of verbal and psychological violence. It destabilises the survivor and invades every corner of their life.
- **Demeaning**: Posting private content, sharing revenge porn, or threatening to "expose" the survivor is all about shame and silence. The psychological impact is profound, it strips away dignity, safety, and autonomy.
- **Coercing**: Abusers pressure survivors to share passwords, engage in video calls on demand, or respond immediately. It's about control disguised as connection. manipulating them into a performance of compliance.
- **Using GPS & Smart Devices**: From location tracking to hacking into smart home cameras or even baby monitors, abusers use technology to erase privacy. It creates a suffocating environment where every move is monitored.
- **Exerting Financial Control**: With access to digital banking, PayPal, crypto, or Amazon Alexa, abusers can block employment, disable cards, or commit fraud. Financial abuse keeps survivors stuck and tech makes it seamless.

***The Psychology Behind Tech Abuse***

Tech abuse is psychological warfare.

From a counselling and trauma therapy lens, it induces a state of *hypervigilance* in the victim. The body and brain begin to expect intrusion at any time. Sleep becomes fractured. Communication becomes filtered. Identity becomes performative. Survivors no longer know what's real, what's private, or who is watching.

Many survivors report symptoms similar to PTSD: flashbacks, anxiety, dissociation, and paranoia. But what looks like paranoia is often real and that's what makes tech abuse so dangerous. It's invisible, yet total.

***Why the Traditional Wheel No Longer Suffices?***

The *Duluth Power & Control Wheel* was never wrong. just incomplete in this digital age.

Today's survivors are navigating a battleground that exists in invisible spaces: apps, devices, screens, and passwords. Yet many professionals, especially those not trained in tech abuse, still fail to screen for or recognise this form of harm.

This new wheel provides:

- A visual language for what survivors are experiencing
- An educational tool for support workers, therapists, and law enforcement
- A validation framework for those who feel unseen or disbelieved

It says: *Your pain is not imagined. Your story matters. And yes, this is abuse.*

***A Tool for Empowerment and Education***

If you are a therapist, caseworker, police officer, legal advocate, or frontline DV responder, please integrate this wheel into your practice. Include it in assessments. Share it with clients. Use it to educate others.

If you are a survivor or think you might be, this wheel is yours, too. Use it to name what's happening. Use it to seek support. And use it to know, deeply, that *abuse is not just what happens in person.*

This is what modern control looks like. And this is how we begin to dismantle it.

***Tech Abuse: Government Responsibilities & Solutions***

As the nature of abuse evolves, so too must the systems designed to prevent it. Technology, once a tool for connection, is increasingly weaponised in intimate relationships used to monitor, manipulate, intimidate, and isolate victims. This digital form of abuse isn't speculative or rare. It's embedded in the everyday tools we all rely on: smartphones, smart homes, social media, and messaging apps. And it's happening silently behind locked screens, under the radar of outdated laws.

Governments have a critical role to play in recognising and responding to this modern frontier of harm. Without systemic intervention, perpetrators will continue to outpace protections, exploiting technological gaps while survivors remain exposed and unsupported.

The first step is updating legislation to reflect the reality that abuse no longer begins and ends in the physical world. Lawmakers must expand the definitions of domestic violence to include tech-facilitated behaviours, such as, GPS stalking, remote installation of spyware, online impersonation, deepfake manipulation, and image-based abuse like revenge porn. Enforcement of existing legislation, including the Domestic

Abuse Act and the Online Safety Bill, must be strengthened with clear directives and digital-specific guidelines. Tech-based coercion and harassment should carry meaningful criminal consequences, with sentencing reflecting the deep psychological and reputational harm these tactics cause.

Governments must also invest in survivor-centred innovation. Technology can just as easily be a shield as a weapon, when it's designed for safety. Funding should be allocated to support the creation of survivor-led digital tools such as encrypted evidence storage, secure messaging platforms, AI-powered emergency systems, and invisible browser modes that leave no trace. Public partnerships with responsible tech companies can drive the integration of safety features like panic buttons, automatic alerts, and privacy resets into the everyday platforms victims already use.

Regulating the tech industry is equally essential. Companies must be held accountable for the misuse of their platforms in domestic abuse cases. That means mandating timely response to abuse reports, enforcing the removal of harmful content, and implementing robust ID verification systems that prevent abusers from re-entering under new aliases. Tech giants have a duty of care and governments must ensure that legal frameworks reflect that.

Frontline professionals must be trained to identify and respond to tech abuse. Survivors shouldn't have to explain spyware, geolocation tracking, or cloud-based coercion to the very people they turn to for help. Mandatory, CPD-accredited training should be rolled out across police forces, the legal system, housing teams, healthcare providers, and social services. These professionals need to know how to sensitively document tech-based abuse, preserve digital evidence, and support survivors in securing their digital environments.

Infrastructure, too, needs to evolve. We must build survivor-centric systems that recognise the realities of the modern world.

That means creating trauma-informed reporting hubs with tech support, offering clean devices or secure digital resets to those fleeing abuse, and ensuring refuges provide protected internet access and digital literacy support. Escaping violence shouldn't mean becoming digitally disconnected from help, community, or opportunity.

Public awareness is another crucial component. Many people still don't understand what tech abuse looks like or even that it's abuse at all. Governments must lead national campaigns that speak plainly, powerfully, and compassionately about digital control, with real-life stories, education, and direct links to support. This awareness must start early with relationship and digital safety education embedded in school curricula, giving young people the language and tools to recognise red flags before they escalate.

Finally, long-term investment in research and responsive policymaking is key. Tech abuse is evolving rapidly, and governments must stay ahead of the curve. This means funding intersectional studies into the psychological and social impact of tech-facilitated coercion, analysing patterns of abuse across platforms and communities, and establishing independent review boards to continually assess national strategy. When policy lags behind technology, victims pay the price.

Technology shouldn't be a weapon, but without modern, responsive governance, that's exactly what it becomes. By updating legislation, investing in innovation, training professionals, and holding platforms to account, governments can disrupt the silent evolution of digital abuse. The future of safeguarding must be digital, because survivors can't afford for the system to keep buffering while perpetrators upgrade.

# Hidden Truths—Domestic Abuse in LGBTQ+ Relationships

Power and Control Wheel for
Lesbian, Gay, Bisexual and Trans Relationships

*"If you're dating a woman and she's half my size, who's going to believe me?"* — Celia Vasquez, recalling the disbelief she faced after seeking help for abuse in a same-sex relationship.

Despite decades of progress in LGBTQ+ rights, domestic abuse in queer relationships remains deeply hidden, misunderstood, and misunderstood. In too many cases, survivors are silenced—

not because their experience isn't real, but because society lacks the frameworks to recognise theirs.

### *Abuse Doesn't Discriminate*

Statistic-heavy does not begin to describe the scale:

- 46% of gay male couples reported intimate partner violence (IPV) in the past year, with nearly a quarter experiencing physical abuse
- According to the CDC, nearly half of bisexual women (61%) and lesbian women (44%) face IPV—compared to 35% of heterosexual women
- Transgender individuals report lifetime IPV rates between 31% and 50%

But the issue goes beyond numbers. The majority of LGBTQ+ survivors never report abuse fearing they won't be believed, judged, or outed.

### *Misunderstood, Ignored, Invisible*

Survivors face a labyrinth of barriers:

- Lack of recognition: Abuse models assume heterosexual relationships. A woman abused by her partner is often seen as radical *"how bad can it be?* "especially if there are no bruises or physical evidence them.us.
- Service gaps: A survey of LGBTQ+ survivors found 70% experienced prejudice or dismissal from agencies when they sought help
- Outing as control**:** Threats to reveal sexual orientation or gender identity become weapons of emotional coercion
- Fear of reinforcing stereotypes: Many survivors hesitate, thinking *"I don't want to give homophobes ammunition"*

***The Psychology Behind LGBTQ+ Abuse***

Understanding this requires unpacking some core psychology:

*Minority Stress Theory*

Meyer's model describes how societal stigma creates distal stressors (e.g., harassment) and proximal stressors (e.g., internalized homophobia), leading to anxiety, depression, and increased relationship conflict

Internalised shame can fuel both victimization and perpetration, a tragic feedback loop visible in bisexual women's higher rates of IPV compared to heterosexual women.

***Power & Control in LGBTQ+ Contexts***

The *LGBTQ+ Wheel of Power & Control* illustrates how abuse adapts in queer dynamics:

- Using isolation**:** Protecting the coming out process by controlling social circles, phone use, or even spaces they enter.
- Using privilege**:** Gendered social power, a more "masculine" partner may assume the authority, emotionally or physically.
- Denial & Minimisation**:** Gas lighting becomes more convincing when societal stereotypes deny the possibility of abuse in "equal" same-sex relationships.

***Lived Experience: Human and Heartening***

I've sat across from queer survivors who shared heart-breaking stories of threats to out them, identity-based taunts, weaponised misgendering, or covert financial control. Many described being stalked online and threatened with exposure. The trauma?

Real. The fear? Justified. And yet the world rarely responds with resources.

***What Works: Counselling with Caring Competence***

To disrupt this cycle, we need interventions that are:

1. Culturally competent**:** Services that don't merely allow queer survivors, but understand them, their nuance, and their trauma.
2. Trauma-informed**:** Aware of how chronic minority stress amplifies IPV risk and complicates trauma responses.
3. LGBTQ+-specific**:** Acknowledging hunger for community, fear of being outed, and unique barriers to formal support
4. Intersectional: Accounting for race, disability, HIV status, all of which heighten vulnerability and marginalise survivors further.

***Tools & Resources***

Here are actionable steps and community lifelines:

- *National Coalition of Anti-Violence Programs* (USA)
- *Galop* (UK)
- Training for providers: Ensure police, therapists, and shelters understand queer abuse dynamics.
- Peer support groups: Safe spaces where survivors can be seen, affirmed, and never silenced again.

***What This Means for You***

If you're a survivor:
You're not alone. Your pain is valid. And this wheels exists to validate you, to give your experience shape, and to light a path to healing.

If you're a practitioner or supporter:
Understand that domestic abuse in LGBTQ+ relationships is not an exception, it's pervasive, nuanced, and needs robust support systems. Validate, learn, believe.

### *A Final Truth*

Abuse doesn't discriminate, nor does it need a specific gender to thrive. The tools we use must evolve to see, hear, and heal all forms of hidden violence. Because everyone deserves the dignity of recognition. Everyone deserves safety. And everyone, absolutely everyone, deserves to be believed.

# The Equality Wheel: Re-imagining Relationships Through Respect, Choice & Trust

### Origins & Purpose

In response to the abusive behaviours outlined in the Duluth Model's Power & Control Wheel, a ground-breaking shift occurred through the creation of the Equality Wheel. Activists and mental health professionals designed this wheel to effectively illustrate what healthy, loving relationships should embody. Its overarching goal is not to imply a flawless partnership but to promote a vision grounded in mutual respect, shared power, and a commitment to cooperation, contrasting sharply with coercive dynamics.

While the Power Wheel delineates the mechanisms of abuse, the Equality Wheel presents the opposite: a framework for healthy relationships built on eight fundamental principles. This framework serves as a constructive blueprint for not only identifying toxic behaviours to avoid but also for discovering and nurturing positive relationship dynamics.

**The Eight Principles Explained**

*Non-Violent Behaviour*
In a healthy relationship, all individuals feel empowered to express their thoughts, emotions, and disagreements without the fear of intimidation or backlash. This means eliminating tactics such as door slamming, silent treatments, or explosive anger, fostering a safe space for open dialogue.

**Respect**

Partners actively listen to one another, ensuring that each person feels heard and validated. This principle emphasizes the importance of empathy and acceptance, acknowledging that differing opinions, needs, and aspirations are inherent to any partnership. Partners honour each other's uniqueness without resorting to ridicule or dismissal.

**Trust & Support**

Supportive partners encourage each other's aspirations and personal growth. They appreciate and nurture individual identities by fostering friendships, hobbies, and interests outside the relationship, effectively combatting any attempts at control or dependency.

**Honesty & Accountability**

In a respectful partnership, individuals take ownership of their mistakes. Trust is built through sincere communication, keeping promises and addressing issues head-on rather than deflecting blame. An emphasis on accountability ensures that any harm inflicted is taken seriously, with a genuine willingness to repair and restore.

**Responsible Parenting**

When it comes to parenting, both partners engage cooperatively, prioritizing their children's well-being and providing positive role models. Healthy relationships avoid using children as pawns in conflicts, fostering a nurturing environment that promotes their growth and development.

**Shared Responsibility**

Healthy relationships thrive on joint decision-making. Both partners participate in discussions regarding chores, finances, and emotional labour, ensuring that expectations are transparent and that responsibilities are equitably shared, challenging traditional gender roles and societal pressures.

**Economic Partnership**

Financial decisions are made collaboratively and transparently. Budgets, expenses, and financial goals reflect the needs and desires of both partners, eliminating power struggles and fostering a genuine partnership in financial matters rather than one partner wielding money as a tool for control.

**Negotiation & Fairness**

Conflict in a partnership is seen as an opportunity for growth rather than something to be avoided. Both partners engage in compromise and negotiation, striving to ensure that each person's voice is acknowledged. The objective shifts from exerting power to fostering genuine connection and understanding.

## Psychology & Counselling Application

*Psychoeducation and Rewiring Beliefs*
Many clients may have internalized abusive dynamics as normal. Introducing the Equality Wheel opens their eyes to what constitutes a healthy partnership. By visualizing these principles through tangible examples, clients can begin to reshape their understanding of relationships.

### Values Clarification

Using the Wheel, individuals and survivors can identify the core values they need to reclaim in their lives. Each time they assert their right to respect, they reinforce their identity and self-worth, creating a foundation of empowerment rooted in psychological principles.

### Cognitive & Emotional Re-patterning

Cognitive Behavioural Therapy (CBT) can assist individuals in replacing self-doubt with affirmations rooted in the Equality Wheel. Phrases like "I deserve honesty" and "I deserve to be heard" help to rewire neural pathways, steering individuals away from patterns of self-blame towards personal affirmation.

### Relational Skills Building

Therapists can guide clients through role-playing exercises to practice assertive communication and shared decision-making. These practical exercises facilitate the transition from theoretical understanding to lived experiences within healthy relationship dynamics.

### Integration with the Power Wheel

One of the most powerful moments in counselling occurs when survivors visualize the stark contrasts between the Equality Wheel and the Power Wheel. This overlay allows individuals to comprehend the differences between abusive tactics and healthy alternatives clearly:

| **Abusive Tactic** | **Healthy Tactic** |
|---|---|
| Intimidation | Non-Violent Behaviour |
| Emotional Abuse | Respect |
| Isolation | Trust & Support |
| Minimising / Blaming | Honesty & Accountability |
| Parental Manipulation | Responsible Parenting |
| Coercion & Threats | Negotiation & Fairness |
| Male Privilege | Shared Responsibility |
| Economic Control | Economic Partnership |

Through this framework, survivors gain insight into the dynamics at play in their relationships and are empowered to envision and strive for a healthier, more balanced partnership.

# The Cycle of Abuse: Recognising the Pattern to Reclaim Control

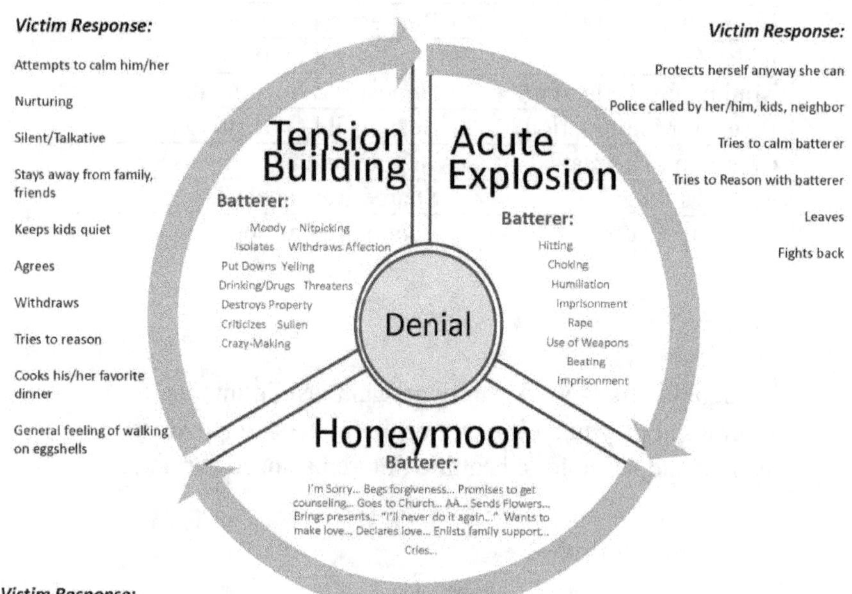


Psychologist Lenore Walker's ground-breaking 1979 work introduced the Cycle of Abuse, a comprehensive model that illustrates how domestic violence evolves into a repeating and entrapping pattern. By understanding this cycle, survivors and practitioners can identify the mechanisms of control that underpin abusive relationships and begin to dismantle them psychologically, emotionally, and practically.

**The Four Phases of the Cycle**

1. *Tension-Building*

The cycle often starts subtly. Survivors may feel an unexplained heaviness in their chest, an increase in irritability, or a lingering sense of dread. During this phase, survivors frequently experience hypervigilance, actively monitoring the abuser's emotional state in an effort to avert conflict. This heightened awareness is reminiscent of early trauma patterns where individuals learned to reduce harm by anticipating and accommodating another's moods or reactions.

1. *Acute Explosion*

As tension escalates, it often culminates in an incident of abuse, which can manifest as verbal assaults, emotional manipulation, physical violence, or sexual coercion. Neuroscientific research indicates that during these confrontations, the brain's amygdala (the fear centre) and hypothalamus trigger a release of stress hormones, such as cortisol, which can overwhelm cognitive functions in the prefrontal cortex. This neurological response can lead to shut down or dissociation, leaving the survivor feeling powerless and confused.

2. *Reconciliation (Honeymoon Phase)*

Following an abusive incident, many abusers engage in a period of reconciliation characterized by displays of affection, heartfelt apologies, gifts, and promises to change. This phase triggers the release of bio-chemicals like dopamine and oxytocin in the survivor's brain, creating feelings of euphoria and re-establishing a sense of connection. Often referred to as "love bombing," this phase can momentarily alleviate the psychological pain inflicted by the abuse and strengthen the survivor's emotional attachment to the abuser, in spite of the harm experienced.

3. *Calm*

The calm phase is marked by a temporary peace and tranquillity. During this time, the abuser may downplay the incident, deny wrongdoing, or shift blame onto the survivor, often leading to further confusion. For survivors, this intermittent affection may serve as validation, persuading them that the relationship is fundamentally intact and discouraging thoughts of leaving.

Over time, the cycle tends to accelerate. Tension builds more rapidly between incidents of abuse, the violence may intensify in severity, and the phases of reconciliation might shorten or vanish altogether. This rapidity increases the survivor's isolation, deepens trauma, and establishes a bond of trauma that fosters psychological dependence on the abuser.

**Why the Cycle Persists**

*Trauma Bonding*

Commonly referred to as intermittent reinforcement, this bonding mechanism is fuelled by the release of dopamine and adrenaline during moments of reunion following abuse. Each cycle of harm followed by seemingly restorative gestures deepens the emotional bond between the survivor and the abuser, even when the survivor recognizes the dangers.

*Neurobiological Conditioning*

The brain learns to anticipate the cycle. With consistent activation of the amygdala, the prefrontal cortex—the centre of rational thought—becomes severely compromised by the onslaught of stress. This learned response can result in symptoms such as anxiety, flashbacks, emotional numbness, and difficulties in establishing trust in new relationships.

*Cognitive Distortion & Learned Helplessness*

Survivors often internalize a sense of blame ("It's my fault"), accept justifications for abusive behaviour ("They can't help it"), or adopt self-deprecating beliefs ("I deserve this"). This cycle can be further reinforced by learned helplessness, where continued exposure to threats diminishes the survivor's belief in their ability to change their circumstances.

**Psychological & Counselling Interventions**

1. *Psychoeducation*

Educating survivors about the cycle of abuse helps them step out of the shadows of shame and allows them to see the repetitive nature of the dynamic clearly. Counsellors guide them to identify and name each stage of the cycle, emphasizing that it's not their fault.

2. *Cognitive Behavioural Therapy (CBT)*

CBT techniques are employed to address distorted beliefs that have been developed under abusive circumstances. Clients learn to question harmful thoughts (e.g., "I deserved it") and work toward constructing healthier alternatives (e.g., "This was violence, not love").

3. *Trauma-Focused Treatment*

Methods such as Eye Movement Desensitization and Reprocessing (EMDR), prolonged exposure therapy, and Trauma-Focused Cognitive Behavioural Therapy (TF-CBT) assist survivors in processing their trauma. These therapies help them revisit and manage painful experiences in a therapeutic context, reducing their hold over time.

4. *Somatic and Grounding Techniques*

Recognizing that the body stores trauma, approaches such as grounding exercises, diaphragmatic breathing, yoga, and somatic experiencing help to recalibrate physiological responses to perceived threats, restoring a sense of safety and equilibrium within the nervous system.

5. *Safety Planning & Skill-Building*

Understanding the cycle empowers survivors to develop precise exit strategies. This may include preparing essential documents, identifying safe locations, and alerting trusted contacts, which in turn helps them reclaim agency and reduce feelings of chaos.

6. *Peer Groups and Support Networks*

Group counselling provides survivors with a platform to validate their experiences, share their stories, and accelerate healing. The sense of community within peer groups fosters empathy and diminishes the feeling of isolation often experienced in trauma-bonded situations.

**Breaking the Cycle: A Practical Blueprint**

| **Step** | **Action** |
|---|---|
| Recognize the Cycle | Identify the phases of tension, incident, reconciliation, and calm in your own experience. |
| Map the Triggers | Document early warning signs such as silent treatment, controlling behaviours, or unwarranted criticism. |
| Challenge Distortion | Utilize CBT to reframe negative beliefs (e.g., "I deserve respect" instead of "I deserve this"). |
| Implement Interventions | Ground yourself in reality using techniques like |

| | |
|---|---|
| | grounding, EMDR, or exposure therapy. |
| Respond with Safety | Activate your safety plan by leaving during the calm phase if necessary and securing essential items. |
| Access Support | Seek out a counsellor, peer support group, or advocacy services for guidance and companionship in your journey to healing. |

By identifying and understanding the Cycle of Abuse, survivors can take significant steps toward reclaiming their control, fostering a path toward healing and empowerment.

# The Frog in the Boiling Pot – How Abuse Creeps In

***The Psychology of Gradual Harm***

Domestic abuse doesn't always start with fists. It often starts with flowers. With charm. With a voice that makes you feel seen for the first time. And by the time you realise something is wrong, you're already tangled in something you can no longer name.

This isn't weakness. It's survival. It's your nervous system doing its job, keeping you safe in an unsafe situation.

***Learned Helplessness***

In 1975, psychologist Dr Martin Seligman coined the term "learned helplessness" to describe what happens when people are exposed to repeated, uncontrollable harm. Over time, they stop trying to escape—not because they don't want to, but because their nervous system has given up. They begin to believe that nothing they do will make a difference.

In domestic abuse, this shows up as silence. As staying. As second-guessing your own instincts. It's not a reflection of weakness, but a sign of psychological exhaustion and survival adaptation.

***Coercive Control***

Professor Evan Stark, a leading expert on domestic violence, described coercive control as the invisible architecture of abuse. It's a slow, calculated erosion of a person's freedom, voice, and safety. It doesn't always leave bruises. Instead, it leaves confusion, isolation, and fear—disguised as love.

You're told what to wear. Who to see. What to think. The choices shrink until your world is no longer your own. And all of this happens gradually, like the temperature rising in a pot of water.

***Trauma Bonding***

Dr Patrick Carnes, a renowned trauma psychologist, explained trauma bonding as the emotional glue that forms when abusers alternate between cruelty and kindness. They punish you, then comfort you. They hurt you, then apologise. These emotional highs and lows create a biochemical trap, where pain is followed by reward, keeping you emotionally hooked.

***Neuroscience of Abuse***

Over time, the brain adapts to this stress. Your "window of tolerance," a term introduced by psychiatrist Dr Dan Siegel, begins to narrow. You stop recognising red flags. Your body adjusts to survive, not thrive. Fear becomes familiar. Safety feels alien. And this is how you stay in the pot long after it starts to boil.

**The Boiling Frog Metaphor**

To understand how abuse escalates unnoticed, we turn to a metaphor that captures this chilling reality.

They say if you drop a frog into boiling water, it'll leap out straight away. It senses the danger. But if you place that same frog in cold water and slowly turn up the heat, it stays. It adapts. It doesn't notice the change, until it's too late.

That's how domestic abuse works.

It doesn't always storm in, fists clenched or voices raised. Sometimes, it walks in softly. Smiling. Telling you everything you've ever longed to hear.

At first, it feels like love.

*The Water Starts Warm*

It begins with passion. Intensity. They can't stop thinking about you. You've never felt so seen, so chosen. They want to be with you all the time. They're protective, attentive, a little jealous—but that just means they care… right?

They text constantly. They need to know where you are. They "don't like" certain friends. They say you're better off without them. They question your choices, your clothes, your tone, your time.

You justify it. You call it love. You shrink a little to keep the peace. You compromise. You adapt.

The water gets warmer. And you stay.

*Slowly, the Rules Change*

It's subtle, at first. A joke that doesn't feel like a joke. An eye-roll when you speak. A sulk when you make a choice they don't like. You stop doing things that make them uncomfortable. You stop speaking up. You stop feeling like yourself.

And somewhere in the middle of all that, without even realising, it stops feeling like love and starts feeling like walking on eggshells.

You tell yourself they're stressed. It's your fault. It'll get better. And sometimes, it does. That's the trick. The cycle spins, good, bad, apology, repeat.

And all the while, the heat keeps rising.

*Why Didn't You Leave Sooner?*

That question cuts. It always comes from people standing outside the pot.

But when you're the one inside it, you don't always realise you're burning. You've been conditioned to survive, not to run. You're holding onto hope. Onto memories. Onto the person they were before the mask slipped.

You make excuses because trauma bonds are real, and fear doesn't always look like terror. Sometimes it looks like silence. Like guilt. Like trying to be good enough so they'll stop hurting you.

You didn't stay because you liked the pain.
You stayed because the pain didn't come all at once.

It crept in. Bit by bit. Until you forgot how cold the water used to be.

*Coercive Control Doesn't Always Leave Bruises*

This is the part society still struggles to grasp.

Abuse isn't always black eyes and broken bones.
Sometimes it's gas lighting—making you question your reality.
Sometimes it's isolation—disguised as protection.
Sometimes it's financial control, sexual coercion, digital surveillance, or a slow, grinding erosion of who you are.

It's the constant walking on eggshells. The feeling that nothing you do is right. The way your confidence withers. The way your voice disappears.

By the time the water is boiling, you're not just scared. You're exhausted.

*Waking Up to the Heat*

Something shifts. Maybe it's a word. A moment. A conversation that cracks the illusion. You start to feel the burns. The scald marks left on your self-worth. You start to realise this isn't love. It's power. It's fear. It's control.

And that knowing? That's the start of freedom.

You may not leap out right away, most people don't. But now you're aware. And once you see the truth, you can't unsee it. The illusion is broken. The heat is real. And you deserve better than to boil alive for someone else's comfort.

*To the Survivors Still in the Water*

You're not weak. You're not naive. You're not to blame.
You're someone who loved, who adapted, who tried.
You stayed because you hoped.
You left, or are trying to, because you finally saw the truth.

If no one else has said this to you today:
You were never meant to be boiled.

You were meant to live. To love freely. To feel safe in your own skin.
And you will again.

**Final Thought**

Abuse doesn't always roar. Sometimes, it whispers.
It wraps itself in romance, in concern, in charm.
But love should never feel like survival.
And safety should never be something you have to earn.

You don't have to leap all at once. But you can start noticing the water.
That's where your power begins.

**You are not the frog.**
**You are the fire escape.**

# Trauma Bonding: The Chain You Didn't Know You Were Wearing

**What Is Trauma Bonding?**

Trauma bonding is a deeply entrenched emotional attachment that develops between a victim and their abuser when periods of abuse are interspersed with moments of kindness, remorse, or affection. This cycle of hot and cold creates confusion, dependency, and a biochemical addiction to the very person causing harm.

It's not about intelligence or willpower. It's not a moral failing. Trauma bonding is survival instinct, hijacked.

**The Psychology Behind the Bond**

*1. Intermittent Reinforcement*

Abuse doesn't happen all at once. It creeps in, wearing different faces. The abuser may insult you one moment and cradle your face the next. One day you're worthless, the next you're their everything. This inconsistency, called intermittent reinforcement, is one of the most powerful behavioural traps studied in psychology.

Just like gamblers who pull a slot machine handle waiting for a win, victims of abuse remain hopeful for the return of the "good" version of their partner. The brain becomes addicted to the dopamine spikes that come with occasional approval, validation, or intimacy. You chase their affection like a fix.

*2. Learned Helplessness*

Coined by psychologist Dr Martin Seligman in the 1970s, learned helplessness describes how individuals subjected to repeated pain or discomfort they cannot escape begin to believe they have no power to change their circumstances.

In domestic abuse, this shows up as a quiet resignation. A belief that no matter what you do, it won't make a difference. You stay because you've been trained to believe that there's no other option. Over time, escape becomes not just impossible, but unimaginable.

*3. Coercive Control*

Professor Evan Stark called coercive control the "invisible architecture of abuse." It is a methodical campaign of domination where the abuser slowly erodes a person's autonomy, identity, and ability to make decisions.

It doesn't require violence. It operates through rules, restrictions, surveillance, gas lighting, and psychological warfare. You begin to second-guess your every move. Your world becomes smaller and smaller until you exist only within the boundaries they set.

*4. Trauma Bond Chemistry*

The emotional push-pull cycle of abuse is not just psychological, it's physiological. Dr Patrick Carnes, a pioneer in trauma research, found that cycles of punishment and reward flood the brain with stress hormones (like cortisol and adrenaline) followed by bonding chemicals (like oxytocin and dopamine).

This creates a biochemical addiction. The brain starts associating relief and affection with the same person who causes the pain. Over time, you become neurologically bonded to your abuser, even as they destroy your sense of self.

**The Voice of the Survivor**

You start believing:

- "Maybe if I'm quieter, they'll calm down."
- "They didn't mean it. They're just under pressure."
- "It's not always like this—they can be so kind."

This is the essence of trauma bonding. You rationalise the abuse. You shrink yourself to fit their needs. You convince yourself that the love is worth the pain.

But in reality, you're not clinging to the abuser. You're clinging to the memory of who they were at the start and to the hope they'll return to that version.

**The Cycle Is the Cage**

*Good moment → Abuse → Guilt → Apology → Affection → Repeat.*

Each loop builds the chain tighter.

It's not the fear that keeps you, it's the hope.

Hope that they'll change.
Hope that love can heal them.
Hope that if you just try harder, it'll all stop.

But the truth is, that hope is part of the trap. The abuse doesn't end. it resets. And every apology becomes another layer of the chain.

**How to Break the Bond?**

Breaking a trauma bond is not an instant event. It's a process, a sacred unlearning. A return to self. A reclamation of truth.

*Step 1: Name the Pattern*

Seeing the cycle is the beginning. Knowledge breaks illusion. When you can identify the abuse for what it is, the hold it has over you starts to loosen.

*Step 2: Reconnect with Yourself*

Abuse erodes identity. It teaches you to distrust your own instincts. Recovery begins by tuning back into your needs, your values, your voice. You start to remember who you were before they rewrote your worth.

*Step 3: Create Safe Distance*

Trauma bonds thrive in proximity. Physical and emotional distance allows your nervous system to stabilise. This could mean a safety plan, a shelter, trauma-informed therapy, or digital disconnection.

*Step 4: Grieve the Illusion*

You're not just losing a partner. You're mourning a fantasy. A future that was promised. A version of them that only existed in the beginning. That grief is valid, and healing demands space for it.

*Step 5: Rewire the Narrative*

Over time, the brain can heal. With trauma therapy, support networks, and consistent safety, your system can unlearn fear and relearn trust. You begin to make decisions from self-worth instead of self-preservation.

**Final Thought**

You didn't stay because you were naive.
You stayed because you loved deeply, survived intelligently, and hoped fiercely.

But now it's time to return to yourself.

Let go of the illusion.
Let go of the idea that you have to be hurt to be held.
Let go of the person who taught you that pain is the price of love.

**You were never broken. You were bound.**
**And now you are unbinding.**
**One truth at a time.**

# The Story of Clare Wood – The Woman Behind Clare's Law

Clare Wood was, like many others, in search of love, connection, and a fresh start. At the age of 36, she was a devoted single mother living in Salford, Greater Manchester. Friends described her as warm, trusting, and open-hearted, someone who radiated positivity and kindness. However, the narrative of hope that surrounded her budding romance with George Appleton concealed a lurking danger, one that would ultimately claim her life and ignite profound changes in how domestic abuse is addressed in the UK.

Clare met George through Facebook in 2007, and, like many relationships that begin online, their connection blossomed rapidly. George appeared to be charming, attentive, and seemingly genuine, drawing Clare into his orbit. Unbeknownst to her, George Appleton harboured a deeply troubling past, one that involved a well-documented history of violence against multiple women. He had previously faced convictions for harassment, making threats, attempted strangulation, and even kidnapping. Unfortunately, this crucial information was not accessible to Clare at the time; there was no formal system in place to alert her to the potential dangers he posed.

As time passed, the initial charm of George began to fade, revealing a darker side marked by control and intimidation. Clare started experiencing a pattern of harassment and threats that escalated in severity. In her desperate attempts to protect herself, she reported George to Greater Manchester Police on five separate occasions, expressing her fears that he would harm her. Despite her brave efforts to seek help, the system remained unresponsive, offering no restraining orders, no intervention, and no warning about his violent history.

Tragically, on 2 February 2009, Clare Wood's life was brutally cut short within the supposed safety of her own home. George Appleton strangled her and then callously set her body on fire, a horrific act that would be followed by his own suicide days later, found lifeless in a derelict pub.

The grief that enveloped Clare’s family was not silent; it transformed into a powerful rallying cry for justice and change. Clare’s father, Michael Brown, became resolutely determined not to allow his daughter’s death to fade into a mere statistic. He actively campaigned for awareness and change, persistently asking a heart-breaking yet fundamental question: Why didn’t my daughter have the right to know about this man’s violent past? Why was the system prioritising his right to privacy over Clare’s right to life and safety?

Michael’s tireless advocacy eventually led to the establishment of the Domestic Violence Disclosure Scheme in 2014, informally known as Clare’s Law. This ground-breaking legislation now empowers individuals in the UK with the legal right to inquire whether their partner has a history of violence, designed to prevent potentially devastating outcomes like Clare’s.

***Clare’s Law consists of two key components:***

- Right to Ask: Individuals who are concerned about their own safety or that of someone they know can make a request to the police to gain information about their partner's past.
- Right to Know: Police have the authority to proactively disclose information if they assess that someone is at risk, even without a request having been made.

Although Clare’s Law may not prevent every tragedy, it fundamentally shifts the power dynamic, providing crucial information to those most vulnerable to charm tactics, coercive control, or manipulative partners who thrive on silence.

# Clare's Law: Understanding Rights and Resources for Safety

1. *The 'Right to Ask'*

Clare's Law empowers individuals to inquire about the potential risk posed by a partner or acquaintance due to their history of abusive behaviour. Notably, you do not need to be the direct victim to make this request. Concerned friends, family members, or professionals, such as social workers or counsellors, can initiate a request if they believe someone may be in danger.

Upon receiving a request, the police conduct a thorough assessment to determine if sharing information is lawful, necessary, and proportionate to safeguard the individual at risk. If a credible threat is identified, police will confidentially share pertinent information directly with the person in danger, typically through a private meeting where support and guidance are offered.

2. *The 'Right to Know'*

This provision allows law enforcement to take proactive measures by disclosing information about an individual's violent or abusive history, even without a formal request. If the police identify a person with a history of abuse who has entered a new relationship, they can reach out to the new partner to inform them of the potential risks involved.

**Why It Matters (Psychology and Safety Context)**

Clare's Law aims to facilitate informed decision-making, an aspect that abuse survivors often lack until they are already in dangerous situations. From a trauma-informed counselling perspective, being aware of potential risks can:

- Interrupt the cycle of coercive control before it potentially escalates into more severe abuse.
- Empower survivors by providing them with factual information rather than leaving them vulnerable to fear and speculation.
- Assist with safety planning, especially during the early stages of relationships where manipulative behaviour may initially be disguised as affection.

**Limitations**

It is essential to acknowledge that not all abusers have a documented criminal history, and many victims may never report their experiences of abuse. Information sharing is subject to legal thresholds, and there are instances where survivors might choose to remain in an abusive relationship despite being aware of the risks. Factors influencing this choice can include trauma bonding, financial dependency, and overwhelming fear.

**How to Apply (UK-wide)**

If you or someone you know seeks to utilize Clare's Law, the process is straightforward:

- Visit your local police station in person.
- Call the non-emergency police number, 101.
- In certain areas, there may also be an option to apply online via your local police force's official website.

Once a request is submitted, law enforcement officers will follow up to discuss the situation and implement safeguarding measures if deemed necessary.

**Why It's Essential**

Clare's Law is a critical tool designed to provide knowledge, not a definitive solution to stop abuse. While it does not eliminate the potential for harm, having access to vital information can be a crucial first step toward achieving safety and autonomy. When combined with supportive counselling, effective safety planning, and trauma recovery strategies, Clare's Law can play a life-saving role in the lives of those at risk.

**Author Reflection: Why Her Story Still Matters**

Clare's story is deeply moving, and it ignites a passionate response in me as a writer. The tragedy lies in the fact that Clare did nothing wrong; she simply chose to trust someone in her pursuit of love. She spoke out about her concerns and bravely sought help, yet in the end, she met a horrific fate at the hands of someone who should never have been a part of her life.

Her narrative exposes the insidious failures present in our systems, highlighting the gaps between police reports, the trivialization of coercive control as mere "relationship issues," and the acute lack of proactive protection for individuals at risk. Clare's Law is not simply a policy; it embodies a promise that speaks to the fundamental right of every individual to know the truth about their partner's potential dangers. It asserts that every person deserves to be safe and informed.

When discussing domestic violence, Clare Wood's name must be at the forefront of the conversation. It's essential we remember her not only for the tragic way her life ended, but also for the courageous fight her father undertook in the aftermath. This is how meaningful change is born, not from detached discussions in boardrooms, but from the transformation of grief into purpose and action.

If you find yourself questioning the intentions of someone in your life, don't hesitate to seek clarity. Use Clare's Law as a resource. It could very well be the key to ensuring your safety and well-being.

# Understanding MARAC: The Power of Partnership in Domestic Abuse Response.

When a survivor of domestic abuse faces immediate or escalating danger, relying on isolated support systems is inadequate. The risks can be too high, and the complexities of the situation often demand a comprehensive, coordinated approach. This is where MARAC (Multi-Agency Risk Assessment Conference) becomes a vital resource. It stands as one of the UK's most effective safeguarding mechanisms, specifically designed to protect high-risk victims of domestic abuse by fostering collaboration among professionals from various services to create a unified response.

**What is MARAC?**

A MARAC is a regular, confidential meeting in which representatives from multiple statutory and voluntary agencies convene to share information and strategize about the highest-risk domestic abuse cases. These agencies commonly involved include:

- Police: Responsible for responding to incidents and gathering evidence.
- Social Services: Ensuring the welfare and safety of any children involved.
- Health Professionals: Including GPs, mental health teams, and maternity services that assess the physical and mental health aspects of the victims.
- Probation Services: Monitoring offenders and providing insights into their behaviour.

- Housing Providers: Helping secure safe accommodations for victims.
- Domestic Abuse Specialists: Such as IDVAs (Independent Domestic Violence Advisors) who advocate for the victims' needs.
- Substance Misuse Services: Supporting those dealing with addiction issues impacting the perpetrator or victim.
- Children's Services: Addressing the needs of minors involved in the domestic abuse situation.
- Education Sector: Ensuring that schools are aware and can provide support.
- Legal Advisors: Offering guidance on legal rights and options for victims.

The primary aim of MARAC is risk reduction. By pooling intelligence from each agency, a detailed understanding of the circumstances surrounding the abuse and the vulnerabilities of the victim are formulated, enabling the creation of a joint safety plan that addresses both immediate and longer-term needs.

**Who Is Referred to MARAC?**

MARACs serve exclusively high-risk domestic abuse cases, where serious threats to safety, including potential homicide, are evident. Victims are usually identified through the DASH Risk Assessment Tool (Domestic Abuse, Stalking, and Honour-Based Violence), which frontline practitioners such as police officers, housing officers, or domestic abuse workers complete.

Common indicators that may qualify a case for MARAC consideration include:

- Escalating Violence: Increasing frequency or intensity of incidents.
- Weapons Involvement: Use or threats regarding weapons.
- Non-Fatal Strangulation: An act that significantly increases risk levels.

- Coercive Control and Stalking: Ongoing manipulation and harassment.
- Threats to Kill: Direct threats indicating intent to harm.
- Pregnancy: A vulnerable state that can exacerbate risk.
- Child Safeguarding Concerns: Risks to any children involved.
- Mental Health or Substance Abuse Issues: Present in either the victim or the perpetrator.
- Multi-Agency Involvement: Cases already recognized by various services.

While any professional working with the victim can initiate a MARAC referral, obtaining the victim's consent is encouraged whenever possible. However, in urgent situations where there are safeguarding concerns, referrals can proceed without consent under established legal frameworks for data-sharing.

**What Happens During a MARAC?**

1. Case Presentation: The lead agency, often the police or an IDVA, presents the case details, including historical context, recent incidents, and identified risks.

2. Information Sharing: Each agency contributes relevant information, such as prior arrests, medical records, children's involvement, housing stability, and other pertinent data.

3. Risk Identification: The group collaborates to identify both known and hidden risks, guided by professional insights and survivor perspectives.

4. Safety Planning: The agencies work together to develop a personalized safety and support plan that may involve:

- Installing target-hardening measures (e.g., enhanced security systems).
- Referring victims to refuge or safe housing options.

- Assigning an IDVA or caseworker to maintain ongoing support.
- Notifying relevant schools or workplaces to ensure awareness and safety.
- Engaging with professionals for substance misuse or mental health services.
- Flagging the case within police systems for prioritised responses.

5. Action Allocation: Specific actions and timeframes are agreed upon by each agency, with progress monitored in subsequent meetings.

**The Psychological and Practical Impact**

From a counselling and trauma-informed care standpoint, MARAC provides survivors with a level of protection and support that many may have lacked previously. Living under coercive control or enduring continuous violence often leads to feelings of isolation, making it difficult for victims to navigate fragmented services. MARAC addresses this isolation by ensuring that survivors are not only seen and heard but also prioritized across all areas of their recovery and protection.

Moreover, engaging multiple agencies fosters wraparound safeguarding. This approach emphasizes that ensuring a victim's safety transcends merely providing refuge; it encompasses securing stable income, access to child support, mental health services, and legal assistance. Research indicates that multi-agency approaches significantly reduce the chance of repeat victimization and can be life-saving.

**Trauma-Informed Considerations**

Trauma counsellors emphasize the importance of involving the victim whenever safe and feasible. Survivors often experience a profound sense of helplessness following abuse, and empowering them, even in safety planning discussions, can help restore a sense of agency. This is why IDVAs, who serve as the survivor's voice at MARAC meetings, play a crucial role.

Counsellors working with survivors post-MARAC are also encouraged to address specific areas, such as:

- Rebuilding Trust: Helping survivors navigate their feelings about previous experiences where they felt their help-seeking was ignored.
- Managing Emotions: Supporting them in processing feelings of fear or guilt that may arise from sharing their experiences without consent.
- Navigating Transitions: Assisting with changes related to rehousing or criminal proceedings stemming from MARAC discussions.

**Limitations and Challenges**

While the MARAC framework stands as one of the most robust tools in UK safeguarding, it is not without its challenges:

- Resource Constraints: Limited resources can lead to inconsistent follow-up and support for victims after initial interventions.
- Data Silos: Fragmented data can hinder agencies from having a complete understanding of a case, thus impeding effective risk assessment and action planning.
- Perpetrator Accountability: MARAC primarily focuses on the victim's safety rather than engaging in the rehabilitation or legal prosecution of the offender, sometimes leaving accountability issues unaddressed.
- Survivor Voice Representation: The potential underrepresentation of the survivor's voice can occur if the IDVA is overburdened or underfunded, significantly impacting the plan's effectiveness.

In light of these challenges, ongoing evaluation and advocacy are essential to ensure that MARAC remains an effective tool in combating domestic abuse and protecting vulnerable individuals.

**Final Thoughts**

MARAC operates as a vital yet understated force in the background, lacking the flashy headlines and courtroom dramas often associated with advocacy work. However, the impact of its efforts is truly profound and far-reaching. This organization exemplifies what is achievable when dedicated professionals, from social workers to law enforcement, come together, not merely to exchange paperwork, but to unite around a shared mission: ensuring the safety and well-being of survivors and helping them reclaim their autonomy.

If you are a survivor, a supportive friend, or a frontline worker, it's essential to understand the core philosophy of MARAC. The commitment here is not to strip individuals of control over their own lives but rather to empower them. The focus is on restoring their sense of agency, providing them with the tools and support they need to navigate their journeys toward safety and healing. In this collaborative environment, every voice is valued, and every decision is made with the survivor's best interests at heart. This collective effort stands as a powerful testament to the difference that can be made when compassion and professionalism intersect.

# The DASH Model – Identifying High-Risk Domestic Abuse

The DASH: Domestic Abuse, Stalking, and Honour-Based Violence, risk assessment model serves as a cornerstone for multi-agency domestic abuse work throughout the United Kingdom. Originally formulated by Laura Richards and her colleagues at CAADA (now known as SafeLives), this model has been embraced nationally since March 2009. The DASH framework equips essential services, including police, social services, healthcare providers, housing authorities, probation officers, and domestic abuse specialists, with a standardized language and method for identifying and managing high-risk domestic abuse cases.

1. *Purpose & Foundations*

The development of DASH aimed to transform the fragmented and inconsistent practices surrounding risk management into a systematic and coherent framework. The primary objectives of the DASH model are:

- Identification of High-Risk Survivors: To effectively recognize individuals who are at acute risk of serious harm, particularly those experiencing stalking or honour-based violence.
- MARAC Referral: To expedite the process of flagging cases for MARAC (Multi-Agency Risk Assessment Conference), ensuring that urgent, coordinated interventions can be implemented when necessary.
- Evidence-Based Decision-Making: To support defensible and informed decision-making grounded in thorough case reviews, which include analyses of domestic homicide cases and instances of "near misses." This structured

method guarantees that all frontline professionals, regardless of their specific roles or training, pose the same 27 critical questions and facilitate essential referrals for next steps.

2. *What is in the DASH Checklist?*

The DASH checklist encompasses 27 items that assess a range of different forms of abuse, including but not limited to the following:

- Physical and Sexual Violence: Direct acts of harm or coercion that pose immediate threats to a survivor's safety.
- Emotional and Psychological Abuse: This includes tactics such as insults, belittling language, and gas lighting, which can profoundly impact the mental well-being of survivors.
- Coercive Control and Isolation: Tactics aimed at restricting a survivor's freedom or ability to operate independently.
- Stalking and Harassment: This category includes actions like monitoring online activity or unwanted constant communication.
- Honour-Based Pressures: Situations involving threats of forced marriage or other culturally rooted forms of pressure.
- Safeguarding Factors: Critical aspects such as pregnancy or ongoing health issues that may heighten the risk.

It is important to note that a response of "Yes" to any question on the checklist does not automatically equate to a diagnosis. Instead, these responses contribute to painting a comprehensive risk picture that practitioners are expected to evaluate through structured professional judgment.

3. *Scoring & Interpreting Risk*

Although DASH does not provide a definitive numerical score, established benchmarks indicate that:

- For the 24–27 item version of the checklist, a threshold of 14 or more "Yes" responses typically warrant a referral to MARAC.
- In the 27-item police version, a MARAC referral is automatically triggered once a red-flag threshold is met.

The expertise of professionals remains crucial in interpreting these risk assessments. It is essential to acknowledge that professional judgment can identify risks that a survivor may not feel comfortable disclosing due to factors such as fear, trauma, or manipulation.

4. *Practical Use in Counselling & Psychology*

A. Psychoeducation & Validation: Counsellors frequently utilize the DASH model to provide survivors with an understanding of their experiences. By framing their trauma within a research-backed risk model, it helps diminish feelings of self-blame and fosters a sense of validation.

B. Structured Disclosure & Safety Planning: The checklist serves as a guide for safe and sensitive questioning, creating a space for survivors to disclose information with the necessary consent and comfort. It allows for repeated assessments that account for evolving risks.

C. Shared Language Across Services: The use of a uniform assessment tool promotes trust among all involved parties—be it counselling, legal, healthcare, or police professionals. This shared understanding ensures that the survivor's voice is amplified and more likely to be believed.

D. Dynamic Risk Management: Importantly, DASH is intended to be a living document; it should be revisited and updated following each new incident. Counsellors are encouraged to monitor shifts in the situation, such as the emergence of stalking behaviours or custody disputes.

5. *Integration with MARAC & Multi-Agency Response*

Frontline professionals are instructed to complete the DASH assessment following any survivor's disclosure or initial contact. Cases deemed high-risk are subsequently referred to MARAC, where the collective sharing of information fosters the development of a coordinated safety plan. Independent Domestic Violence Advocates (IDVAs) often take the lead in this process, ensuring that survivors receive comprehensive support that encompasses all dimensions of their lives, including mental health, legal protection, housing issues, and financial stability. This collaborative approach transforms isolated disclosures into a cohesive multi-agency response, proactively preventing the escalation of harm.

6. *Psychological & Trauma-Informed Perspective*

Adopting a trauma-informed approach, the DASH model offers a range of significant advantages:

- Validation of Lived Experience: It affirms that abuse and trauma are real and not merely the result of the survivor's perception or mental state.
- Restoration of Agency: By equipping survivors with knowledge about risk factors, they can make more informed decisions concerning their own safety and wellbeing.
- Trust Building: When multiple services utilize the DASH model, survivors are more likely to cultivate trust in the system and believe in its ability to provide protection.
- Empowerment through Knowledge: Understanding that the subtle forms of abuse they endure are taken seriously can be profoundly empowering for survivors.

Clinicians often weave DASH into ongoing therapeutic work, aligning practical responses with trauma-focused therapeutic objectives such as safety planning, boundary setting, and survivor empowerment.

### 7. *Challenges & Considerations*

Despite the compelling evidence base and broad acceptance of the DASH model, certain challenges persist:

- Variability in Implementation: Research indicates that the application of DASH can be inconsistent across various frontline settings, often due to gaps in training and understanding.
- Loss of Contextual Nuance: While DASH serves as a valuable guide, it cannot replace the deep professional insight required to understand the complexities of each individual case.
- Threshold Limitations: The predefined thresholds may not fully encapsulate the range of risks that a survivor may face, highlighting the importance of ongoing vigilance and professional judgment.

In sum, while the DASH model represents a vital tool in the identification and management of high-risk domestic abuse, it is paramount for practitioners to approach each case with a nuanced understanding of the broader context, ensuring that survivors' needs are met comprehensively and compassionately.

# The Dash Form Explained

The DASH Risk Checklist—short for Domestic Abuse, Stalking, and Honour-Based Violence, is a structured 27-question assessment used by professionals across the UK to identify the level of risk a victim is facing. Designed with input from frontline services and behavioural psychology, the form allows practitioners to consistently evaluate immediate and ongoing danger, including emotional, physical, sexual, and coercive abuse. It helps determine whether a case should be referred to a Multi-Agency Risk Assessment Conference (MARAC), which coordinates protection and support from police, housing, health, and social care. While originally developed for use by trained professionals such as police officers and Independent Domestic Violence Advisors (IDVAs), the DASH form also empowers victims by validating their lived experiences in a trauma-informed way. Answering "yes" to certain high-risk indicators, such as threats to life, strangulation, stalking, or control, can trigger urgent intervention. Including this form here is not just about paperwork; it's about reclaiming voice, visibility, and safety. For many survivors, it is the first time their fragmented fears are seen as serious, patterned, and actionable.

Risk Identification for Trained Front Line Practitioners (Please refer to the DASH (2009-2024) Practice Guidance on Risk Identification in full)

A number of high risk factors and more recently high risk clusters have been identified as being associated with serous violence and murder through researching many cases. Any professional using the DASH (2009- 2024) must be trained in its use. This is crucial to understanding what the high risk factors are and how they apply in each situation, and what needs to be done to keep the victim safe.

This form should be completed for ALL cases of domestic abuse by front line staff. Initial risk identification must be undertaken by asking ALL the questions on this checklist, as well as searching appropriate databases, such as the intelligence databases. First response staff and their supervisor should identify risk factors, who is at risk and decide what level of intervention is required.

Details of children resident at the address must be provided. Consider the nature of the information and what it means in terms of public protection - preservation of life, reduction, and prevention of harm to victim and others.

Please ensure that when you ask these questions the victim is comfortable and understands why you are asking them – it is about their safety and protection. Particular sensitivity and attention are required when asking about whether the victim has been assaulted, physically and/or sexually by the perpetrator. The vulnerability of victims cannot be overstated. This could be further compounded by issues such as traditional gender roles, literacy, language and/or immigration or refugee status. Please take into consideration the victim's perception of risk.

Please ensure you ask the victim about the abuser's behaviour when stalking and honour-based violence are present. Do not just tick the box 'yes'. You must identify what is happening. There are specific risk factors that relate to these areas as well. Assessment of risk is complex and NOT related to the number of risks appearing alone. Rather, the risk posed to the victim or others in a particular situation will be dependent upon what they are and how they apply in that context. Refer to the full DASH (2009-2024) Practice Guidance on Risk Identification.

Record what steps you have taken to ensure the immediate safety of the victim(s) and any children. Ask yourself 'Am I satisfied that I have done all I can?' Everything you do must be recorded.

The risk identification process must remain dynamic. Events and circumstances may undergo rapid and frequent change. Where this is the case, the assessment must be kept under review. Risk identification is based on structured professional judgement. This model is most effective when undertaken by professionals who have been fully trained in its use. High risk cases may well require a multi-agency response and should be referred to the relevant risk management panel i.e. the Multi-Agency Risk Assessment Conference (MARAC) or Multi

Agency Public Protection Panel (MAPPP). MARACs are for the most serious and high risk cases.

| CURRENT SITUATION<br>THE CONTEXT AND DETAIL OF WHAT IS HAPPENING IS VERY IMPORTANT. THE QUESTIONS HIGHLIGHTED IN BOLD ARE HIGH RISK FACTORS. TICK THE RELEVANT BOX AND ADD COMMENT WHERE NECESSARY TO EXPAND. | YES ☑ | NO ☑ |
|---|---|---|
| 1. Has the current event resulted in injury? (please state what and whether this is the first injury) | ☐ | ☐ |
| **2. Are you very frightened?**<br>Comment: | ☐ | ☐ |
| **3. What are you afraid of? Is it further injury or violence? (Please give an indication of what you think (name of abuser(s)..... might do and to whom)**<br>Kill: Self ☐ Children ☐ Other (please specify) ☐<br>Further injury and violence: Self ☐ Children ☐ Other (please specify) ☐<br>Other (please clarify): Self ☐ Children ☐ Other (please specify) ☐ | ☐ | ☐ |
| 4. Do you feel isolated from family/ friends i.e. does (name of abuser(s).....) try to stop you from seeing friends/family/Dr or others? | ☐ | ☐ |
| 5. Are you feeling depressed or having suicidal thoughts? | ☐ | ☐ |
| **6. Have you separated or tried to separate from (name of abuser(s)....) within the past year?** | ☐ | ☐ |
| 7. Is there conflict over child contact? (please state what) | ☐ | ☐ |
| **8. Does (.....) constantly text, call, contact, follow, stalk or harass you? (Please expand to identify what and whether you believe that this is done deliberately to intimidate you? Consider the context and behaviour of what is being done. Ask 11 additional stalking questions*)** | ☐ | ☐ |
| CHILDREN/DEPENDENTS (If no children/dependants, please go to the next section) | YES | NO |
| **9. Are you currently pregnant or have you recently had a baby in the past 18 months?** | ☐ | ☐ |
| 10. Are there any children, step-children that aren't (.....) in the household? Or are there other dependants in the household (i.e. older relative)? | ☐ | ☐ |
| **11. Has (.....) ever hurt the children/dependants?** | ☐ | ☐ |
| 12. Has (.....) ever threatened to hurt or kill the children/dependants? | ☐ | ☐ |
| DOMESTIC VIOLENCE HISTORY | YES | NO |
| 13. Is the abuse happening more often? | ☐ | ☐ |
| **14. Is the abuse getting worse?** | ☐ | ☐ |
| **15. Does (.......) try to control everything you do and/or are they excessively jealous? (In terms of relationships, who you see, being 'policed at home', telling you what to wear for example. Consider honour based violence and stalking and specify the behaviour)** | ☐ | ☐ |
| 16. Has (.....) ever used weapons or objects to hurt you? | ☐ | ☐ |

| | | |
|---|---|---|
| **17. Has (.....) ever threatened to kill you or someone else and you believed them?** | ☐ | ☐ |
| **18. Has (.....) ever attempted to strangle/choke/suffocate/drown you?** | ☐ | ☐ |
| **19. Does (....) do or say things of a sexual nature that makes you feel bad or that physically hurt you or someone else? (Please specify who and what)** | ☐ | ☐ |
| **20. Is there any other person that has threatened you or that you are afraid of? (If yes, consider extended family if honour based violence. Please specify who. Ask 10 additional HBV questions*)** | ☐ | ☐ |
| 21. Do you know if (.....) has hurt anyone else ? (children/siblings/elderly relative/stranger, for example. Consider HBV. Please specify who and what)<br><br>Children ☐ Another family member ☐ Someone from a previous relationship ☐ Other (please specify) ☐ | ☐ | ☐ |
| **22. Has (.....) ever mistreated an animal or the family pet?** | ☐ | ☐ |
| ABUSER(S) | Yes | No |
| 23. Are there any financial issues? For example, are you dependent on (.....) for money/have they recently lost their job/other financial issues? | ☐ | ☐ |
| 24. Has (.....) had problems in the past year with drugs (prescription or other), alcohol or mental health leading to problems in leading a normal life? (Please specify what)<br><br>Drugs ☐ Alcohol ☐ Mental Health ☐ | ☐ | ☐ |
| 25. Has (.....) ever threatened or attempted suicide? | ☐ | ☐ |
| 26. Has (.....) ever breached bail/an injunction and/or any agreement for when they can see you and/or the children? (Please specify what)<br><br>Bail conditions ☐ Non Molestation/Occupation Order ☐ Child Contact arrangements ☐<br>Forced Marriage Protection Order ☐ Other ☐ | ☐ | ☐ |
| 27. Do you know if (........) has ever been in trouble with the police or has a criminal history? (If yes, please specify)<br><br>DV ☐ Sexual violence ☐ Other violence ☐ Other ☐ | ☐ | ☐ |
| Other relevant information (from victim or officer) which may alter risk levels. Describe: (consider for example victim's vulnerability - disability, mental health, alcohol/substance misuse and/or the abuser's occupation/interests-does this give unique access to weapons i.e. ex-military, police, pest control) or is there serial offending? | | |
| Is there anything else you would like to add to this? | | |

In all cases an initial risk classification is required:

| RISK TO VICTIM: | | |
|---|---|---|
| STANDARD ☐ | MEDIUM ☐ | HIGH ☐ |

**DASH (2009-2024) Additional HBV Risk Questions**

**Q20. Is there any other person who has threatened you or who you are afraid of?*** (If yes, please specify who and why. Consider extended family if HBV)

**Practice Point: If the victim is subject to HBV and answers 'yes' to this question, ask the following questions:**

- ✓ Truanting – if under 18 years old is the victim truanting?

  ...........................................................................................................................................

- ✓ Self-harm – is there evidence of self-harm?

  ...........................................................................................................................................

- ✓ House arrest and being 'policed at home' – is the victim being kept at home or their behaviour activity being policed(describe the behaviours)?

  ...........................................................................................................................................

- ✓ Fear of being forced into an engagement/marriage – is the victim worried that they will be forced to marry against their will?

  ...........................................................................................................................................

- ✓ Pressure to go abroad – is the victim fearful of being taken abroad?

  ...........................................................................................................................................

- ✓ Isolation – is the victim very isolated?

  ...........................................................................................................................................

- ✓ A pre-marital relationship or extra marital affairs – is the victim believed to be in a relationship that is not approved of?

  ...........................................................................................................................................

- ✓ Attempts to separate or divorce (child contact issues) –is the victim attempting to leave the relationship?

  ...........................................................................................................................................

- ✓ Threats that they will never see the children again – are there threats that the child(ren) will be taken away?

  ...........................................................................................................................................

- ✓ Threats to hurt/kill – are there threats to hurt or kill the vitcim?

  ...........................................................................................................................................

**DASH (2009-2024) Additional Stalking and Harassment Risk Questions**

**Q8. Does (......) constantly text, call, contact, follow, stalk or harass you?*** (Please expand to identify what and whether you believe that this is done deliberately to intimidate you? Consider the context and behaviour of what is being done)

**PRACTICE POINTS: Stalking is pattern of unwanted, fixated and obsessive behaviour which is intrusive and causes fear of violence or serious alarm or distress.**
**If the victim answers 'yes' to this question then you must ask the following as they are risk factors for future violence:**

- ✓ Is the victim very frightened?
  ..............................................................................................................................
- ✓ Is there previous domestic abuse and harassment history?
  ..............................................................................................................................
- ✓ Has (insert name of the abuser....) vandalised or destroyed property?
  ..............................................................................................................................
- ✓ Has (insert name of the abuser....) turned up unannounced more than three times a week?
  ..............................................................................................................................
- ✓ Is (insert name of the abuser....) following the victim or loitering near the victim?
  ..............................................................................................................................
- ✓ Has (insert name of the abuser....) threatened physical or sexual violence?
  ..............................................................................................................................
- ✓ Has (insert name of the abuser....) been harassing any third party since the harassment began (i.e. family, children, friends, neighbours, colleagues)?
  ..............................................................................................................................
- ✓ Has (insert name of the abuser....) acted violently to anyone else during the stalking incident?
  ..............................................................................................................................
- ✓ Has (insert name of the abuser....) engaged others to help (wittingly or unwittingly)?
  ..............................................................................................................................
- ✓ Is (insert name of the abuser....) been abusing alcohol/drugs?
  ..............................................................................................................................
- ✓ Has (insert name of the abuser....) been violent in past? (Physical and psychological. Intelligence or reported)
  ..............................................................................................................................

| MARAC REFERRAL | |
|---|---|
| **Do you believe that there are reasonable grounds for referring this case to MARAC?** | **Yes / No** |
| If yes, have you made a referral? | **Yes/No** |

| CONSENT | |
|---|---|
| If the case is high risk and you are referring it to the MARAC, please explain to the victim what the MARAC is and that it is there to help them, giving them options and choices to keep them and their children safe. | |
| **Has the victim given verbal consent to share information with partner agencies?** | **Yes/No** |
| **Officer's signature**............................................... | **Date:**.................. |

**Risk Assessment Categorisation**

This is *based* on the Offender Assessment System (OASys) developed by the Prison and Probation Services definitions of what constitutes standard, medium, high risk. Please use your professional judgement to categorise the risk level:

| **Standard** | Current evidence does not indicate likelihood of causing serious harm. |
|---|---|
| **Medium** | There are identifiable indicators of risk of serious harm. The offender has the potential to cause serious harm but is unlikely to do so unless there is a change in circumstances, for example, failure to take medication, loss of accommodation, relationship breakdown, drug or alcohol misuse. |
| **High** | There are identifiable indicators of risk of serious harm. The potential event could happen at any time and the impact would be serious.<br><br>Risk of serious harm (Home Office 2002 and OASys 2006):<br>'A risk which is life threatening and/or traumatic, and from which recovery, whether physical or psychological, can be expected to be difficult or impossible'. |

**Risk Management Framework**

Use the RARA model when compiling safety plans for victims. What are you planning to do?

| Remove the risk: | By arresting the suspect and obtaining a remand in custody. |
|---|---|
| Avoid the risk: | By re-housing victim/significant witnesses or placement in refuge/shelter in location unknown to suspect. |
| Reduce the risk: | By joint intervention/victim safety planning, target hardening, enforcing breaches of bail conditions, use of protective legislation and referring high risk cases to Multi-Agency Risk Assessment Conference (MARAC). |
| Accept the risk: | By continued reference to the Risk Assessment Model, continual multi-agency intervention planning, support and consent of the victim and offender targeting within Pro-active Assessment and Tasking Pro forma (PATP), or Risk Management Panel (such as Multi-Agency Risk Assessment Conference (MARAC) or Multi-agency Public Protection Panel (MAPPP). |

# Economic Abuse: The Silent Chain

Economic abuse stands as one of the most insidious and often overlooked forms of domestic violence. Unlike the more overt manifestations of physical violence or verbal threats, economic abuse operates in the shadows, often unnoticed by those outside the relationship. It may lack visible markings, no bruises or raised voices, yet it exerts just as much control, and often more, over a victim's life. This form of abuse is quiet, methodical, and devastatingly effective in undermining a person's sense of self and autonomy.

At its essence, economic abuse is designed to strip a victim of their financial independence and autonomy. It involves a deliberate manipulation of money, employment, access to resources, and decision-making processes, fostering a dependency that can be incredibly difficult to escape. This is not merely incidental abuse; it is a calculated strategy aimed at maintaining power and control. The ramifications of such abuse are significant, as it not only restricts a survivor's freedom and choices but effectively shackles them to their abuser, often making it nearly impossible to leave the abusive situation.

*What Economic Abuse Looks Like?*

Economic abuse manifests in various subtle and overt behaviours:

1. Controlling Access to Money: The abuser may take complete control of all household finances, managing income that may even be earned by the victim. This often involves refusing to provide access to joint accounts or even personal funds that belong to the victim.

2. Sabotaging Employment: An abuser may actively disrupt their partner's employment prospects by making them late to work, creating chaos at home that distracts from job responsibilities, or instilling fear that affects job performance.

3. Taking Out Debt: Abusers often force their partners to take out loans or credit cards in their name, deliberately plunging them into debt. This burdens the victim with financial obligations that can take years to resolve and severely damage their credit score.

4. Forcing Financial Dependence: By monopolizing financial decisions, down to the minutiae of grocery spending or utility payments, abusers can create a sense of financial paralysis for their victims, leaving them feeling incapable of making even minor financial choices.

5. Stealing or Withholding Benefits: Abusers may intercept benefits or child maintenance payments, effectively cutting off the survivor's access to vital financial support, thus depriving them of the means to care for themselves or their children.

According to the organization Surviving Economic Abuse UK, a staggering 95% of domestic abuse cases involve some aspect of economic abuse. It often begins with subtle manipulations, such as suggesting who should manage the bills, but can escalate to total financial domination. While instances of physical violence may cease with separation, the scars of economic abuse can linger long after a survivor leaves.

*The Psychological Impact*

The emotional and psychological toll of being economically controlled is profound and can lead to lasting trauma. Survivors of economic abuse frequently experience chronic anxiety, feelings of helplessness, and a profound loss of identity. Many report feeling like prisoners within their own lives—unable to make even the most basic financial decisions without explicit permission. Economic abuse also cultivates isolation; lacking the means for transport, communication, or secure housing can leave survivors feeling entrapped in their situation.

This psychological impact can lead survivors to internalize the abuse, blaming themselves for being "bad with money" or "too dependent" on their abuser. Counsellors often report that victims of economic abuse may develop complex post-traumatic stress disorder (PTSD), particularly when their sense of self-worth has been intricately tied to their financial autonomy. In therapeutic settings, rebuilding confidence involves not only restoring a sense of self but also fostering a regained competence and control over personal finances.

*Survivor Stories*

Survivor stories poignantly illustrate the harsh reality of economic abuse. One woman shared her experience, describing how her ex-partner forced her to quit her job and restricted her to a daily grocery allowance of just £5. "If I asked for more," she recounted, "he'd accuse me of being ungrateful and trying to bankrupt him." Another survivor, Clare*, was coerced into signing loan applications that ultimately burdened her with £30,000 in debt. "Even after I left him," she reflected, "his control lingered in my credit file, making it impossible for me to rent or forge ahead. I still felt as if I were owned."

*Leaving Isn't Free*

A significant barrier to escaping abusive situations is the lack of financial resources. Many survivors find themselves remaining in or returning to abusive relationships due to economic hardship. Relocating entails expenses such as deposits, transport, time off work, childcare arrangements, and sometimes legal fees. Without savings, stable employment, or a good credit score, a realistic escape may feel unattainable.

Access to safe housing, emergency funds, and legal assistance becomes critical in these situations. Organizations like Women’s Aid, Refuge, and Surviving Economic Abuse advocate for better financial protections, including options for benefit advances, rent-free periods, and debt relief for survivors.

*Rebuilding Financial Autonomy*

Recovery from economic abuse is a multi-layered process that demands time, patience, and support. Engaging in financial counselling, trauma-informed care, and support groups can be invaluable in this journey. Many survivors must work to rebuild their financial literacy, not due to a lack of intelligence, but rather because they were deliberately kept in the dark about financial matters. They require access to secure banking options, credit repair resources, and budgeting skills. Above all, they need a supportive community that understands that financial entrapment can inflict wounds just as deep as any physical bruise.

Survivors of economic abuse carry invisible scars that often manifest in their bank statements, unpaid bills, and lost opportunities over the years. It's imperative that we recognize that abuse extends beyond a slap or a scream; it sometimes resides in the silence at the checkout, the anxiety of opening a bank app, or the forced choice between staying in a harmful situation and facing starvation.

Economic abuse thrives on secrecy and isolation. Yet, by naming it, we can begin to break the silence. And breaking that silence is the essential first step toward reclaiming freedom.

# Post-Separation Abuse – The Other Half of Survival

Abuse rarely concludes with the end of a relationship. For many survivors, the threat continues or even intensifies after separation, a phenomenon known as post-separation abuse. This form of abuse involves former partners exerting control through various means, including ongoing coercion, psychological manipulation, child exploitation, stalking, and complex legal manoeuvring. A comprehensive review of studies conducted in North America between 2011 and 2022 reveals that post-separation abuse frequently encompasses a wide array of psychological, legal, economic, and mesosystem tactics. Survivors often face the weaponisation of children, economic sabotage, inappropriate court filings, and persistent stalking. Alarmingly, up to 90% of women report experiencing ongoing harassment, stalking, or other forms of abuse following separation.

One of the most prevalent strategies employed by abusers is legal coercion and custody manipulation. Former partners often weaponised child contact arrangements, making use of court applications and disputes or engaging in parental alienation to exert emotional and logistical control over survivors. This creates a climate of emotional confusion, pervasive guilt, and disrupted parenting roles, which can persist even when child welfare agencies such as CAFCASS intervene. Furthermore, financial abuse is a significant factor in post-separation control strategies, where perpetrators may withhold child support, initiate expensive legal action, or threaten eviction and homelessness to destabilize the survivor's independence and autonomy.

Stalking and intimidation are hallmark behaviours patterns associated with post-separation coercive control. Survivors may find themselves subjected to repeated unwanted contact through phone calls, text messages, or the uninvited presence of their ex-partner at their home or workplace. These relentless actions aim to provoke fear, disrupt daily life, and reassert power over the survivor. Additionally, abusers often exploit children as tools for emotional manipulation, coaching them to deliver threatening messages, challenge the survivor's authority, or misrepresent their parent's character during court proceedings.

Psychologically, post-separation abuse creates a persistent state of threat that triggers the body's chronic stress response, significantly undermining the survivor's mental health. Common psychological effects include heightened anxiety, post-traumatic stress reactions, severe depression, self-doubt, and a continuous feeling of powerlessness. The compounded impact of navigating legal battles, disrupted parenting dynamics, and stalking amplifies the experience of complex trauma, which profoundly affects the survivor's recovery process.

Counsellors and therapists play a crucial role in addressing the multifaceted nature of post-separation abuse. The initial step involves conducting a thorough risk and safety assessment, utilizing structured tools to evaluate the risks of lethality, stalking, and child safety. Effective safety plans must be tailored to encompass digital, physical, legal, and emotional vulnerabilities, often developed in collaboration with law enforcement, housing authorities, and social services.

Establishing and maintaining clear boundaries is vital for survivors to regain a sense of control over their lives. Therapists support survivors in setting no-contact boundaries, maintaining detailed records of incidents, navigating court communications, and fostering confidence in their decisions. Legal literacy and advocacy are also fundamental components of the support process. Survivors require comprehensive guidance concerning protective orders, such as non-molestation and occupation orders, in addition to strategies on how to accurately document incidents to support their claims. Partnering with Independent Domestic Violence Advisors (IDVAs) or legal advocates ensures that survivors are not navigating this challenging terrain alone.

Cognitive-behavioural and trauma-informed therapies are essential aspects of the healing journey. Interventions such as Cognitive Behavioural Therapy (CBT) and Eye Movement Desensitization and Reprocessing (EMDR) are effective in addressing distorted beliefs and trauma responses, while attachment-based care fosters emotional regulation and the rebuilding of trust. For those involved in co-parenting situations, emotionally focused family therapy can be beneficial in establishing secure emotional frameworks that reduce conflict and promote healthier interactions. Children affected by post-separation abuse require specialized support; therapeutic techniques such as play therapy, trauma-informed CBT, and school-based liaison services are crucial for fostering emotional healing and resilience.

Community and systemic engagement are equally important in addressing the challenges posed by post-separation abuse. Family courts and child welfare agencies must receive training to recognize the indicators of coercive control and child manipulation. Expanding the roles of IDVAs and advocacy services to specifically target post-separation dynamics can enhance support for survivors and their children across various systems. Schools and youth services also play a pivotal role in preparing children with knowledge of personal boundaries, coping mechanisms, and strategies for self-protection.

Consider the story of Lisa, who separated from her partner five months prior. Following her separation, her ex-partner consistently missed custody exchanges while bombarding her with harassing emails and making frequent threats of legal action. Initially feeling overwhelmed by the ongoing situation, Lisa sought therapy focused on boundary-setting and collaborated with an IDVA for both legal and emotional support. As time progressed, she learned to minimize contact, enhancing her child's school experience and gradually restoring her sense of agency. Her case underscores the necessity for trauma-informed, multidisciplinary support in post-separation contexts.

Post-separation abuse is not merely an adjunct to domestic violence; it is a strategic and calculated extension of it. The survivor's journey towards liberation frequently begins only after they leave. A comprehensive, multi-layered response that includes rigorous risk assessment, safety planning, legal empowerment, trauma-informed therapy, and child-centred support is imperative for helping survivors reclaim their lives and rebuild a future free from the shadow of their past.

For many survivors of domestic abuse, the act of leaving a relationship is often perceived as the end of their struggles, a moment of liberation and hope for a new beginning. However, for countless others, this departure marks the onset of a new and often more perilous phase known as post-separation abuse. This form of abuse is a frequently underestimated extension of control, manipulation, and violence that continues long after the survivor has taken steps to exit the relationship.

Abuse does not always come to a halt when a relationship ends; rather, it shifts its tactics. Research reveals a disturbing truth: the risk of severe harm or homicide spikes significantly in the months following separation. According to the Femicide Census, an alarming 41% of UK women who were killed by a partner experienced their fatal assault after the end of the relationship, with many casualties occurring within the first year. The trauma for survivors does not simply end with a final argument or a slamming door; for many, it intensifies as the abuser, having lost their immediate grip on power, becomes more desperate and erratic in their attempts to reclaim control.

This ongoing cycle of abuse is rarely about "love gone wrong." Instead, it revolves around a fundamental struggle for power and the lengths an abuser is willing to go when that power is perceived to be under threat.

In today's technologically advanced world, post-separation abuse can manifest through various forms of digital stalking and surveillance. Survivors frequently report experiences such as GPS trackers hidden in personal belongings, spyware installed on devices, and exploitation of smart home technology to monitor their activities. Social media harassment, impersonation, and use of listening devices further contribute to a constant sense of being watched, eroding survivors' sense of safety even in their own homes.

For those survivors with children, the family court system can become a new battlefield. Abusers may file frivolous lawsuits, make repeated court applications, or falsely accuse survivors of parental alienation. These tactics drain survivors emotionally, financially, and mentally, and can even result in dangerous co-parenting arrangements enforced under the guise of "child's best interest."

Economic sabotage persists in the aftermath of separation. This includes the non-payment of child support, job interference, coerced debt, and mismanagement of joint accounts, all designed to entrap survivors in financial instability and dependence.

The impact on children is profound. Abusers may coach children to turn against the survivor, ignore parental authority, and instil confusion and fear. These tactics contribute to emotional and behavioural problems, anxiety, and developmental trauma.

Survivors frequently live in a state of prolonged hypervigilance. Complex PTSD, flashbacks, sleep disturbances, and depression are common. Healing requires more than time, it demands trauma-informed support, legal advocacy, safety planning, and systemic reform.

To truly support survivors of post-separation abuse, systems must acknowledge that leaving does not equal freedom. Empowering survivors requires understanding the nuanced and continued nature of abuse, and meeting it with holistic, consistent, and compassionate responses.

# Trapped by Care – Disability and Domestic Violence

Domestic violence is a multifaceted issue that manifests differently across various demographics. For individuals living with disabilities, whether those disabilities are physical, sensory, intellectual, or cognitive, the experience of abuse can take on particularly insidious forms. Often concealed behind the facade of "care," such abuse becomes a reality that is seldom acknowledged, yet profoundly felt. It represents a silent cruelty that silences, immobilizes, and isolates individuals under the guise of dependency. Alarmingly, the very systems designed to protect disabled survivors frequently fail to recognize or address their unique challenges.

Research conducted in the UK and globally reveals a troubling statistic: people with disabilities are significantly more prone to experience domestic abuse compared to their non-disabled peers. Reports from Public Health England and Women's Aid indicate that disabled women are nearly twice as likely to encounter domestic violence. Furthermore, this violence tends to be more severe and prolonged. Despite the gravity of these findings, the stories of disabled survivors remain strikingly underreported, and their access to necessary support is often hindered by a combination of physical barriers and systemic shortcomings.

*Weaponising Disability*

In the context of abusive relationships, disability is frequently weaponized as a means of control and manipulation. This form of abuse often diverges from more traditional forms in that it may not always be overtly violent. Instead, it encompasses a range of behaviours, including:

- Withholding essential resources: Abusers may restrict access to vital tools such as wheelchairs, communication aids, or medication, using these as forms of punishment or mechanisms of control.

- Manipulating care routines: When the abuser is also a designated caregiver, they may sabotage necessary support, limit access to healthcare services, or cut off external contact—all under the pretext of providing care while effectively increasing isolation.

- Mocking and belittling disabilities: Abusers may humiliate their partners through derogatory name-calling or by framing them as "incapable," systematically eroding their confidence and fostering dependency.

- Financial manipulation: Many abusers control or exploit benefits, misuse Direct Payments, or outright steal disability-related financial support, often without raising suspicion among outsiders.

- Sexual coercion and exploitation: Individuals with learning disabilities face an alarmingly high risk of sexual abuse, particularly from those in positions of trust or authority.

- Isolation from essential services: Abusers may intervene in communications, accompany survivors to appointments, or speak on their behalf to prevent them from disclosing the abuse they are experiencing.

These forms of abuse can be particularly difficult to identify, as they tend to manifest not through physical violence but rather through persistent psychological manipulation. Such coercive control undermines the basic needs, routines, and dependencies of disabled individuals, creating an environment of chronic oppression.

*The Psychological Toll*

Enduring this style of oppression inflicts a substantial psychological toll on survivors. Trauma research indicates that disabled individuals subjected to prolonged abuse often internalize harmful ablest narratives. Over time, this may lead them to develop beliefs that they are unworthy of love, incapable of achieving independence, or undeserving of support.

This toxic mind-set can result in:

- Learned helplessness: A state where continuous abuse and limited pathways to escape foster a belief that liberation is impossible.

- Chronic mental health issues: Survivors may develop PTSD, depression, and anxiety, with those having sensory or cognitive disabilities showing symptoms such as extreme withdrawal, self-harm, or behavioural outbursts—reactions that are frequently misinterpreted by support services.

- Loss of self-identity: Many survivors describe feeling invisible, defined solely by their disability and their abuser's narrative, which diminishes their sense of self.

`The intersection of disability and abuse leads to compounded trauma, wherein survivors experience harm not only from their abusers but also from systems that are not equipped to meet their specific needs.

*Systemic Barriers*

Despite increasing awareness of these issues, the support infrastructure available for disabled survivors remains deeply problematic:

- Inaccessibility of refuges: Fewer than 10% of refuges in the UK are fully wheelchair accessible, and many lack appropriate visual or auditory support systems for survivors with sensory impairments.

- Inadequate communication support: Survivors who are non-verbal or who require sign language interpreters often find themselves overlooked during critical assessments or police investigations.

- Professional ignorance: Frontline staff in domestic abuse services may not have the training necessary to recognize abuse directed at disabled individuals, especially when that abuse diverges from physical violence.

- Financial challenges: Austerity measures, benefit caps, and cuts to social care budgets have exacerbated the situation, making it increasingly difficult for disabled individuals to escape abusive environments without compromising their basic needs.

These systemic barriers not only delay potential escape but also actively trap victims in harmful situations.

*Counselling and Therapeutic Support*

To effectively support disabled survivors, counselling must be tailored to be both trauma-informed and accessibility-focused. Therapists should consider the following strategies:

- Utilise multi-modal communication: This includes integrating visual supports, employing simplified language, and ensuring access to interpreters where needed.

- Avoid assumptions: Practitioners should not conflate disability with incapacity. While survivors may require assistance, they are often the experts in their own experiences and needs.

- Prioritize empowerment: Counselling should focus on helping clients regain their autonomy by supporting their choices regarding personal care, communication methods, and planning for the future.

- Collaborate with advocates: To create a coordinated and effective care plan, therapists should engage with disability organizations, caseworkers, and trusted caregivers.

Understanding that trauma manifests differently in disabled individuals, particularly those with learning difficulties, is key to providing the necessary support and intervention they deserve. By acknowledging the complexities of their experiences, we can create a more inclusive and responsive support system for all survivors of domestic violence.

*Real-Life Voices: Sarah's Story*

Sarah is a 34-year-old woman living with cerebral palsy, a condition that has shaped her experiences but not defined her strength. For years, she endured a devastating cycle of abuse at the hands of her long-term partner and carer, who manipulated her vulnerabilities to exert control over her life. He systematically withheld her essential medication, depriving her of the tools she needed to manage her condition effectively. When she expressed her basic needs, such as requesting food, he would berate her for asking "too often," further eroding her sense of self-worth. To isolate her from support, he convinced friends and family that she was "mentally unstable" whenever she attempted to voice her concerns.

After reaching a breaking point, Sarah bravely sought help by contacting a domestic abuse helpline. However, the response she received was disheartening. The worker informed her that the organization did not provide accessible accommodation, leaving Sarah feeling trapped and hopeless. "I stayed," she recounted, her voice filled with pain. "Because no one believed me. They thought he was helping. He was killing me slowly."

Sarah's experience is tragically emblematic of countless others. When disability is used as a mask for coercive control, society must be more vigilant and responsive, listening not less.

*A Path Forward*

To effectively support disabled survivors like Sarah, domestic violence services and public health systems must take significant steps to adapt and improve:

1. Accessibility: All refuges and services must be designed to be physically accessible communicatively inclusive, ensuring that survivors with diverse needs can seek help without barriers.
2. Dedicated Services: Funding must be allocated to create specialized services for disabled survivors, including targeted outreach programs and peer support initiatives that resonate with their unique experiences.
3. Professional Training: It is crucial to train professionals across various sectors to recognize the signs of abuse in caregiving relationships. This training would help ensure that survivors are taken seriously and receive appropriate support.

Social Care Reform: Reforming existing social care laws to prioritize the autonomy and safety of survivors is essential. These reforms should empower individuals to make informed choices about their care without fear of coercion.

On a policy level, stronger enforcement of the Equality Act is necessary, coupled with increased funding for inclusive services tailored to the needs of disabled individuals. Additionally, developing comprehensive domestic violence strategies that specifically address the intersections of disability and abuse is vital for meaningful change.

*Closing Thoughts*

Disability should never equate to vulnerability to abuse, yet in the current system, it often does. Survivors with disabilities confront a perfect storm of isolation, disbelief, and systemic neglect that can leave them feeling powerless. Their experiences of abuse are real, their stories are crucial, and their needs must be prioritized in the fight against domestic violence.

By sharing these powerful narratives, we illuminate the hardships faced by survivors like Sarah. In giving voice to their struggles, we take a step toward creating a world where no one, regardless of ability, is left behind. Together, we can build a society that supports and uplifts all individuals, ensuring that every survivor has the opportunity to live free from abuse and fear.

# Behind Closed Doors: Domestic Violence in Later Life

When we envision domestic violence, our thoughts often gravitate towards younger couples engulfed in turmoil: the harsh sounds of slamming doors, heated arguments echoing through a home, and bruises obscured by clothing. It's rare to think of the frail figures living in care homes or senior citizens trapped in familiar, yet suffocating, environments. However, for many older adults, domestic abuse not only persists but can intensify over time. Veiled by ageism, generational stigma, and physical frailty, the reality of their suffering remains hidden behind closed doors.

*Silent Suffering*

For survivors over 60, the journey out of an abusive relationship is far from straightforward. It involves navigating a complex labyrinth filled with disbelief, shame, and numerous practical challenges. In England and Wales, approximately 3.2% of individuals aged 60–74 and 1.4% of those over 75 report experiencing domestic abuse annually, a statistic that likely obscures a much bleaker reality. Many older victims have endured mistreatment for decades before they can even articulate the concept of abuse, influenced by cultural norms that dictate private suffering should be borne in silence and not aired in public discussions.

*Different Faces of Abuse*

As physical dependency grows and health deteriorates, the nature of abuse often transforms from overt violence to subtler, insidious forms:

- Physical violence can manifest as pushing, slapping, or rough handling by caregivers or spouses, often cloaked in the guise of assistance.
- Emotional cruelty includes belittling remarks, gas lighting, and threats of being placed in a care home, creating a climate of fear.
- Sexual abuse may involve non-consensual acts, frequently perpetrated by family members or professional caregivers who exploit their positions of trust.
- Financial coercion can take the form of theft, misuse of pensions, or forced alterations to wills and banking arrangements, effectively stripping individuals of their financial autonomy.
- Neglect entails the deliberate denial of essential needs such as medication, food, hygiene, or medical care, further isolating and endangering vulnerable individuals.

This multifaceted cruelty not only isolates older survivors but also exploits them, erasing their autonomy, often perpetrated by those they trust most.

*Barriers to Speaking Out*

For older adults, the obstacles to revealing their abuse are particularly daunting:

- Generational beliefs perpetuate the notion that "this is a family matter," creating a societal code that venerates silence as an unspoken virtue.
- Fear of losing independence looms large; many older adults fear that reporting abuse could lead to involuntary placement in a care home, a prospect they often view with greater dread than the abuse they currently face.
- Physical vulnerability related to health issues like chronic illness, hearing loss, or dementia can render the act of seeking help feel insurmountable.

- Social isolation compounds their suffering, as dwindling friendships, distant children, and limited mobility leave many survivors trapped without the necessary support to seek help.

Counselling psychology highlights how this complicated interplay of shame, fear, and dependency often intertwines, perpetuating cycles of abuse that survivors find nearly impossible to escape.

*Margaret's Story*

At 82, Margaret's life had been dominated by emotional control and financial restrictions imposed by her husband for over fifty years. After his death, her adult son moved in, demanding she surrender her independence. She was relegated to the role of an emotional ATM, her dignity withheld as she was manipulated by the one she should have been able to trust. The weight of guilt and shame rendered her voice, a once brilliant silver, barely a whisper.

It wasn't until an observant doctor noticed the bruises on her arms and listened to her halting words that the invisible chains began to break. "I thought I was to blame," she confessed with vulnerability. "I was so loyal." Through dedicated therapy and supportive housing, Margaret began to reclaim a piece of herself that had long been relegated to the shadows her dignity and sense of self-worth.

*Psychological Consequences*

Older survivors frequently bear the profound burden of lifetime trauma. Confronting decades of silent suffering necessitates a deep, often painful journey toward rediscovery of their self-worth during their twilight years. This healing process typically involves:

- Reframing internal narratives, shifting the focus from "I must endure" to "I deserve peace and happiness."

- Processing compounded trauma, where the echoes of past and present pains intertwine, making recovery challenging yet necessary.
- Reclaiming lost identities and autonomy, which may have been steadily eroded over many years of manipulation and abuse.

Therapeutic approaches such as EMDR (Eye Movement Desensitization and Reprocessing), CBT (Cognitive Behavioural Therapy), and narrative therapy, which is mindful of age and health specifics, can prove transformative in these situations.

*Systemic Failures and Needed Change*

The existing structures designed to support survivors, refuges, social care systems, healthcare, are frequently inadequate for the unique challenges older individuals face:

- Less than 10% of refuges in the UK are wheelchair-accessible or equipped to meet the needs of older survivors, leaving many with few options.
- Frontline professionals may misinterpret signs of abuse as symptoms of confusion or dementia, thereby silencing those who need advocacy and support the most.
- Significant policy gaps exist, leaving older survivors with limited access to justice, safe housing, or financial independence.

These systemic failures urgently call for comprehensive reform to better serve this vulnerable population.

*Creating a Safer Future*

To foster a safer environment for older survivors, we must develop support networks that truly address their needs:

- Establishing accessible and safe housing equipped to accommodate both physical needs and personal care requirements should be a priority.
- Implementing specialized training for healthcare and social care professionals can equip them to identify signs of abuse effectively and respond with sensitivity.
- Engaging and mobilizing local communities, harnessing the resources of organizations like Age UK and SafeLives, can enhance outreach and empower older survivors to speak out and seek help.
- Advocating for robust policy frameworks ensures that no survivor is forced into a care home or faces financial destitution after fleeing violence.

*Final Thoughts*

Abuse is not confined by age; it doesn't simply fade with time. Healing is not automatic when oppression remains concealed and voices are silenced. We cannot afford to look away from this reality. The survivors are not merely frail, they are resilient warrior's worthy of every resource, compassionate ear, and moment of peace.

If you or someone you know is an older adult experiencing domestic violence, it's crucial to remember: it's never too late to seek freedom. Strength, hope, and safety are within reach for every individual, at any stage of life.

# The Silent Wounds – Male Survivors of Domestic Abuse

James didn't fit the stereotype most people envision when they think of a domestic violence survivor. A former soldier, he was broad-shouldered and calm by nature, believing firmly in the role of protector. His definition of strength was mired in silence; he thought emotions were a weakness. That all changed one frigid night when, after refusing to hand over his debit card to the woman who had once promised him love and loyalty, he found himself locked outside in the bitter cold, barefoot and bleeding.

It was only much later that James came to understand the deeper truth of his situation: he had become one of the staggering 1 in 6 men in the UK who experience domestic abuse over the course of their lifetimes. Unfortunately, his story, like those of countless others remained unheard for far too long.

*Redefining the Narrative*

When discussions on domestic abuse arise, they often revolve around female survivors. While this focus is entirely justified, considering the high prevalence and severity of violence directed at women, this narrative creates an unintended consequence: it renders male victim's invisible. Society continues to struggle with the idea of men as vulnerable individuals who can be controlled or abused. As a result, for many male survivors, this cultural silence can feel as imprisoning as the abuse itself.

A staggering number of male survivors don't even recognize their victimhood. They are often trapped by pervasive and damaging myths like:

- “Men can’t be abused.”
- “He must have done something to provoke it.”
- “If he really wanted to leave, he would.”

These misconceptions are not just erroneous; they are perilous. They contribute to a system where male survivors are less likely to report their abuse, less likely to be believed when they do seek help, and far less likely to receive appropriate support. Many internalize the damaging belief that their pain is not valid or worthy of attention.

However, domestic abuse is indiscriminate; it affects individuals of all genders, including men, trans men, and non-binary individuals. Abuse transcends size, strength, or gender—it is fundamentally about control.

*What Abuse Looks Like for Men*

The experience of abuse among male survivors often manifests differently than it does for female victims, yet is no less destructive. Many men undergo psychological and emotional manipulation long before any physical violence occurs. This can include:

- Constant criticism or belittlement
- Threats of false accusations related to abuse or child neglect
- Deliberate separation from children or family
- Financial exploitation, where their wages are controlled or their access to funds is impeded
- Physical harm, followed by ridicule or dismissal when they seek assistance
- Sexual coercion, which inflicts deep emotional wounds yet remains a rarely discussed topic

In their quest for help, men frequently face ridicule or disbelief from police, friends, and professionals. One survivor recounted, “They treated me like a joke. Like I was the abuser.” This kind of reaction leads many men to remain silent, prolonging their suffering until trauma engulfs their sense of self.

*The Psychological Toll*

Domestic abuse severely erodes identity. For male survivors, this process is often intensified by societal expectations to "man up" or project an image of being unaffected. However, the human brain does not differentiate by gender when processing trauma.

Abuse engages the amygdala, the brain's fear centre, resulting in a cascade of survival responses—fight, flight, freeze, or fawn. This continuous state of activation over time rewires neural pathways, leading survivors to experience hypervigilance, anxiety, depression, emotional numbness, and Complex PTSD.

Common reports from male survivors include:

- Intrusive thoughts or flashbacks
- Feelings of low self-worth or profound guilt
- Emotional detachment from loved ones, causing rifts in relationships
- Physical symptoms manifesting as migraines, insomnia, or gastrointestinal distress
- Engagement in addictive behaviours such as substance abuse, sexual escapism, overworking, or bouts of unmanageable rage

In therapy, many male survivors confront a painful realization: "I didn't know it was abuse until someone else said it out loud." Therapeutic support, especially trauma-informed counselling, EMDR (Eye Movement Desensitization and Reprocessing), or group therapy, can facilitate the reconnection with their experiences, enabling them to piece through the chaos. Importantly, it allows them to redefine masculinity—not as unyielding stoicism—but as resilience born from vulnerability.

*Barriers to Help*

Even when men muster the courage to leave abusive situations, they often find that the support system is ill-equipped to meet their needs. In England and Wales, only 4% of refuge spaces are accessible to men. Few support services explicitly include male survivors, and institutions like social services and courts frequently struggle to recognize male coercive control.

In LGBTQ+ relationships, abuse is often mischaracterized as "mutual conflict," further complicating avenues for help. A persistent fear of not being believed looms large. One father disclosed the mockery he faced from his ex-partner, who taunted him, "Go ahead, tell the police. Who are they going to believe: you or me?" Fears of child custody loss, community shame, or professional stigma contribute to a cycle that keeps many men ensnared in their abusive relationships.

*James's Journey*

James's path to healing began only after a violent episode led him to the hospital. In a quiet moment, a compassionate nurse asked if he felt safe at home. "No," he replied, and she handed him a leaflet from the Mankind Initiative.

That simple, pivotal moment changed everything. He took the brave step to join a support group for male survivors. Although it felt awkward at first to sit in a circle of men discussing their fears, James gradually regained something that abuse had stripped away: dignity without conditions. Through therapy, he unpacked years' worth of trauma and silence, finding solace in journaling, exercising, and reconnecting with his children. Over time, he began to build a life not governed by someone else's control.

Now, James volunteers with a charity that supports male survivors, using his experience to provide hope and encouragement to others who have faced similar struggles. He is a living testament that healing is possible, and together, survivors can rewrite their stories.

*Changing the System*

We need a comprehensive support system that recognizes male survivors of abuse, listens to their stories, and provides the same level of compassion, support, and funding that is often directed toward female victims. Acknowledging the struggles of male survivors does not diminish the very real experiences of female victims; instead, it fortifies our collective efforts to combat all forms of abuse more effectively.

To achieve this, we must:

1. Expand Male Refuge Spaces: Increase the number of safe havens specifically available for men, ensuring they have accessible environments where they can seek refuge and receive care without stigma.

2. Integrate Male-Focused Language in Domestic Violence Campaigns: Develop outreach materials and campaigns that include language and imagery that resonate with men, making it clear that help is available for all survivors, regardless of gender.

3. Provide Specialized Training for Professionals: Equip police officers, legal professionals, and mental health therapists with the knowledge and skills to understand and effectively respond to male trauma responses, thereby fostering an environment of trust and safety.

4. Address Abuse in Same-Sex and Trans Relationships: Approach the issue of domestic violence in same-sex and transgender relationships with the nuance and sensitivity it deserves, recognizing the unique challenges faced by these communities.

5. Fund Dedicated Helplines and Peer Support Groups: Establish and finance helplines and peer support groups specifically for men, creating platforms where they can share their experiences and receive support from others who understand their journeys.

Because abuse is not a failure attributable to gender; it is a profound human violation that impacts individuals across the spectrum.

*To Every Silent Survivor*

To every man reading this who has been told to remain silent, to toughen up, or to dismiss his pain:

Your experience is valid, your pain is real, and your healing journey is entirely possible. You are not alone; many have walked a similar path and found their way to recovery.

Remember, surviving does not signify weakness. On the contrary, it takes immense strength to endure such hardships. It demonstrates courage to confront this reality and, even more so, to decide that the cycle of abuse ends with you. You deserve support, understanding, and the opportunity to heal.

# When Faith Silences – Cultural and Religious Barriers in Domestic Abuse

For many individuals, faith serves as a haven—a sacred space for prayer, a source of trust in a higher power, and guidance from community leaders during tumultuous times. However, for others, faith morphs into a quiet imprisonment: beliefs are contorted into shackles, and traditions are weaponized to enforce silence and compliance.

In our previous discussions on domestic violence, we've examined coercive control, honour-based violence, and the various cultural barriers that hinder survivors. Now, we delve deeper into the intricate relationship between faith and abuse: how religious and cultural structures can both uplift and restrain those who endure violence.

*The Double-Edged Sword of Faith*

Religion is steeped in rituals, rites, and profound meanings that have the potential to provide solace. In therapeutic settings, spiritual communities often emerge as anchors amid life's storms. Yet, paradoxically, these very rituals can become chains that bind individuals when they are applied without compassion or understanding.

Research conducted within UK Bangladeshi, Eritrean, and Ethiopian communities reveals a duality. While religious and community institutions often offer essential resources—such as emotional support and a sense of belonging—they frequently lack trauma-informed approaches. This oversight leaves worshippers vulnerable and silenced precisely when they need protection the most.

Faith can be a powerful force for salvation, but it can just as easily perpetuate silence:

- "God desires for families to remain united."
- "Divorce is an affront to God's will; you'll jeopardize your standing with Him."

Moreover, community leaders may actively discourage the reporting of "family issues" to secular authorities, framing such actions as betrayals of trust against the community. Individuals raised in collectivist traditions often carry heavy burdens of honour, shame, and duty—emotional weights that can imprison them in abusive relationships far longer than others may endure.

*Narratives of Control: Honour, Shame, and the Fear of Ruin*

Consider the concept of izzat, or family honour, a dynamic that resonates across numerous cultures. When individuals contemplate speaking out against abuse, they recognize that their outcry may not only tarnish their reputation but could also sully the honour of their entire community. Guilt becomes a pervasive emotion:

- "If I remain silent, I safeguard our family's honour."
- "If I reveal the truth, I could destroy everything."

This guilt is a psychological tool that abusers exploit. It erodes self-worth and ensnares survivors in a web of deeply internalized shame.

To facilitate healing for such survivors, counselling may integrate several approaches:

- Cultural humility: valuing faith as an integral part of identity while actively challenging its misuse as a tool of oppression.
- Narrative therapy: allowing individuals to disentangle themselves from the problems they

face, viewing their experiences through a different lens.
- Cognitive reframing: assisting survivors in understanding that their suffering does not equate to sinfulness.

*Case Study: Kiranjit Ahluwalia*

In 1989, Kiranjit Ahluwalia, an Indo-Canadian woman living in London, ignited a fire that changed her life forever after enduring a decade of relentless abuse. Despite her desperate pleas for assistance, her in-laws and religious advisors pushed her to sustain the marriage, even as she faced starvation, physical violence, and threats to her life for resisting intimacy.

Convicted of murder, she ultimately gained her freedom in 1992 with the support of organizations like Southall Black Sisters. Her case redefined legal understandings in the UK around "battered woman syndrome" and coercive control, illustratively demonstrating how cultural and faith-based pressures can manifest as lived terror.

*Psychological and Counselling Insights*

The intersection of faith and abuse creates a distinct kind of trauma which encompasses:

- Spiritual abuse: where faith becomes a complex entanglement characterized by fear and the imposition of conditional love.
- Internalized guilt: leading to thoughts such as, "If God truly wished for my happiness, I wouldn't feel this suffering."
- Social isolation: as leaving an abusive situation may expose survivors to ostracism or homelessness.
- Cultural PTSD: a profound fracture that affects faith and personal identity concurrently.

Trauma-informed interventions may include:

- Involving trusted religious leaders in therapy—only with the survivor's consent.

- Reinterpreting spiritual texts to emphasize themes of liberation and justice instead of subjugation.
- Highlighting faith figures who have historically resisted injustice to inspire current survivors.

*Barriers to Finding Help*

Shockingly, only about 15% of survivors within minoritised communities report experiences of abuse. Barriers often include:

- Fear of cultural or faith-based repercussions: disclosing abuse may lead to the loss of marriage, community standing, or both.
- A fundamental misalignment between secular services and the realities of faith-based life, including differences in language, cultural norms, and gender roles.

*The Role of Religious Institutions*

When faith leaders engage with sensitivity and accountability, survivors can discover both refuge and purpose. However, it is crucial that these leaders are adequately equipped with knowledge and training, not merely well-intentioned.

Initiatives such as "Safe in Faith" are working towards change by offering:

- Training workshops focused on recognizing and addressing coercive control.
- Confidential "faith spaces" where survivors can safely express their experiences.
- Collaborative pathways that connect survivors with Independent Domestic Violence Advocates (IDVAs) and legal advocates.

Yet, these vital pockets of hope need to expand and permeate broader communities.

*A New Path: When Faith Sets You Free*

Imagine a scenario where faith serves to uplift rather than hinder. Graduates of training programs that blend scriptural study with safeguarding principles act as vital bridges between survivors and sanctuaries. Survivors report feeling seen and validated—redeemed rather than erased.

*From Silence to Sanctuary*

To genuinely support survivors, we need to establish key landmarks that address their unique challenges:

- Clerical Training: Must prioritize education around the recognition of domestic violence and its implications.
- Peer Groups: Formulate faith-based, survivor-led support circles to foster connection and shared understanding.
- Culturally Safe Therapy: Develop counselling services that honour and respect individual rituals, language, and beliefs.
- Secular–Faith Partnerships: Create co-designed resources that ensure confidentiality, foster trust, and align with community values.
- Public Messaging: Implement sermons and public campaigns that affirm the message #YouAreNotSin, empowering survivors to reclaim their narratives and truths.

By prioritizing these essentials, we can begin to dismantle the barriers that silence survivors and pave the way for healing and liberation.

# Kiranjit Ahluwalia – A Life Broken, Then Reclaimed

"I decided to show him how much it hurt." These powerful words, spoken by Kiranjit Ahluwalia, emanate not from a place of malice, but from decades of deeply ingrained pain and trauma. Her harrowing journey not only transformed her own life but also catalysed a profound change in the legal and social landscape surrounding domestic abuse in the UK.

*A Marriage Arranged, A Life Entrapped*

Born in 1955 in Punjab, India, Kiranjit emigrated to the UK in 1979, stepping into an arranged marriage with Deepak Ahluwalia. Initially, the union held the promise of a new beginning filled with hope and aspirations. However, this optimism quickly unravelled. Within just forty-eight hours, Deepak's facade of affection was stripped away, revealing a dark reality characterized by violence, manipulation, and degradation. For the next decade, Kiranjit endured a relentless cycle of abuse.

Deepak isolated Kiranjit from her friends and family, enforcing an oppressive regime that dictated every aspect of her life, from the foods she could eat—restricting her even from drinking tea—to the people she could associate with. As the years rolled on, the abuse escalated, culminating in heart-wrenching scenarios where he raped her repeatedly and threatened her life with chilling regularity, often in front of their two young sons. Kiranjit lived in a state of constant dread, her spirit eroded to a point of near obliteration until one fateful day when she reached her breaking point.

*A Moment of Sociopath History*

On the evening of May 9, 1989, Kiranjit made a fateful decision. In a desperate bid to escape the unrelenting torment, she procured petrol and caustic soda, concocting a volatile mixture she then poured over Deepak as he slept. The horrifying act burned over 40% of his skin, leading to his death ten days later from sepsis. This was not merely an act of aggression; it was a culmination of years of suffering. Deepak's past attempts to inflict harm on her, including threats to burn her with a hot iron and brutalize her physically, loomed large in her mind as she carried out her desperate act.

When Kiranjit was later tried for murder, the prosecution painted a picture of premeditated malice, citing her knowledge of hazardous materials and the calculated timing of her attack as evidence of a cold-blooded killer. Tragically, her story of torment went unheard; instead, she found herself sentenced to life in prison, her trauma overlooked in the face of legal scrutiny.

*Trauma Strangled by the Law—Then Freed*

In prison, Kiranjit often felt invisible, a sentiment she later articulated in her memoir, 'Circle of Light'. However, her plight caught the attention of the Southall Black Sisters, a group dedicated to supporting women facing domestic violence. They rallied public support and gathered vital evidence of the abuse she had endured over the years. By 1992, the Court of Appeal recognized that her original legal counsel had failed to adequately inform her of her right to plead diminished responsibility, and the initial trial had dismissed the psychological impact of years of cumulative abuse on her actions.

With fresh medical evidence revealing her severe depression and unstable psychological state, Kiranjit's conviction was eventually downgraded from murder to manslaughter. After serving the time for a crime borne out of desperation rather than malice, she walked free, a profound moment of liberation.

*The Aftermath: Voice, Reform, and Recognition*

Following her release, Kiranjit dedicated herself to rebuilding her life. She took on night shifts at Royal Mail and, through sheer determination, purchased her own home. In recognition of her courage and resilience, she received the Asian Women of Achievement Award in 2001 from Cherie Booth, a pivotal acknowledgment of her journey.

In 2006, her compelling narrative was adapted into the film 'Provoked', featuring prominent actress Aishwarya Rai, and it premiered to international audiences. Kiranjit transformed her personal ordeal from one of victimhood into a powerful advocacy, paving the way for important legal precedents. The landmark case, R v Ahluwalia, changed the understanding of self-defence in the context of domestic abuse, establishing that a decade of sustained abuse could override the immediate triggers of provocation, emphasizing the psychological trauma that often accompanies such violence.

*Psychological Dimensions*

From a counselling perspective, Kiranjit's actions represent the devastating impact of cumulative trauma, a response not born of a single moment of rage but instead a breaking point resultant from sustained violence. Her experiences resonate with the mechanisms of learned helplessness and complex PTSD, conditions that reflect the psychological consequences of prolonged abuse. The willingness of the court to accept this evidence marked a radical shift in legal attitudes from moral condemnation to a framework of psychological empathy, granting survivors a form of agency over their narratives that had been previously denied.

*Legal and Cultural Ripples*

The ripples of Kiranjit's case extended far beyond her personal reprieve. It set precedents that influenced subsequent significant legal cases, such as R v Thornton (1996) and R v Humphreys (1995). Furthermore, it contributed to the 2009 Coroners and Justice Act, which replaced the archaic provocation defence with the more nuanced concept of "loss of control." This legal shift acknowledged the psychological aspects of domestic abuse, validating theories such as Battered Woman Syndrome and embedding trauma's role into both legal frameworks and counselling practices.

*Reflection: Survival and Justice*

Kiranjit Ahluwalia's story compels us to confront critical questions: What happens when faith, culture, and societal expectations bind an individual in fear? How can legal, medical, and social systems evolve to recognize and respond to the unseen scars of psychological trauma? What language and support do we need to offer survivors who have suffered through years of silent agony?

Her journey is not merely a case in law; it serves as a powerful mirror to the realities faced by many survivors, highlighting the necessity of listening to their experiences. It reminds us of the significance of recognizing and validating trauma to foster understanding and support for those who have endured long-standing abuse.

*Voice Reclaimed*

Today, Kiranjit lives a quieter life in Slough, taking pride in her two sons, both of whom are pursuing their education at university. She has built a life characterized by independence, having purchased her home through determination and hard work. Once rendered invisible by her circumstances, Kiranjit has emerged as a crucial voice in the conversation surrounding domestic abuse. Her story has not only transformed legal precedents but has also reshaped public empathy and awareness, opening avenues for survivors of all backgrounds and genders.

Kiranjit's life serves as a poignant reminder that justice extends beyond legal definitions; it encompasses the learning and growth of society as it seeks to understand the deeper implications of trauma and the human experience.

# Honour-Based Violence and Killings: The Hidden War on Autonomy

Honour-based violence (HBV) represents one of the most deeply entrenched and complex forms of abuse, characterized by its cultural entwinement and silent operation within families, communities, and institutions. At its most extreme manifestation, honour-based violence culminates in honour killings, the premeditated murder of a family member, overwhelmingly female, who is perceived to have brought shame or dishonour upon her family or community. These acts are neither crimes of passion nor momentary lapses of control; instead, they are calculated and intentional expressions of power meant to restore perceived lost honour through irreversible harm and violence.

A critical point to understand about honour-based violence is that it does not find its roots in any specific religion, ethnicity, or nationality. Rather, it transcends ethnic, cultural, and geographic divides, revealing itself to be fundamentally about power and control. Often veiled under the guise of tradition, cultural obligation, or alleged religious values, HBV can encompass a broad spectrum of abusive behaviours, including physical violence, forced marriages, emotional manipulation, financial control, and social confinement. Unlike other forms of domestic violence, honour-based violence frequently involves collusion among multiple perpetrators, not merely the intimate partner, but also parents, siblings, extended family members, or even broader community actors, who collectively reinforce patriarchal norms and social expectations.

The psychological underpinnings of HBV are intricately linked to the collective identity of the family or community. When an individual's personal choices, such as declining an arranged marriage, adopting Western lifestyle practices, or pursuing a romantic relationship contrary to cultural expectations, challenge established social norms, they can be perceived as threats to the communal fabric. This perception often elicits not merely individual retaliation, but collective punishment, as the community reasserts control to send a resounding message: dissent and nonconformity will not be tolerated.

From a counselling and psychological perspective, honour-based violence presents unique challenges for intervention. Victims often grapple with profound loyalties to their families, feelings of cultural shame, and an overwhelming fear of social ostracism. Perpetrators frequently frame their abusive actions as protective, moral, or redemptive, leading to a distortion in the victim's understanding of right and wrong. This manipulation can leave victims feeling paralysed, caught between cultural expectations and their personal safety.

The most harrowing expression of HBV is the honour killing. In the UK, several high-profile cases, such as those of Heshu Yones, Shafilea Ahmed, and Banaz Mahmod, have brought to light the tragic consequences of this form of violence. For instance, Heshu was murdered at the age of 16 by her father for the perceived dishonour of dating a boy outside her ethnic group. Similarly, Shafilea, also just 17, faced suffocation at the hands of her parents for resisting an arranged marriage that contradicted her desires. Banaz Mahmod, after voicing her fears and reporting threats to the police multiple times, was ultimately murdered by her family for daring to leave an abusive husband.

The psychological aftermath of honour-based violence on victims can be profound and debilitating. Survivors often exhibit symptoms indicative of complex trauma: hypervigilance, dissociation, a shame-based identity distortion, and profound internalised guilt. In therapeutic settings, these individuals require culturally competent and trauma-informed care that acknowledges both the personal and collective dynamics of their abuse. Methodologies such as narrative therapy, grounding techniques, and identity-rebuilding work are essential to facilitating their healing journey.

Moreover, children who witness or are subjected to HBV experience enduring developmental harm. Their cognitive and emotional growth is hindered by chronic fear and a skewed understanding of social relationships. This environment can later manifest in adulthood as anxiety disorders, depression, deteriorated relational functioning, and even the perpetuation of abusive behaviours.

In the UK, honour-based killings are prosecuted under standard homicide laws. However, significant legislative developments like the Domestic Abuse Act 2021 have broadened the definitions of abuse to explicitly include coercive control, emotional abuse, and familial violence. Legal instruments such as Forced Marriage Protection Orders (FMPOs), the criminalisation of Female Genital Mutilation (FGM), and multi-agency frameworks like Multi-Agency Risk Assessment Conferences (MARAC) and the DASH (Domestic Abuse, Stalking and Harassment) model are crucial for effectively identifying and responding to instances of HBV.

A pivotal resource in the prevention of honour-based violence is the Power and Control Wheel, which maps the various ways in which control is enforced across emotional, economic, and cultural dimensions. Its counterpart, the Equality Wheel, delineates the characteristics of healthy and equitable relationships, serving both as an educational tool and a resource for therapy.

Organisations such as Karma Nirvana, Halo Project, and IKWRO provide urgent frontline support, advocacy, and safe housing for individuals at risk. However, effective service provision must extend beyond crisis intervention. Prevention requires proactive engagement with schools, community leaders, healthcare professionals, and policymakers to challenge the cultural narratives that perpetuate honour-based violence.

Ultimately, honour-based violence is not a question of culture; it is a matter of control. It represents a profound violation of human rights that must be identified, confronted, and eradicated with the same urgency accorded to other forms of systemic abuse. At the centre of this critical work must be the voices of survivors—restored, validated, and safeguarded.

To envision a world devoid of honour-based violence is to assert that no individual should ever have to choose between their cultural identity and their safety. Autonomy, dignity, and freedom are fundamental rights that belong to every human being, regardless of gender, faith, or familial legacy.

# Heshu Yones – The Price of Honour

There are some names that should never be remembered solely through tragedy but instead through their dreams, laughter, and the vibrant lives they never got to fully live. Heshu Yones is one of those names, symbolizing both the potential of youth and the harsh realities of cultural oppression.

At just sixteen, Heshu was a bright and spirited young woman with a life full of possibilities ahead of her. She loved music, excelled in school, and cherished her time spent with friends. Her intelligence was matched only by her warm heart and enduring optimism. However, in October 2002, her hope was brutally extinguished. Heshu became the first recorded victim of an honour killing in the UK, an act that transcends mere explanation, revealing profound betrayal, heartbreak, and an irremediable loss.

*Behind Closed Doors*

Heshu Yones was a British teenager of Kurdish-Iraqi heritage, living in Acton, West London, where the blend of cultural expectations shaped her daily life. Outwardly, she was like many girls her age, navigating the labyrinth of adolescence, forging friendships, and exploring her burgeoning identity. Behind her family's closed doors, however, she was subjected to an oppressive environment dominated by her father, Abdalla Yones. This man, who had fled the oppressive regime of Saddam Hussein, nevertheless embodied a deeply entrenched patriarchal mind-set that dictated every aspect of Heshu's life.

During a visit to Iraqi Kurdistan that summer, her family imposed a horrific violation upon her by subjecting her to a forced virginity test, an appalling assault on her bodily autonomy used to "verify" her honour. She was threatened by relatives that her life would be claimed if she were found to be "impure." Such threats were not mere conjecture; they were manifestations of a belief system in which a daughter's perceived morality was inextricably linked to her family's honour, where control was maintained through intimidation and fear.

*The Day Everything Changed*

On the fateful day of 12 October 2002, in the midst of rising tensions instigated by her growing independence and suspicions surrounding her relationships, Heshu's father turned to violence. In an act of premeditated brutality, he stabbed her multiple times and ultimately slit her throat. Heshu's life came to a painful end in the bathroom of their family home, the very place that should have been her sanctuary. Following his heinous act, her father attempted to take his own life. When interrogated by authorities, he chillingly stated, "My daughter was bringing shame on the family." This was not an outburst fuelled by rage but rather an expression of calculated control, cold, systematic, and deeply embedded in a patriarchal societal structure.

In 2003, Abdalla Yones was sentenced to life in prison. His case represented a pivotal moment in the UK's legal landscape, marking the first time honour-based violence was publicly acknowledged not as an aberration, but as a severe and targeted form of domestic abuse deserving of serious legal consideration.

*Psychological Undercurrents*

What transpired in Heshu's life was not an isolated incident; rather, it marked the tragic culmination of a prolonged pattern of coercive control. Psychological research and counselling practices indicate that many victims of honour-based abuse endure complex PTSD, stemming from the chronic stress of living under constant surveillance, threats, and psychological manipulation from their own families. For children like Heshu, life often becomes a delicate balancing act, externally conforming to societal expectations while internally yearning for autonomy. This ongoing self-monitoring leads to hypervigilance, fragmented identities, and profound internal conflict.

In therapeutic settings, survivors grapple with intense feelings of guilt, torn between love for their families and the fear that permeates their lives. These dynamics often create trauma bonds that normalize abuse and make the prospect of escape fraught with the fear of betraying one's cultural roots or community.

Heshu, like countless teenagers, sought to navigate her identity and forge her own path. Tragically, the price she paid for this exploration was her very life.

*Systemic Failures*

Heshu had voiced her fears to friends, confided her desire to escape, and documented her distress in a video diary. She even entrusted her passport to a friend, seeking safety. Despite these clear cries for help, the warning signs went unnoticed or unaddressed.

It is imperative for schools, social workers, and healthcare professionals to be equipped to recognize the signs of honour-based abuse, which often do not align with conventional models of domestic violence. Key indicators may include:

- Sudden and unexplained changes in behaviour or attendance
- Increased anxiety regarding family obligations, particularly concerning trips abroad
- Discomfort when discussing home life or familial relationships

- Secrecy surrounding romantic interests or friendships

In Heshu's case, the presence of these red flags was evident, yet they were not interpreted with the cultural sensitivity or urgency necessary to prevent her tragic end.

*Counselling Implications*

Effectively supporting survivors of honour-based abuse necessitates a culturally sensitive approach grounded in trauma-informed care and a deep sense of patience. The profound betrayal of being harmed by one's own family introduces layers of grief, identity confusion, and pervasive isolation.

Survivors need:

- Safe, non-judgmental spaces where they can express themselves openly
- Recognition that their experiences are valid and that cultural differences do not excuse abuse
- Assistance in navigating conflicting emotions such as love, grief, anger, and guilt
- Practical tools to aid in rebuilding trust, autonomy, and self-worth

Peer support emerges as a vital component of healing, as many survivors find solace and empowerment through connections with others who have faced similar challenges.

*Honouring Heshu*

The tragedy of Heshu Yones ignited a national conversation about honour-based violence, leading to important developments such as the UK's Forced Marriage Unit and the formulation of protocols for handling honour-based violence within law enforcement and safeguarding frameworks. Though her life was tragically cut short, she became a catalyst for change, driving the dialogue surrounding gender, culture, and domestic abuse forward.

However, the push for change must endure. Schools must evolve into more than mere educational institutions; they should transform into safe havens where young individuals like Heshu feel seen, heard, and protected. Responsibility must extend to families, regardless of cultural background, and society at large must amplify its collective voice, affirming that there is no honour in violence, and that every child's right to safety and autonomy must be upheld.

# Shafilea Ahmed – A Voice Crushed in the Name of Honour

Seventeen-year-old Shafilea Ahmed stood on the brink of adulthood, vibrant and ambitious, harbouring dreams of becoming a solicitor. However, beneath her warm personality lay a life shadowed by fear, control, and the weight of cultural expectations—demands she courageously refused to accept, a defiance that tragically led to her untimely demise.

*From Promise to Pressure*

Born in Bradford in 1986 to British-Pakistani parents, Shafilea was primarily raised in Warrington and became known for her academic brilliance and gentle spirit. She flourished in school, expressing her creativity through fashion and poetry, eagerly envisioning a future sculpted by her own choices.

However, as she began to explore her identity through Western clothing, hairstyles, and friendships, her family's traditional values began to clash violently with her burgeoning independence. Shafilea's parents perceived her evolving self-expression as a source of shame. Her mother reacted harshly, forcibly removing her false nails and hair dye, and subjecting her to derogatory insults, repeatedly calling her a "slut." These invasive actions were not mere disciplinary measures, but rather calculated tools of coercive control designed to suppress her autonomy and conform her to a restrictive cultural paradigm.

*Attempts at Escape*

At the tender age of 11, Shafilea initiated her first escape from the oppressive environment of her home. This act of defiance became a pattern over the next two years as she fled repeatedly, desperately seeking refuge. She confided in social services about the physical and emotional abuse she endured and articulated her fears of being forced into an arranged marriage in Pakistan. Unfortunately, the institutional barriers she faced thwarted her attempts at a lasting solution, leading her back into the constraints of her family life.

In February 2003, after being compelled to travel to Pakistan, she resorted to swallowing bleach, a desperate bid to escape the reality of marrying a stranger, a plight her family dismissively labelled as an accidental incident rather than recognizing the depths of her despair.

*Warning Signs Ignored*

After this harrowing episode, Shafilea was hospitalized due to her damaged throat and the visible scars of trauma etched on her spirit. However, despite the acute danger she faced, no long-term protective measures were implemented. Although her school identified bruising and listened to her pleas for help, they were ill-equipped with culturally sensitive protocols. Ultimately, social services closed Shafilea's case, blind to the urgent nature of her situation.

By September 2003, Shafilea vanished without a trace. Alarmingly, her parents did not report her missing, and it took a week of silence before her concerned teachers raised the alarm.

*A Hidden Tragedy*

Shafilea's body was discovered five months later, decomposed and concealed in the River Kent in Cumbria. Forensic examinations suggested that her death was akin to suffocation, leading police to suspect the involvement of honour motives; yet they lacked the concrete evidence necessary to charge her parents. The breakthrough came only when Alesha, her sister, summoned the courage to come forward eight years later to share the harrowing truth.

Alesha testified that she witnessed their father suffocate Shafilea with a plastic bag, spurred on by their mother's chilling declaration, "Let's finish it here." Following this, Alesha endured threats that forced her into silence, haunted by the fear of familial retaliation.

*Justice Delayed and Delivered*

In 2012, after Alesha's courageous testimony, Shafilea's parents were finally convicted and sentenced to life in prison, with a minimum of 25 years to serve. Nevertheless, the case illuminated systemic failures within institutions meant to protect vulnerable individuals highlighting cultural misunderstandings, institutional oversights, and the tragic delay in securing much-needed protection for Shafilea.

*Psychological & Counselling Insights*

Complex Trauma & Betrayal:

Shafilea endured cumulative trauma, ranging from earlier abuse to forced medical interventions, and threats that infiltrated every aspect of her life. These experiences manifested in self-harm, dissociation, and overwhelming feelings of helplessness, which became her psychological survival mechanisms.

Coercive Control & Honour-Based Violence:

The hostilities she faced, threats, punitive measures, coerced silence, and deliberate isolation, created a psychological prison that stripped her of the right to live freely.

Institutional Betrayal:

The lack of response to her SOS calls deepened her solitude and scepticism towards authority figures. For effective safeguarding, it is essential to foster cultural responsiveness and acknowledge the potential for parental harm, even within seemingly protective family structures.

Survivor Courage Amidst Shame:

Shafilea's poetry, her secret friendships, and her repeated escape attempts represented her indomitable spirit in the face of adversity. Many survivors of abuse echo that these seemingly small acts of defiance are laden with immense emotional risks, and they warrant protection, not punishment.

*Counselling Approaches*

Cultural Empathy & Validation:

Survivors like Shafilea navigate a tapestry of layered trauma, cultural expectations interwoven with familial harm. Therapeutic practices must validate their pain and respect their survival instincts rather than pathologise them.

Confidential & Non-Judgmental Spaces:

Support services should offer confidential disclosure channels, peer feedback avenues, and culturally savvy mediators to ensure that victims' voices are not silenced and crucial risk signals are not overlooked.

Early Intervention & Safety Planning:

Utilizing established tools like DASH and MARAC is critical, but these must be adapted specifically for honour-based violence risks. Acknowledging that the warnings of children may not easily conform to established checklists is paramount.

Supporting Sibling Witnesses:

Alesha's bravery in breaking her silence underscored the urgent need to support siblings who find themselves complicit witnesses to harm perpetrated under threats of coercion.

*Legacy of Change*

Shafilea's tragic death has spurred national reflection on honour-based violence. The UK established the National Day of Memory for Honour-Based Violence, and organizations such as Karma Nirvana advocate for the One Chance Rule the principle that victims may often have only a singular opportunity to disclose their abuse.

Her poignant words resonate through her poetry:
"I feel trapped so trapped … Will this ever go away?"
These lines remind us that captivity is not merely a physical state; it encompasses emotional, cultural, and systemic dimensions.

*What We Must Do Next*

Educate staff in educational and healthcare settings about culturo-behavioral signals that indicate risks such as forced marriage, secrecy, and the dynamics of honour and shame.

Create safe communication channels for adolescents, incorporating text messages, codes, and trusted allies, ensuring that they have a reliable pathway to seek help without fear.

*Reflection Prompt*

In our communities and institutions, the voices of teenagers often go unheard, silenced by the very structures that are meant to support them. This silence can manifest in various forms, from cultural expectations to systemic barriers that stifle their expression. It is vital to identify specific areas, like schools, community centres, and family settings, where teenagers may feel voiceless.

Creating safe moments for teenagers to express themselves requires intentional actions. We can establish listening circles where their perspectives are valued, or mentorship programs that empower them to share their experiences without fear of judgment. Additionally, fostering an inclusive environment that celebrates diversity can encourage teenagers from different backgrounds to speak up, knowing they will be heard and respected.

The tragic story of Shafilea Ahmed exemplifies the dangers of ignoring these voices. Her death was not merely a personal loss but a failure of cultural understanding, family dynamics, and institutional responses. Yet, amid this tragedy, Shafilea's small acts of defiance and her sister's brave emergence as a spokesperson shine through as powerful reminders that resistance exists even in the darkest of circumstances.

Her narrative is more than just one among many; it serves as a crucial beacon for change. By committing to listen, taking action, and holding institutions accountable, we can create a future where the next teenager who voices feelings of entrapment, be it emotional, cultural, or social will find open ears and supportive hands. In doing so, we pave the way toward their autonomy and freedom, transforming silent struggles into powerful movements for change.

# Banaz Mahmod – Buried by Blood, Remembered by Truth

Banaz Mahmod was only twenty years old when her life was tragically cut short in an act that would reveal the pervasive and harrowing reality of honour-based abuse in Britain. To many outsiders, she was merely a British-Iraqi woman from a Kurdish Muslim family in South London. Yet, behind the façade of her suburban home lay a young woman who had endured immense suffering, survivor of forced marriage, familial violence, and systemic neglect, tirelessly advocating for her right to live and love freely.

Her narrative is not solely a tale of a life extinguished prematurely; it is also a poignant illustration of how cultural expectations, fear, coercion, and institutional failures can converge, creating a silence that ultimately leads to deadly consequences.

*A Childhood in the Shadow of Control*

Banaz arrived in the UK from Iraq in 1998 at just ten years old, entering a new life in a foreign land with hopes of experiencing freedom and educational opportunities. However, her adolescence became marred by constant fear and oppression. At the tender age of seventeen, she was coerced into marrying a much older man, a decision orchestrated by her family under the guise of preserving cultural integrity and familial reputation. This marriage, like many forced unions, soon descended into a nightmare; Banaz faced not only rape and physical violence but also emotional degradation at the hands of her husband.

In a courageous attempt to escape this torment, Banaz returned to her family seeking refuge and support, hoping to find safety in the arms of those she loved. Instead, she faced betrayal and manipulation. Her parents, prioritizing cultural honour over her autonomy, pressured her to return to her husband. In the suffocating context of their beliefs, her desire for independence was misconstrued as a dishonour to the family.

*Coercive Control in Its Most Chilling Form*

What Banaz suffered was not simply domestic violence; it was a terrifying manifestation of coercive control exacerbated by honour-based violence. This type of abuse consists of a relentless pattern of intimidation, isolation, and psychological manipulation intended to in still a sense of helplessness in the victim. In Banaz's situation, this coercive control was enforced not merely by one individual but by an entire familial unit intent on maintaining a façade of honour.

Banaz was subjected to constant monitoring, silencing, and intimidation whenever she attempted to assert her own choices. Her budding relationship with another man, Rahmat Sulemani, based on mutual respect and shared aspirations, ignited furious reprisals from her family. Her father, Mahmod, and uncle, Ari Mahmod, conspired to murder her in a desperate effort to "restore" the honour they believed was irreparably lost through her quest for autonomy.

*Warning Signs and Systemic Failures*

In a valiant effort to seek help, Banaz reached out to the police on five different occasions. On one alarming occasion, she meticulously penned a letter naming those she feared would take her life, her father and uncle among them. Shockingly, her pleas for assistance were dismissed; officers belittled her, viewing her as an attention-seeker or melodramatic. This tragic misjudgement, fuelled by institutional ignorance regarding the complexities of honour-based violence, further compounded her anguish.

When survivors are not believed, their paths to safety are thwarted. For Banaz, the chasm between refuge and peril narrowed alarmingly quickly. On January 24, 2006, she was abducted from her family home. In a brutal and unfathomable act of violence, her cousin strangled her with a shoelace for over five agonizing minutes as she fought valiantly for her life, clawing at the walls in desperation. Her lifeless body was ultimately concealed in a suitcase and buried in a Birmingham garden.

It took three harrowing months before her remains were discovered.

*The Aftermath: Fighting for Justice*

Detective Chief Inspector Caroline Goode spearheaded the investigation into this horrific murder. What ensued was one of the most intricate honour killing cases in British history, entailing not only hidden mobile phones and intercepted communications but also international efforts to extradite suspects who had fled to Iraq.

After a protracted fight for justice, her father, uncle, and three accomplices were convicted and sentenced to life in prison. This case became a historical landmark, representing the first instance in the UK where individuals implicated in an honour-based killing were extradited from overseas. Moreover, it ignited a critical national dialogue concerning the dangers of cultural sensitivity overshadowing the urgent need to confront systemic abuse.

*The Psychology of Honour-Based Abuse*

At its essence, honour-based abuse springs from distorted collectivist values, where the family or community's reputation is prioritized over the individual's rights. Women are often objectified as embodiments of purity and obedience, and any pursuit of autonomy whether in love, expression, career, or individuality invites severe repercussions.

Psychologically, survivors of honour-based abuse confront a unique and harrowing double trauma: the violence itself and the deeply painful betrayal from family members who are typically seen as trusted protectors. Mental health professionals assisting such survivors must employ culturally informed trauma frameworks, acknowledging not just the violence endured but also the identity disintegration that occurs when the concepts of safety and family begin to clash.

Banaz's trauma was profound and multi-layered. Experts propose that she may have suffered from complex PTSD, a condition arising from repeated, inescapable abuse compounded by systemic failures and an absence of therapeutic resources. With her nervous system perpetually on high alert, her final attempts to seek help can be viewed as incredible acts of bravery from a young woman who had been systematically silenced and marginalised.

*Lessons in Prevention and Protection*

Banaz's tragic murder was avoidable, and her story imparts vital lessons:

1. We must believe survivors: When someone confides in us about their perception of danger, we must take their concerns seriously.
2. Enhance training for law enforcement: Officers must receive education on recognizing the signs of honour-based violence and coercive control.
3. Empower community dialogue: Conversations around cultural norms and their implications on personal freedoms need to be more widespread and honest.
4. Provide resources: Survivors of honour-based violence require access to comprehensive support

networks, including legal assistance and mental health services that are sensitive to cultural contexts.

Banaz Mahmod's story is a powerful reminder of the urgent need for cultural sensitivity combined with unwavering commitment to protect the fundamental rights of individuals, particularly women, who may suffer at the intersection of tradition and modernity. Her legacy calls for an ongoing dialogue about honour, autonomy, and the means to ensure that no one else endures the same fate.

# Female Genital Mutilation (FGM): Understanding and Supporting Survivors

### What Is FGM?

Female Genital Mutilation (FGM), commonly referred to as cutting, circumcision, or female genital cutting entails the partial or complete removal or alteration of the external female genitalia for non-medical purposes. This deeply rooted cultural practice has no health benefits and is recognized globally as a violation of women's rights, dignity, and bodily autonomy. The World Health Organization (WHO) reports that more than 200 million girls and women worldwide have suffered from FGM, with approximately 3 million girls at risk annually. In the United Kingdom, it's estimated that over 100,000 women and girls between the ages of 15 and 49 are living with the physical and psychological consequences of FGM.

### Health & Psychological Impact

The ramifications of FGM are severe and multifaceted, causing both immediate and long-term physical health complications. These include excessive bleeding, increased susceptibility to infections, infertility, complications during childbirth, and, in extreme cases, death. The psychological toll is equally significant, as studies indicate that survivors of FGM have a markedly increased likelihood of developing Post-Traumatic Stress Disorder (PTSD), depression, anxiety, and various somatic disorders. This risk is amplified in cases where more extensive forms of FGM are practiced. A review conducted in the UK revealed that over 80% of survivors reported experiencing trauma-related disorders. Additionally, survivors who underwent FGM during childhood often carry lasting emotional scars, manifesting as profound shame, anxiety, and difficulties in establishing trust with others.

## Legal Framework in the UK

FGM has been illegal in the UK since the enactment of the Prohibition of Female Circumcision Act in 1985. This was followed by the introduction of the Female Genital Mutilation Act in 2003, which was further strengthened by the Serious Crime Act in 2015. The legal framework encompasses several critical provisions, such as:

- Extraterritorial Jurisdiction: Individuals based in the UK can be prosecuted for facilitating FGM abroad.
- Mandatory Reporting: Professionals working with minors are obliged to report any suspicions regarding FGM.
- FGM Prevention Orders: Specific legal measures that can impose penalties, including up to 14 years in prison, for individuals involved in FGM practices.
- Family Court Considerations: Recent amendments to the Children Act ensure that cases related to FGM are addressed within family court settings.

Despite these legal protections, the prosecution rate remains alarmingly low. The first successful prosecution for the practice of FGM in the UK occurred in 2019, with a ground-breaking conviction for arranging an FGM procedure following in 2024.

## Trauma-Informed Counselling & Support

For survivors, receiving trauma-informed care is imperative. Many experience feelings of shame and guilt, and it's crucial for therapists to validate their experiences, affirming that FGM is a form of non-consensual abuse that leads to lasting trauma.

- Cognitive Behavioural Therapy (CBT): This therapeutic approach has proven effective in treating mental health conditions such as PTSD, depression, and anxiety. The WHO recommends CBT as a key intervention both before and after deinfibulation (surgical reversal of FGM) to help survivors cope with their experiences.

- Pre- and Post-Deinfibulation Support: Providing counselling before and after surgical intervention aids survivors in navigating the significant physical and emotional transitions, addressing concerns related to fear, identity, and intimacy.

- Somatic and Body-Integrated Approaches: Therapeutic practices that focus on mindful movement and body-centred therapies help survivors regain confidence in their bodies, facilitating a sense of safety and autonomy.

- Cultural Sensitivity and Community Engagement: Interventions should respect the cultural nuances of the communities they serve while actively challenging harmful practices. Initiatives such as the Orchid Project focus on fostering community-led efforts to abandon FGM. Support groups like Daughters of Eve play a critical role in integrating survivor narratives with advocacy, particularly within diaspora communities.

**Clinical & Systemic Responsibilities**

Healthcare and education professionals, including midwives, general practitioners, teachers, and social workers are vital in identifying and addressing FGM:

- Recognizing signs of FGM and the risk of "vacation cutting" when families travel abroad.
- Complying with mandatory reporting laws for underage individuals.

- Offering confidential, trauma-informed counselling and facilitating medical referrals for effective treatment, including reconstruction or deinfibulation.
- Specialist NHS clinics established since 2014 provide comprehensive medical and psychological support tailored to the needs of FGM survivors.

**A Survivor's Journey to Healing**

Nimco Ali, a survivor of FGM who underwent the procedure at just seven years old, now advocates fervently for those affected by this practice. Her journey emphasizes that healing is achievable through psychological therapy, robust community support, empowerment, and concerted advocacy efforts. Ali highlights the importance of reclaiming one's voice, resilience, and identity as integral to the healing process.

# Breaking the Silence – Nimco Ali and the War on FGM

Female Genital Mutilation (FGM) is an issue that is often whispered about, if it is discussed at all. It is frequently framed as a "cultural tradition" or a "rite of passage," which obscures the profound violence and trauma it imposes on millions of girls across the globe. At its essence, FGM is not about hygiene, morality, or femininity; it is fundamentally about control. Control over a woman's body, autonomy, and identity. Among those brave enough to confront this silence is Nimco Ali, an extraordinary advocate fighting against this deeply ingrained practice.

Nimco Ali was born in Somaliland and raised in the UK. At the tender age of seven, she underwent FGM during what she believed to be a family holiday in Djibouti. The procedure was brutal and traumatic, performed without anaesthetic in a makeshift clinic. A woman, armed with a razor blade, inflicted immediate and excruciating pain, leaving Nimco with long-lasting psychological and physical health issues. Years later, she collapsed due to an infection stemming from the procedure, requiring reconstructive surgery that served as a painful reminder of her past. Yet, it wasn't solely her physical body that needed repair; her voice, self-worth, and ability to trust were also fractured in a world that often prefers to ignore such realities.

The World Health Organization recognizes FGM as a violation of human rights and a form of gender-based violence. It is classified into four distinct types, all involving the alteration or injury of the female genitalia for non-medical reasons. The psychological and emotional repercussions can be severe and enduring. Survivors of FGM are often burdened with complex trauma, PTSD, anxiety, depression, sexual dysfunction, and feelings of betrayal. For many women, the pain of their experience is not something confined to memory; it persists as a living wound, resurfacing in relationships, during medical examinations, and amidst the pervasive silence surrounding the issue.

Nimco's experience reflects a broader crisis; over 200 million women and girls globally have experienced FGM. In the UK, it is estimated that tens of thousands of girls are at risk, frequently being subjected to “cutting holidays” overseas. The psychological manipulation surrounding FGM is often insidious. Girls are taught that undergoing this act is the price of being deemed “pure,” “marriageable,” or “honourable.” Those who resist face severe consequences, such as social ostracisation or even violence.

However, Nimco Ali chose a different narrative. Rather than remain silent, she emerged as one of the most prominent voices advocating against FGM. In 2010, she co-founded Daughters of Eve, a non-profit organization dedicated to supporting survivors and raising awareness in communities about the devastating effects of FGM. Nimco broke through social taboos by publicly sharing her story through interviews, speeches, and even donning a giant "vagina costume" to highlight the absurdity of enduring such silence. While her outspokenness led to death threats, social isolation from parts of her community, and political backlash, it also inspired healing, not only for herself but for countless others.

Nimco’s activism is deeply informed by her experiences of trauma. She frames FGM not merely as an act of violence but as a systemic betrayal of bodily autonomy. Understanding that true healing for survivors involves more than just physical recovery, Nimco emphasizes the need to reclaim one’s body, voice, and narrative. This approach aligns with concepts in therapy and trauma psychology, particularly the idea of post-traumatic growth. This concept suggests that individuals can emerge from suffering not simply as victims but as transformed individuals, possessing a renewed sense of identity and purpose.

In her ongoing commitment to end FGM, Nimco co-founded The Five Foundation, an organization dedicated to eradicating FGM worldwide by supporting survivor-led initiatives, influencing public policy, and shifting the focus from victimhood to empowerment. In 2020, she was appointed as the UK Government's Independent Adviser on Tackling Violence Against Women and Girls, where she played a crucial role in shaping national strategies, advocating for intersectional approaches, and framing FGM as both a safeguarding issue and a mental health concern rather than purely a legal matter.

Nimco often states that speaking out essentially saved her life. Her voice became a formidable weapon against silence, illuminating the dark corners of institutional neglect. She authored "What We're Told Not to Talk About," a compelling anthology featuring real stories from women around the globe on taboo subjects such as sex, menstruation, abuse, and shame. Her mission is to cultivate a world in which girls are not coerced into "being good" but are empowered to embrace their freedom.

Survivors of FGM frequently contend with what psychologists define as complex PTSD, a form of trauma resulting from ongoing abuse rather than a singular event. Healing requires going beyond the removal of physical scar tissue; it necessitates shedding internalized shame, rebuilding trust in interpersonal relationships, and fostering a new connection with one's body. Many survivors, Nimco included, find comfort and healing through storytelling, community advocacy, body-centred healing practices, and trauma-informed therapies like EMDR and sensorimotor psychotherapy.

Nimco Ali's legacy is still unfolding, but its significance is undeniable. She has transformed her personal trauma into a powerful catalyst for global reform, opening discussions on issues that were once considered untouchable. She has challenged the complicity of silence and compelled policymakers, healthcare professionals, and communities to pay attention and act.

Nimco's resounding message is clear: FGM is not a cultural practice; it is a crime. Survivors are not weak; they are warriors.

**Reflection**

As we reflect on Nimco's story, we are invited to engage with deeper inquiries:
What injustices thrive in silence around us?
What taboos prevent survivors from sharing their stories and seeking justice?

**Key Takeaways**

- FGM constitutes a grave human rights violation with profound physical, psychological, and emotional consequences for survivors.
- While UK law provides essential frameworks for protection, prevention, and legal recourse, actual enforcement remains lacking.
- Access to trauma-informed, culturally sensitive mental health care (including CBT, somatic therapies, and narrative counselling) is crucial for fostering recovery among survivors.
- Community-driven initiatives that empower individuals and challenge the normalization of FGM practices are essential for dismantling the cycle of harm.

# First Loves, First Bruises – Understanding Teen Dating Abuse

Adolescence is a tumultuous time when many young people experience first love, but it can also be a period marked by profound emotional and psychological challenges. Teen dating abuse (TDA) is not merely a minor issue that affects a few individuals; it is a serious and multifaceted form of domestic violence that is intricately linked to the developmental stage of teenagers, the dynamics of peer relationships, and the pervasive influence of digital culture.

*1. The Hidden Landscape*

In the UK, the prevalence of teen dating abuse is alarmingly high. Recent statistics reveal that 25% of girls and 17% of boys aged 13 to 17 report having experienced physical abuse in their romantic relationships. Even more concerning is the prevalence of emotional or psychological abuse, which affects around 72% of girls and 51% of boys in this age group. Among those who have dated in the past year, nearly 49% have encountered violent or controlling behaviour in their relationships.

Despite these staggering figures, many teenagers endure these experiences in silence, often perceiving such behaviour as a normal aspect of teenage romance. This normalization of abuse is a significant factor that allows it to persist and escalate.

*2. Why Teens Are Vulnerable*

A. Identity in Formation

Teenagers are in a critical phase of developing their identity and often view their first romantic relationships as essential indicators of their self-worth. They may confuse jealousy for love and interpret controlling behaviour as a sign of care and devotion.

B. No Relational Map

Most teens lack previous relationship experience, making it difficult for them to establish healthy boundaries. Without clear examples to reference, they may not recognize coercion when it arises, leaving them vulnerable to manipulative dynamics.

C. Brains Under Construction

The adolescent brain is still developing, particularly the prefrontal cortex, which is responsible for impulse control and decision-making. As a result, teens are more likely to act on emotion rather than reason, increasing their susceptibility to coercive tactics from partners.

D. Digital Coercion

In today's digital age, technology serves as a double-edged sword. While it facilitates communication, it can also become a tool for control. Constant messaging, location tracking, and demands for password sharing are just some of the methods abusers use to maintain power in a relationship.

*3. Patterns of Abuse*

Teen dating abuse typically unfolds in stages, each building upon the last:

- Love-bombing: The relationship often begins with overwhelming attention and affection, characterized by frequent texts and compliments.
- Control: This phase introduces a shift in tone, where jealousy and criticism begin to surface, making the victim feel guilty or insecure.

- Emotional Manipulation: The abuser may isolate the victim from friends and family, using tactics like gas lighting to distort their perception of reality.
- Physical or Sexual Coercion: This stage may involve explicit acts of physical or sexual violence, sometimes occurring without consent.
- Secrecy and Entrapment: Over time, victims may find themselves trapped in a cycle of abuse, marked by silence and fear.

The impact of such experiences can lead to long-lasting trauma, manifesting as PTSD, depression, self-harm, and substance misuse, potentially affecting survivors well into adulthood.

*4. Alice's Story*

Seventeen-year-old Alice thought Rory's intense attention was a sign of love until it crossed a line. At a party, Rory physically pinned her down and kissed her forcefully. When she struggled and cried, he twisted her emotional response, insisting that her refusal was proof of a lack of love.

Afterwards, Rory's obsessive need for control surfaced, as he frequently checked her phone and bombarded her with angry texts when she didn't reply immediately. It wasn't until Alice encountered awareness-raising campaign posters at her school that she recognized her experience as abuse rather than affection. Now at 20, Alice reflects on the lasting scars this relationship left on her ability to trust others. She advocates for awareness, hoping her story resonates with those experiencing similar situations.

*5. Psychological & Counselling Approaches*

To effectively address and mitigate the effects of teen dating abuse, several therapeutic interventions can be utilized:

A. Psychoeducation: It's crucial to help teens identify and normalize their feelings, recognizing that jealousy is not love and restrictions are not acts of care.
B. Cognitive Restructuring: This involves challenging harmful beliefs, such as "If he loved me, he wouldn't be jealous," helping teens reframe their thinking.
C. Somatic Relief: Techniques such as mindfulness, body-awareness practices, and yoga can assist in releasing trauma that may be stored within the nervous system.
D. Group Therapy: Participating in peer-led support groups can foster trust among participants and help dismantle feelings of shame associated with abuse.
E. Family Involvement: Equipping parents with the tools and language to support their teens without placing blame is essential.

These approaches align with trauma-informed care principles and adolescent developmental psychology.

*6. Role of Schools and Community*

A. Operation Encompass

In efforts to provide sensitive support, police notify schools when domestic incidents involving students occur. This proactive approach allows schools to offer trauma-informed responses as soon as the students arrive on campus.

A. PSHE and Prevention Programmes

Programs like Pretty 'n' Pearly and the Youth Endowment Fund toolkit are examples of effective curriculums that teach consent, healthy boundaries, and the digital dimension of control. Such education has been shown to reduce the incidence of abuse among teens.

B. DSL Training

Designated Safeguarding Leads (DSLs) in schools that receive specialized training report feeling more confident in identifying and responding to instances of abuse, indicating the importance of proper training in safeguarding practices.

*7. After Escape: Healing and Hope*

For those who have escaped abusive relationships, effective post-abuse interventions are essential to foster healing and resilience:

- Referrals to CAMHS or Child line can provide specialized trauma care tailored for young people.
- Peer support programs can help combat isolation and promote emotional resilience.
- Restorative justice initiatives, where safe and voluntary, can enable teens to process the harm they've experienced and begin to rebuild trust.
- School-wide awareness campaigns ensure that survivors are visible and supported, rather than erased or silenced.

*8. Long-Term Impact*

The echoes of teen dating abuse do not simply fade away—it leaves a lasting imprint on the lives of those affected.

- It shapes expectations for future relationships, often leading individuals to carry their trauma into adulthood.
- Survivors may face an increased risk of experiencing abuse in later relationships.
- The impact on education, mental health, and self-concept can be profound and pervasive.

Recognizing that "first love" need not equate to a first wound is vital. With appropriate support, teens can heal, learn valuable lessons, and emerge stronger.

*Reflection & Action*

Consider the following questions regarding the mental and emotional health of the teens in your life:

- Who is monitoring your teen's psychosocial health both online and offline?
- What boundaries and communication guidelines have you established concerning digital interactions?
- Does your school's safeguarding policy incorporate teen dating education and guidelines for disclosure?

*Empowerment for Survivors*

To anyone reading this, either at home or in school, know the following:

You deserve respect. You deserve trust. If your partner is making you feel small or insignificant, remember that you have the right to seek help. You are not alone, and there are resources available to support you in recognizing your worth and reclaiming your voice.

# Between the Lines – Police & Justice System Responses

Even after the difficult decision to leave an abusive situation, many survivors find themselves ensnared in a second harrowing ordeal: navigating the criminal justice system. Unfortunately, this system, which is supposed to offer protection and support, often ends up re-traumatizing survivors through various mechanisms, including initial police responses, court hearings, and the overall treatment they receive. In these environments, survivors may find themselves reliving their trauma amid silences, dismissals, delays, and failures by a system meant to shield them.

1. When the First Responder Fails

Survivors frequently report having to disclose their abuse multiple times before receiving any meaningful intervention. Research from Victim Support indicates that ethnic minority victims face a staggering 50% rate of dismissal upon their first reports, with many only being taken seriously after repeated attempts to seek help. This pattern fosters feelings of frustration and helplessness.

Compounding the issue, survivors often experience a troubling inversion of blame during their interactions with first responders. Phrases like, "What did you do to make them hit you?" are not uncommon, illustrating how victims may be treated as the perpetrators of their own circumstances. Such questions and attitudes perpetuate a damaging narrative of self-blame and shame.

In cases where police officers themselves are accused of domestic violence, the situation becomes even more alarming. Findings from the Centre for Women's Justice reveal that abusive officers often receive protection from within the ranks, leading to their continued employment or promotions, sometimes even to roles that involve handling domestic violence cases. This reality severely undermines survivors' confidence in law enforcement and the justice system overall, making them feel isolated and unsupported.

2. Secondary Victimization in the System

The concept of secondary victimization, where victims experience further harm through their interactions with the justice process is alarmingly prevalent. When a survivor's account is met with scepticism, their fragmented memories are dismissed, or their emotional responses are invalidated, the initial trauma is often exacerbated rather than alleviated. This dynamic is particularly troubling when considering symptoms associated with PTSD, such as emotional numbness and fragmented recall. Instead of being met with compassionate and understanding questioning, many survivors encounter suspicion and disbelief, reinforcing feelings of shame and inadequacy, and leading some to withdraw from the quest for justice entirely.

3. Family Courts: A Different Battlefield

The family court system poses additional challenges for survivors seeking justice. A review by the Ministry of Justice has highlighted that nearly 90% of survivors receive no support during family court hearings, and a staggering 71% report a total lack of support within criminal or civil courts. The prevailing judicial norms that prioritize "parental equality" can lead to situations where victims are forced into unsafe living arrangements, further perpetuating their trauma.

Expert analyses in counselling psychology characterize this as a form of re-traumatization, whereby survivors find themselves back in the court environment, often facing their abusers directly during cross-examinations an experience that can feel suffocating and controlling, reminiscent of their previous trauma.

4. Small Victories: Special Measures & IDVAs

Despite these challenges, there have been some important reforms that can offer critical protection for survivors:

- Special Measures: Established under the Youth Justice and Criminal Evidence Act 1999, these measures include the use of screens, video-link testimony, and the ability to exclude the abuser from the same courtroom, helping to create a safer environment for survivors during legal proceedings.

- Victims' Code of Practice: This code guarantees certain rights for victims, including clear updates on their cases, referrals to support services, and entitlement to compensation for their suffering.

- Independent Domestic Violence Advisors (IDVAs): These professionals provide personalized and survivor-centred support, helping victims navigate the complexities of the legal system from the crisis point to stability, ensuring that their needs are prioritized throughout the process.

While these reforms represent significant steps forward, they are not universally applied, leaving many survivors without the protection they need.

5. Where the System Still Falters

Despite the positive changes that have been made, considerable gaps continue to exist:

- Inconsistent Implementation: Not all survivors are afforded the benefits of special measures, with reports of delays and outright refusals still occurring far too frequently.

- Restricted IDVA Access: Alarmingly, over 20% of survivors in family courts report being denied access to IDVA support, leaving them without essential guidance during their legal battles.

- Judicial and Police Culture: Institutional inertia often results in survivors being judged based on outdated stereotypes rather than trauma-informed principles, further alienating them from the justice process.

- Lack of Accountability: The absence of accountability for abusive professionals within the system continues to erode survivors' trust in law enforcement and legal authorities.

6. Psychological Insights: Supporting Through the Process

To more effectively support survivors navigating the justice system, several key considerations need to be addressed:

- Validation and Education: Survivors must be made aware that their experiences of trauma do not signify weakness; rather, they are indicative of the profound effects that abuse can have on an individual.

- Holistic Support: Collaboration among IDVAs, mental health professionals, and legal advisors is critical to providing comprehensive support for survivors.

- Trauma-Informed Spaces: Both courts and police stations should strive to create environments that feel safe and welcoming for survivors, reducing feelings of hostility and anxiety.

- Empathy Training for Staff: It is essential that staff working within the justice system receive training focused on trauma, particularly how it impacts memory, emotional responses, and communication.

- Counselling psychology emphasizes that when we respect and listen to survivors' voices, we begin to restore the power that was taken from them through abuse.

7. Systemic Reform Roadmap

To achieve meaningful reform, targeted changes are required across various areas of the justice system:

- Police: Implement mandatory training for officers and establish external oversight for abuse cases involving law enforcement professionals to ensure accountability.

- Courts: Guarantee automatic access to IDVAs and special measures for all survivors, and limit the ability of abusers to cross-examine their victims.

- Victims' Code: Increase public awareness of the rights outlined in the Victims' Code and establish feedback mechanisms for survivors to report instances of non-compliance.

- Judicial Review: Commit to tracking and publishing data on the time taken for case resolution and the satisfaction levels of victims involved.

- Cultural Overhaul: Embed trauma-informed, gender-aware, and diversity training within all agencies involved in the justice process, fostering a more supportive framework for survivors.

Addressing these issues is essential to create a justice system that truly protects and empowers survivors rather than further victimizing them.

# When the Law Steps in – Protective Orders Against Abuse

For many survivors of domestic violence, the experience of entering a courtroom can feel just as isolating as the moment they dial 999 for emergency help. However, for those who find themselves in such perilous situations, a protective order acts as a legal shield—a vital lifeline that can offer a degree of safety and peace of mind. This chapter delves into the mechanics of protective orders, how they serve to safeguard survivors, their limitations, and the critical importance of accompanying psychological support.

*Understanding Protective Orders*

In England and Wales, the Family Law Act 1996 provides two primary forms of civil orders designed to protect individuals from abuse:

1. Non-Molestation Order (NMO):

An NMO is specifically formulated to prevent various forms of abuse that can range from physical and emotional to sexual, financial, and psychological harassment. This order legally prohibits the abuser from making any form of contact with the survivor, from entering their shared residence, or approaching them and their children. Courts have the option to include a power of arrest clause, which allows police to arrest the abuser if they breach the order. Breaching an NMO is classified as a criminal offense that could lead to imprisonment for up to five years.

2. Occupation Order:

This order governs the living arrangements of individuals involved in a domestic setting, determining who may reside in the home or return, who should be excluded, and sometimes outlining access to shared areas. This is especially beneficial in situations where relationships have undergone a dramatic transformation, thereby necessitating a reallocation of living spaces.

In addition to these traditional orders, the Domestic Abuse Act 2021 introduced two new forms of protective measures aimed at enhancing immediate safety for survivors:

1. Domestic Violence Protection Notices (DVPN):

   These are temporary emergency notices issued by police, allowing for the immediate removal of a perpetrator from the victim's home. They are designed to provide rapid response and protection during critical situations when risk levels may be elevated.

2. Domestic Abuse Protection Orders (DAPO):

   Currently in a trial phase, DAPOs aim to streamline and unify the protection process under one enforceable court order. This new type of order seeks to simplify the legal framework that victims must navigate, although its implementation remains uneven and primarily limited to pilot areas.

*Who Can Apply—and How?*

Survivors of domestic violence, or a trusted individual acting on their behalf, can apply for Non-Molestation Orders and Occupation Orders at no cost. The application process requires the completion of specific forms, and applicants must establish a connection to the respondent, this can include relationships such as spouses, fiancés, family members, cohabitants, or parents of shared children.

Courts can grant interim orders on an ex parte basis, meaning they do not need to notify the abuser beforehand to provide immediate protection. These interim measures can be revisited within approximately two weeks for a full hearing to establish longer-term arrangements. Most protective orders are typically valid for a duration of six to twelve months, although extensions can be sought if threats persist.

*Psychological Effects & Re-traumatization*

A Mixed Blessing

For many survivors, obtaining a protective order can represent a significant step towards empowerment and self-advocacy, serving as the first official recognition of their experiences with abuse. However, the court environment can often exacerbate feelings of trauma. The process of recounting their fears, presenting evidence, or encountering their abuser during hearings can feel akin to reliving some of the most distressing moments of their lives.

As a result, survivors may experience increased levels of anxiety, sleeplessness, and emotional fatigue. Therefore, it's crucial that support systems include trauma-informed counselling that not only acknowledges but actively addresses these psychological impacts. Effective support should involve a combination of grounding techniques, psychoeducation about legal rights, and emotional validation to help survivors navigate this challenging terrain.

*When Orders Protect and When They Don't*

Successes:

- The immediate exclusion of the perpetrator and the police's power to arrest for breaches can provide crucial safety measures in real-time.
- Occupation Orders allow survivors the necessary time and space to establish new living

circumstances, fostering a sense of stability and control.

- Limitations:
- Enforcement remains inconsistent; numerous media reports and survivor testimonials indicate a troubling pattern of breaches occurring with little to no police action.
- Some courts may omit the power of arrest in certain situations, thereby diminishing the effectiveness of the protective measures.
- The rollout of DAPOs is still in its infancy and remains limited to a few areas, resulting in unequal access to protective solutions across the country.

Professional Insight

Counsellors emphasize that while legal mechanisms for protection are essential, they are insufficient on their own. Survivors require clear explanations of the legal process, preparation for court proceedings, and emotional care post-hearing to help them process their experiences.

Moreover, therapeutic approaches should address the unrealistic fears surrounding “failure” when abusers may attempt to manipulate the situation or when delays occur in the court process. Safety planning should also incorporate practical support measures, such as emergency funding, advice on technology safety, and options for safe housing.

*Systemic Gaps & Proposed Reforms*

Area Needs:

- Consistency: It is imperative to establish power-of-arrest clauses in all Non-Molestation Orders to enhance enforcement and deterrence.

- Enforcement: There should be a mandate for police follow-up on breaches of protective orders to ensure accountability.
- DAPOs Rollout: The implementation of Domestic Abuse Protection Orders should expand beyond pilot programs to a nationwide standard.
- Survivor Pathways: Automatic offers of Independent Domestic Violence Advocates (IDVA) should accompany orders, alongside coordinated guidance from courts and police to streamline the support process.
- Training: There is a warrant for enhanced training for magistrates, police officers, and legal staff to adopt trauma-informed procedures, enhancing the overall experience for survivors engaging with the legal system.

In conclusion, while protective orders serve as crucial tools in the fight against domestic abuse, their effectiveness is often contingent upon consistent enforcement, comprehensive support for survivors, and systemic reforms aimed at addressing existing gaps within the legal framework.

# When the Justice System Turns Its Back

We turn to the police and courts with the expectation that they will serve as our protectors, acknowledge our experiences, and ultimately deliver justice. However, for numerous survivors of abuse, that promise remains tragically unfulfilled.

Take the case of Shana Grice, a 19-year-old woman from Sussex whose life was cut short in a horrific manner. Shana endured a profound ordeal, facing relentless stalking by her ex-partner, Michael Lane. She reported a series of alarming incidents: damage to her car, unwanted gifts, persistent phone harassment, and even a terrifying intrusion into her bedroom while she slept. Instead of receiving the help she desperately needed, Sussex Police initially penalized her with a fine for "wasting their time," claiming she hadn't specified the details of her relationship history clearly enough. Despite Shana's repeated appeals for help and the fact that thirteen other women had reported Lane for similar behaviour, investigators tragically treated her case as low-risk. Ultimately, her file was closed, overshadowed by systemic assumptions and biases that trivialized her plight. On July 5, 2016, Shana was murdered by Lane. At the trial, the judge characterised the police response as "woefully inadequate," leading to disciplinary proceedings against three officers in 2019, though the police force initially dismissed the failure as a minor issue.

Shana's harrowing story is emblematic of a broader trend across England and Wales, where police and judicial systems repeatedly fail survivors. Many experience minimizations of their abuse, non-recognition of controlling behaviour, neglect of repeated calls for help, and poor management of protective measures. A report by the Domestic Abuse Commissioner, Dame Nicole Jacobs, found alarming inefficiencies in the enforcement of protective orders, highlighting that convictions are infrequent, breaches often go unnoticed, and referrals for specialized victim support are inconsistent. Research from Victim Support reveals a troubling pattern: victims, especially from marginalized communities, frequently report their abuse multiple times before action is taken, sometimes only being heard after several attempts.

The challenges extend into the courtroom, where the atmosphere can re-traumatize survivors. Trials can extend over lengthy periods, and the questioning process often brings back painful memories without any sensitivity to the individual's emotional state. Court waiting areas provide little comfort or privacy, and while the presence of Independent Domestic Violence Advocates (IDVAs) can be life-saving, many survivors find this support unavailable despite its intended status as a universal right under the Victims' Code.

Even legislative efforts like Clare's Law, which is designed to grant individuals insight into their partner's history regarding abuse, have revealed systemic failures. For instance, Wiltshire Police acknowledged that two women suffered harm due to "catastrophic" failures in their handling of disclosure applications, errors linked to mismanagement and a lack of personalized care.

The Supreme Court has upheld a disturbing reality: victims lack the ability to sue the police for negligence even when there are glaring missteps, such as downgrading a high-risk call. This means that a woman threatened by an ex-partner who stalks or orchestrates harm may find herself without recourse when the system fails to protect her.

This situation transcends mere incompetence; it represents institutional cruelty that is often rooted in systemic issues such as sexism and racism. Such dynamics silence survivors, diminish their suffering, and send a deeply troubling message: your voice is insignificant.

Yet, amidst this disheartening landscape, there is a glimmer of hope. Reformative measures are underway. Specialist Domestic Violence Courts are being introduced, featuring separate waiting areas, video links for testimonies, emotional support, and trauma-informed approaches to questioning. The Victims' Code was restructured in 2024 to enhance the rights of survivors, ensuring timely updates and guaranteed access to IDVAs. Moreover, the Domestic Abuse Commissioner is striving to eliminate a "justice lottery," advocating for a system in which geographic location or personal prejudice does not dictate a survivor's access to justice.

However, such policy changes must translate into real-world application. To demand your rights effectively, it's crucial to be informed about them. Don't hesitate to ask critical questions such as, "Can I have an IDVA present during court proceedings?" "Can I utilize a video link for my testimony?" "Will I receive regular case updates?" Hold the system accountable for its responsibilities. Maintain thorough records of every interaction, including dates, names, and status updates. If you experience failure within the system, escalate your concerns: file formal complaints, engage with organizations like Victim Support or the Parliamentary and Health Service Ombudsman, and consider seeking assistance from an Independent Domestic Abuse Advocate. You have every right to dignity, clarity, and protection.

Shana Grice tragically lost her life because the justice system did not recognize the reality of her vulnerability. She deserved far more than what she received. And, so do you.

**Toolkit**

Reporting Checklist

- Request an IDVA at the very first point of contact, whether at a police station or by phone.

- Clearly express your fears about potential future harm, don't allow your situation to be minimized.
- Collect and retain all physical documents related to your case, including court documents, letters, and disclosures, don't rely solely on memory.
- Utilize the Victims' Code to challenge any lack of support or updates you experience.

If the System Fails, You

- Write a letter referencing the Victims' Code and request a referral for your case.
- File a formal complaint with the police force or the Crown Prosecution Service (CPS).
- If your complaint remains unanswered, escalate the issue to the Independent Office for Police Conduct or the Ombudsman.
- Seek parallel support from organizations such as Women's Aid, Victim Support, or the Centre for Women's Justice.

**Reflective Questions**

- Did you feel believed and adequately protected when you reached out for help or applied for an order?
- Was IDVA support accessible to you at the police station or in court?
- How might the outcome have changed had the police taken your last report with the seriousness it deserved?

The law is designed to safeguard your rights and ensure justice. However, time and again, it falls short of fulfilling this promise. Many individuals find themselves facing formidable challenges within a system that often appears indifferent or even hostile to their needs. By understanding the specific gaps in legal protections and learning how to assert your rights effectively, you can reclaim a measure of power in situations where you may feel vulnerable.

It's important to recognize that the legal system is not inherently broken; rather, it is currently facing a crisis that demands our attention and action. This crisis manifests in various forms, whether through unequal representation, systemic biases, or inadequate support for those in need. Yet, there is hope. With increased awareness, dedicated advocacy, and a united community voice, meaningful change is possible.

Such change can lead to enhanced safety and a more equitable pursuit of justice for all individuals. By working together to address these issues, we can transform the legal landscape into one that truly protects and empowers everyone.

# Intersectional Survivorship – When Identities Intensify Trauma

Intersectionality, a term introduced by scholar Kimberlé Crenshaw, highlights the complex ways in which overlapping identities, such as race, gender, immigration status, disability, and LGBTQ+ identity, interact to amplify the effects of domestic abuse. Survivors facing these intersecting identities often endure heightened risks and encounter compounded barriers, making it essential to understand the unique challenges they face and the limited access they have to available resources and support.

**A Case Study: "Adriana" – A Migrant Survivor's Crucible**

Adriana (name changed) arrived in the UK on a spousal visa filled with promise; she secured a new job, formed friendships, and nurtured hope for a better future. However, her partner soon began to isolate her, controlling her finances and subjecting her to both physical and sexual violence. The most insidious form of manipulation involved threats to report her to immigration authorities, which could jeopardize her custody rights over their children.

Faced with "No Recourse to Public Funds" (NRPF) status, escaping her abuser was fraught with peril. The fear of homelessness, destitution, and potential deportation loomed large. Even after police and other support services were alerted, she found herself repeatedly drawn back into her abusive situation, trapped in a cycle of fear and dependency. It was only after five arduous years, supported by community advocates, that Adriana could finally secure refuge, legal representation, and ultimately, a domestic violence visa through the Domestic Violence Concession. Her journey to safety was not merely an escape from violence but also a desperate flight from an immigration system that had effectively imprisoned her.

*Intersectional Barriers at Play*

1. Immigration Status & No Recourse to Public Funds (NRPF)

- Statistics indicate that approximately 32,000 survivors annually in the UK could receive crucial support if NRPF pathways were expanded. Without these pathways, many survivors remain tethered to their abusers, leading to situations of homelessness, poverty, and economic manipulation.

2. LGBTQ+ & Trans Identity

    - Survivors who identify as transgender or non-binary face heightened risks of stigmatization, misgendering, and threats of being outed by their abusers. Alarmingly, around 43% of trans and non-binary individuals report experiencing family violence, yet many struggle to find inclusive shelters and appropriate counselling services tailored to their needs.

3. Disability & Economic Control

    - Survivors with disabilities are often isolated by caregivers who may also be their abusers, denied access to independent financial resources, and frequently excluded from traditional shelters. Additionally, institutional financial frameworks may prevent them from opening bank accounts, reinforcing their dependency on their abusers.

*Psychological Impact of Intersectional Abuse*

- Layered Trauma: For Adriana, the trauma was not only the physical assault but also the chronic stress associated with being undocumented and feeling invisible within society.

- Structural Betrayal: The very systems that were supposed to protect her—such as immigration authorities, law enforcement, and welfare programs—often reinforced her feelings of isolation and fear, further entrenching her victimization.

- Shattered Trust and Self-Efficacy: Each time Adriana faced denial of support or assistance, whether legal or practical, it eroded her sense of agency. She described her experience of abuse as akin to a "jail sentence," suffering not just at the hands of her partner but also from a system that viewed her as expendable.

*Counselling & Safeguarding for Intersectional Survivors*

A. Use Inclusive, Open Questioning
   - It is vital to ask survivors comprehensive questions, such as:
   - "Do you have secure immigration status?"
   - "Are you able to access funds?"
   - "Do you have a safe place to stay where the abuse isn't known?"
   - These factors are as critical as physical safety in assessing their risk and resilience.

B. Facilitate Legal Empowerment
   - Connect migrant survivors with organizations like Rights of Women or Southall Black Sisters, which specialize in navigating the Domestic Violence Concession and other forms of NRPF relief.

C. Bridge to Specialist, Peer-Led Services
   - Establish connections with organizations such as Galop, LGBT Foundation, and Survivors' Network, which provide essential resources for LGBTQ+ survivors. Southall Black Sisters and Lawrs are also key sources of support for migrants.

D. Layered Safety Planning
   - Safety planning should include concrete steps such as:
   - Assisting in filing immigration applications.
   - Helping survivors open basic bank accounts.
   - Securing affordable housing through local services.
   - Ensuring access to counselling and trauma-informed therapies.

Systemic Reform: How We Move Forward

| Area | Action |
|---|---|
| Policy | Expand NRPF exemptions and separate reporting from enforcement to protect vulnerable survivors. |
| Funding | Invest in specialist services. Recognizing that each survivor's needs are unique, a one-size-fits-all approach is inadequate. |
| Training | Provide comprehensive education on intersectionality for police officers, healthcare staff, and refuge workers. |
| Outcomes Tracking | Collect and disaggregate data to ensure that services effectively reach and support minority survivors |
| Survivor Leadership | Involve survivors from diverse backgrounds in |

| | |
|---|---|
| | advisory roles and the development of policies to ensure their perspectives inform systemic changes. |

By acknowledging and addressing the complexities of intersectional trauma, we can take significant steps toward creating a more equitable and supportive system for all survivors.

# Technology-Facilitated Abuse – Control by Digital Design

In an era dominated by smartphones, smart homes, and pervasive social media, the landscape of domestic abuse has transformed dramatically, moving from physical spaces into the digital realm. This shift raises critical questions about the implications of having control exerted through technology, whether it's in the palm of your hand, via smart devices in your home, or on social networking platforms. Technology-Facilitated Abuse (TFA) is not a theoretical future scenario; it is a present-day reality that is increasingly concerning, with its scope expanding rapidly each day.

*What Is Technology-Facilitated Abuse?*

TFA refers to the misuse of various digital technologies, including GPS systems, spyware, smart devices, and social media to monitor, intimidate, manipulate, or otherwise exploit individuals, particularly survivors of domestic abuse. Although discussions about TFA are becoming more prevalent in recent times, the phenomenon itself is not new. For years, perpetrators have weaponized technology, adapting their tactics in line with advancements in connectivity and the proliferation of "smart" devices that are now commonplace in many households.

Recent research conducted in the UK has revealed alarming statistics: up to 72% of domestic abuse survivors reported experiencing some form of technology abuse, with incidents particularly surging during lockdown periods. More than one in three women faced online abuse, while 40% of individuals victimized by cyberstalking reported enduring the harassment for over two years. Additionally, the use of spyware escalated by 51% during the pandemic, shedding light on how abusers have increasingly turned to technological means to exert control and in still fear.

*The Main Forms of Tech Abuse*

1. Digital Stalking & Surveillance

    - This includes the use of GPS tracking through smartphone applications or Bluetooth-enabled devices such as Apple's AirTags. Abusers can monitor their victims' locations without their consent, creating an environment of constant watchfulness.
    - Spyware, sometimes referred to as "stalker ware," can infiltrate smartphones to capture every interaction texts, calls, and even private conversations.
    - Everyday smart devices, ranging from doorbell cameras to home assistants and fitness trackers, can be manipulated by abusers to access sensitive information and track routines. Studies have documented instances where perpetrators deployed numerous tracking devices and scrutinized cloud data to maintain control over their victims.

2. Revenge Porn & Image-Based Abuse

    - This category involves the non-consensual sharing of intimate images or videos, which is often aimed at humiliating or threatening the survivor while reclaiming a sense of power over their privacy.
    - Data from 2019 indicates that 83% of prosecutions related to revenge pornography in England were linked to domestic violence cases, underscoring how widespread this abuse is.

3. Control via Shared Devices & Accounts

- In many cases, abusers take advantage of shared digital resources by changing passwords, locking survivors out of their own accounts, reading messages without consent, and altering privacy settings.
- By exploiting shared calendars, emails, and contact lists, they can manipulate their victims' schedules and communications, further isolating them from potential support networks.

***Psychological Harm & Counselling Insight***

Chronic Hypervigilance

- Platforms like TikTok, while initially intended for social engagement, have become tools for tracking. The threat of tech abuse creates a persistent state of fear in survivors, as they live in uncertainty over when they might be surveilled again. This constant state of anxiety can trigger the amygdala, undermining higher-order cognitive functions and perpetuating a cycle of survival instinct.

Gas lighting & Emotional Manipulation

- Actions such as deleting emails, changing locks, and erasing digital evidence contribute to a phenomenon known as psychological sabotage. Survivors often find themselves caught in a web of doubt and confusion, questioning their reality and experiences.

Isolation & Identity Theft

- The experience of being evicted from personal devices often parallels the removal of supportive social connections. When abusers gain control over calendars, messages, and even financial applications, survivors can be left feeling stripped of their autonomy and community ties.

*Counselling & Safe Practice*

A. Awareness & Tech Mapping

- Survivors should ask critical questions: Where is your phone located? What smart devices are you using? Who has administrative access to these devices? Engaging in a comprehensive mapping of digital vulnerabilities covering emails, social media accounts, and location services is essential for creating a safe environment.

B. Take-Back Plan

- Implementing strategies like using burner phones, creating new email addresses (such as ProtonMail), and changing passwords away from the abuser's knowledge can help establish a secure connection. Devices and sensitive data should be safeguarded in secure locations, such as counselling centres or trusted friends' homes.

C. Evidence Gathering

- Survivors are encouraged to document abuses discreetly by taking screenshots, capturing metadata, and logging communications and GPS data, all while remaining vigilant not to alert the abuser.

D. Tailored Safety Planning

- This should include a tech audit as a fundamental tool in safety planning. Coordination with tech-savvy NGOs, such as Refuge's Tech Abuse team and the Digital Poverty Alliance, can provide crucial support. Implementing two-factor authentication and fostering tech literacy are also vital components.

E. Neuropsych & Emotional Repair

- Therapy tailored for survivors of TFA should address the unique challenges posed by betrayal trauma and help rebuild a safe perception of their digital and physical environments. Therapeutic approaches such as EMDR and grounding techniques can be particularly beneficial.

*Policy & Systemic Response*

The UK's Domestic Abuse Act 2021 has taken a significant legal step by applying regulations to the threats surrounding the sharing of intimate material, commonly known as revenge porn. However, the rapid advancement of Internet of Things (IoT) technology, evident in devices like smart doorbells and trackers, often outpaces relevant legislation, leaving survivors vulnerable. Unfortunately, prosecutions of spyware manufacturers are exceedingly rare, and many platforms continue to shield abusers under their policies.

*Case Example*

Consider the experience of Julie, who was monitored via her phone by her partner before and during COVID-19 lockdowns. Upon discovering that her movements were tracked through livestreaming spyware and doorbell footage, she sought assistance from the police and tech advisors at Refuge. With guidance, she transitioned to new, secure devices, changed her passwords, and effectively severed digital ties with her attacker. "It clicked when they handed me a burner phone," she recalls. "I realized I was being watched nonstop and finally, I knew how to stop it."

*Chapter Takeaway*

Technology is inherently neutral; its impact can vary significantly based on who wields it. For survivors of domestic abuse, planning for digital safety is just as crucial as establishing a plan for physical safety. Accurate awareness and response strategies are essential to navigate the complex interplay of technology and personal autonomy in today's world.

# When Trust Becomes a Weapon – The Georgia Harrison Story

In an age dominated by smartphones and reality TV, betrayal can often manifest in subtler, yet profoundly damaging ways. For Georgia Harrison, known for her appearances on 'Love Island' and 'The Only Way Is Essex', her intimate betrayal unfolded online, casting a long shadow over her life. In 2020, she became one of the UK's most prominent victims of image-based sexual abuse, commonly referred to as revenge porn. Her abuser was Stephen Bear, a man she once trusted deeply.

This is not merely a celebrity scandal; it embodies a deeply human narrative that explores the intricate dynamics of consent, power, and psychological trauma within the digital age.

*A Private Moment, Publicly Violated*

Georgia and Bear had a tumultuous relationship defined by moments of passion and mistrust. One fateful afternoon, during a private sexual encounter in Bear's garden, a hidden CCTV camera captured what was meant to be a confidential moment. Unbeknownst to Georgia, this violation of privacy ignited a series of events that would alter her life forever. Despite her explicit requests for Bear not to share the footage, he later uploaded the video to his Only Fans account, capitalizing on her vulnerability and the trust she had placed in him.

The fallout was immediate and devastating. Within hours, the video began to circulate online, exposing Georgia's most intimate moments to strangers who had no regard for her dignity or consent. She learned that Bear profited immensely from her violation, earning thousands of pounds from the video.

Georgia later reflected on the experience, saying, “I was completely broken. I honestly thought I might not get through it.”

*The Legal Fight: Setting a Precedent*

In a significant turn of events, 2022 marked a pivotal moment in Georgia’s journey for justice. Stephen Bear was found guilty of voyeurism and distributing private sexual footage without consent. In a landmark ruling, he received a 21-month prison sentence and was ordered to pay £5,000 in compensation to Georgia, along with over £22,000 in profits derived from the video. This marked a ground-breaking moment, as Bear became the first individual in the UK to face imprisonment for revenge porn linked to Only Fans, bringing much-needed attention to the evolving challenges of digital consent.

Georgia’s decision to waive her right to anonymity was a courageous act that empowered countless others to come forward with their own experiences of abuse. Nevertheless, the path to justice was fraught with obstacles. Bear's brash demeanour included posting jokes on social media while awaiting sentencing, demonstrating a stark lack of remorse. Georgia faced relentless online harassment that not only re-traumatized her but exposed the harsh realities many survivors endure while seeking justice.

*A Survivor’s Psychological Journey*

Looking closely at Georgia’s experience from a psychological perspective reveals multiple layers of trauma.

- Betrayal Trauma: When someone a person trusts deeply violates their boundaries, the brain can interpret this as a severe threat. Survivors like Georgia often face symptoms akin to PTSD, including hyper-vigilance, intrusive thoughts, and profound identity struggles. The betrayal shatters a sense of security, leaving an indelible mark on one's mental well-being.

- Violation of Consent: The absence of physical violence in this situation does not diminish the severity of the abuse. Georgia never consented to being filmed, and Bear's actions stripped her of agency. The emotional toll she experienced stemmed from the humiliation of being publicly exposed and the ongoing violation of her trust.

- Secondary Victimization: The trauma inflicted by Bear's actions was compounded by an avalanche of backlash. Georgia faced trolling, court delays, and a media frenzy that mirrored the struggles faced by many survivors when they seek help. This secondary victimization often exacerbates their distress, making recovery feel even more elusive.

Despite these overwhelming challenges, Georgia's resilience shone through. She not only fought back legally but also embarked on a personal journey of emotional healing. By publicly sharing her story and advocating for change, she worked tirelessly to reclaim her narrative.

*Beyond the Courtroom: Turning Pain into Power*

In 2023, Georgia's advocacy was recognized when she was awarded an MBE for her services to charity and her tireless campaign against image-based abuse. Her efforts have significantly shaped public awareness, pushing for more robust digital safety laws in the UK.

Through her ITV documentary, Revenge Porn: Georgia vs Bear, Georgia facilitated a vital conversation about trauma, shame, and survival, demonstrating what it truly means to reclaim one's story. She poignantly stated, "I felt like I was drowning. But the moment I spoke out, I took my power back," symbolizing a crucial turning point in her journey.

*The Psychological Cost of Digital Abuse*

The rise of technology-facilitated abuse is alarming, and Georgia's case is far from an isolated incident. Survivors of revenge porn frequently report a range of severe psychological ramifications, including:

- Chronic anxiety and suicidal ideation: The persistent anxiety stemming from public exposure can lead to dire mental health outcomes, including suicidal thoughts.

- Loss of employment, housing, or relationships: The fallout from such abuse often extends beyond emotional distress, disrupting various aspects of survivors' lives.

- Fear of future relationships and intimacy: The violation of trust can instill deep-seated fears that hinder individuals from engaging in future relationships.

- Long-term PTSD and dissociation: Many survivors struggle with ongoing symptoms of PTSD, including dissociation from their experiences and feelings of unreality.

The trauma inflicted by image-based abuse is not merely emotional; it often has lasting neurological effects. The relentless sharing of abusive content online keeps survivors in a state of hyper arousal, overwhelming their ability to process the trauma effectively. Counsellors are increasingly recognizing image-based abuse as a distinct subtype of trauma, necessitating specialized therapeutic approaches such as trauma-focused cognitive behavioural therapy (CBT), Eye Movement

Desensitization and Reprocessing (EMDR), and somatic therapies.

*Reclaiming the Narrative*

Today, Georgia is thriving, expecting her first child and embracing a healthy relationship. Her journey underscores a critical truth: recovery from abuse is not about erasing the past but about rebuilding a new future on one's terms.

Georgia continues to amplify her voice for those who feel voiceless, reframing what survival looks like: it is not silence but strength, not shame but advocacy, and not brokenness but rebirth.

*Reflective Takeaway*

Georgia Harrison's story transcends the realm of scandal; it illuminates how abuse can lurk beneath the surface of modern intimacy, how predators exploit technology's reach, and how survivors reclaim their narratives in the pursuit of justice. By bravely sharing her experiences, Georgia has unequivocally reminded us of an essential truth: your body, your story, and your dignity belong to you alone. No one, regardless of past trust has the right to take that away from you.

# The Impact Domestic Violence Has on Children

*Emotional, Cognitive & Developmental Consequences*

Witnessing or experiencing domestic violence can have a devastating impact on a child's emotional and neurological development. The early years of a child's life are critical for brain development, and exposure to violence, especially during infancy, can disrupt the normal growth of key brain structures responsible for stress regulation, emotional processing, and sensory perception. Notable areas affected include the amygdala (which plays a role in emotional responses), the hypothalamic-pituitary-adrenal (HPA) axis (involved in stress responses), and the visual and auditory cortices (which process sensory information).

Children living in a violent household often exhibit immediate signs of distress, including heightened anxiety, depression, bed-wetting, nightmares, chronic headaches, and stomach pains, alongside difficulties in concentrating. They can exist in a perpetual "fight-or-flight" state that diminishes their coping abilities and disrupts executive functions critical for planning, attention, and problem-solving. This chronic stress can contribute to lower IQ scores and academic struggles, creating a cycle that inhibits their ability to succeed in school.

As time progresses, these children may develop more significant psychological issues that are classified into two main categories: internalized and externalized problems. Internalized problems can manifest as social withdrawal, low self-esteem, and depression, while externalized behaviours may include aggression, defiance, and antisocial behaviour. Research indicates that boys are more likely to exhibit externalized issues, while girls tend to internalize their feelings.

Over time, some children may start perceiving violence as a normative element of life, potentially leading them to replicate abusive behaviours in future relationships. Furthermore, developmentally, they may regress; behaviours might include increased clinginess, distrust of caregivers, and feelings of confusion, guilt, or abandonment.

*Intergenerational Trauma & Long-Term Outcomes*

The ramifications of abuse during childhood do not cease when the child reaches adulthood. Longitudinal studies indicate that children who endure domestic violence or maltreatment face an increased likelihood of developing chronic mental health conditions such as post-traumatic stress disorder (PTSD), anxiety disorders, depression, and issues with substance misuse. These children are also at a higher risk of encountering long-term physical health problems, potentially jeopardizing their overall well-being.

Boys may be more prone to become perpetrators of violence as adults, while girls might find themselves in the role of victims, perpetuating a disturbing cycle of violence. Both genders often struggle with forming secure, healthy relationships, experiencing difficulties in emotional regulation. This may lead to the development of maladaptive coping mechanisms that further entrench them in the cycle of intergenerational trauma, adversely affecting their future families and relationships.

*Healing Tools for Parents & Carers*

Evidence-Based Therapies

- Trauma-Focused Cognitive Behavioural Therapy (TF-CBT): This robust, evidence-based intervention encompasses multiple components including psychoeducation, relaxation techniques, cognitive coping strategies, trauma processing, and joint sessions for parents and children. Research has shown this therapy to be highly effective across various age groups (ranging from 3 to 18 years), leading to significant reductions in symptoms of PTSD, anxiety, and depression, as well as behavioural problems. It also equips parents with improved parenting skills, vital for supporting their children's healing.

- Parent-Child Interaction Therapy (PCIT): PCIT primarily focuses on enhancing the quality of the parent-child relationship. By strengthening attachment bonds and reducing problematic behavioural issues, this therapy aids non-abusive caregivers in rebuilding emotional attunement after experiences of trauma, fostering a nurturing environment for healing.

*Supportive Interventions*

- Safe, Supportive Environments: Educational institutions and community settings that actively teach children coping skills, establish safe boundaries, and promote healthy relationship dynamics serve as protective factors against the adverse impacts of domestic violence.
- Psychoeducation for Parents/Carers: Equipping caregivers with knowledge about typical trauma responses and effective behaviour strategies can help them regulate their emotional responses. This, in turn, enhances maternal sensitivity, which is crucial for shielding children from the detrimental effects of toxic environments.
- Early Detection Systems: Training for teachers, healthcare providers, and social service professionals is essential to identify signs of distress early, which facilitates timely referrals and interventions.

*Real-Life Case Studies*

1. Case Study 1: Ava, Age 9

Ava witnessed repeated instances of physical abuse directed towards her mother, which led to severe separation anxiety and a resurgence of bed-wetting. Through a series of TF-CBT sessions, alongside support for her mother from a women's refuge and parenting guidance, Ava was able to rebuild her confidence, cease bed-wetting, and regain her focus at school.

2. Case Study 2: Malik, Age 14

After enduring years of emotional abuse and witnessing coercive control within his household, Malik exhibited aggressive behaviours at school, which nearly resulted in his exclusion. Following a referral from a school-based safeguarding team, he participated in a local trauma-informed mentoring program while his family received comprehensive support. Over time, Malik learned to express his anger in safe ways, displaying significant improvements in trust, boundaries, and engagement in his academic environment.

*Guide Plans for Schools and Agencies*

- Implement comprehensive, whole-school trauma training to ensure staff can recognize and respond effectively to signs of domestic abuse in students.
- Integrate social-emotional learning (SEL) into the curriculum, promoting emotional literacy, empathy, and conflict resolution strategies among students.
- Ensure that safeguarding leads receive specialized training in trauma-informed practices and understand the necessary referral protocols.
- Develop referral partnerships with local women's refuges, Child and Adolescent Mental Health

Services (CAMHS), and early intervention services.
- Establish dedicated support spaces or counselling drop-in sessions within schools to offer safe havens for children affected by domestic violence.

*Community-Level Prevention Strategies*

Local councils are encouraged to invest in family intervention services that provide comprehensive therapy, parenting classes, and advocacy to support families in need.

- Community centres should offer after-school programs specifically focused on cultivating emotional resilience and promoting concepts of healthy relationships.
- Training for faith-based and cultural organizations is vital for empowering them to identify signs of domestic abuse and effectively guide families towards appropriate support services.
- Public health campaigns should include targeted messaging directed at children, informing them about recognizing safe adults and avenues to seek help.
- Multi-agency forums, comprising health, education, police, and social care sectors should coordinate care plans and continuously monitor outcomes to ensure comprehensive support for affected families.

By implementing these strategies, we can better protect, heal, and empower children who have been exposed to domestic violence, ultimately breaking the cycle of trauma and fostering healthier future generations.

# Why We Stay: The Complex Psychology of Abuse

Abuse is not merely an emotional experience; it profoundly alters the way our body operates. It creates new neural pathways in our brain, rewires our responses to stress, and imprints trauma deep within our nervous system. Over time, the cumulative effects of this trauma manifest physically, as the body begins to bear the burden of what the mind is unable to contain.

Living under the threat of constant fear or unpredictability triggers the brain's survival mechanisms, commonly referred to as the fight, flight, freeze, or fawn response. In a nurturing environment, this sophisticated system is designed to alert us to genuine threats, guiding us to safety. However, in an abusive relationship, this alert system never turns off. You find yourself perpetually on guard, continually analysing your surroundings, and adjusting your behaviour in an attempt to prevent the next explosion of rage or manipulation. The delicate art of reading moods becomes second nature, and you navigate your life on a tightrope, constantly aware of potential repercussions. The absence of true relaxation leaves you feeling as though peace is an elusive dream, always just out of reach.

This state of hypervigilance takes a toll on cognitive functions, impairing your memory, your ability to concentrate, and your decision-making skills. It's common for survivors to feel disoriented, as if they are "losing their mind." This experience is a result of your brain being inundated with cortisol and adrenaline, hormones designed for short-term survival. When subjected to prolonged exposure, these chemicals disrupt the balance of your nervous system and hinder your capacity to function optimally.

Physically, the repercussions of abuse can be severe and varied. Many survivors report suffering from an array of health issues, including persistent migraines, gastrointestinal problems, chronic pain, and autoimmune disorders. Trauma does not merely pass through the body; it takes root and manifests in physical symptoms that linger long after the abusive situation has ended. Even when the immediate threat has dissipated, many continue to experience debilitating panic attacks, vivid nightmares, emotional numbness, or a pervasive sense of distrust in others. Some individuals describe a haunting sensation of being outside their own bodies, as if they are watching life unfold rather than participating in it.

It is crucial to understand that this response is not a sign of weakness but a biological reaction an instinctive effort by your body to protect you, even in the absence of danger. Therefore, healing from such trauma involves more than simply processing past events; it requires a concerted effort to teach your nervous system that it is safe to exist in the present. This journey of healing necessitates patience and self-compassion, as you work to reclaim your sense of security and reconnect with your body and emotions.

**The Many Faces of Abusers**

Abusers often defy conventional villain archetypes; they don't always appear menacing or dangerous. In fact, they frequently resemble the everyday people in our lives: loving parents, devoted partners, revered pastors, or successful CEOs. They might be the well-meaning individual who surprises you with flowers, offers comforting words during tough times, or tenderly tucks your child in at night. This deceptive charm can make recognizing abusive behaviour incredibly challenging.

Society often teaches us to envision abusers as overtly angry or physically violent, but the reality is that many abusers are calculated individuals who meticulously orchestrate their actions. They engage in grooming, not only targeting their victims but also manipulating the perceptions of their social circles. By crafting an appealing public persona, they create a barrier that complicates the process of speaking out. When victims do summon the courage to share their experiences, they may face disbelief due to the abuser's cultivated reputation.

Abusers can exhibit a spectrum of behaviour. Some resort to overt violence, resorting to physical intimidation to maintain power and control. Others prefer more insidious, psychological tactics that are less recognizable and harder to articulate. These might include gas lighting, where the victim's perception of reality is consistently
undermined; manipulation, which twists circumstances to suit the abuser's narrative; or guilt trips, which make the victim feel responsible for the abuser's unhappiness. Silent treatment can also be a form of psychological abuse, leaving the victim in a state of confusion and longing for reconciliation. Some abusers weaponised love, wielding kindness like a double-edged sword, using affectionate gestures to disrupt the victim's ability to feel stable or secure. Additionally, some may adopt a victim mentality, making their partners feel that their actions are the true source of the problems, that they are the ones harming the relationship.

Abusers vary widely in their backgrounds and motivations. Some are deeply wounded individuals grappling with their own traumas, while others may embody traits of entitlement, narcissism, or sociopathy. There are instances where abusers genuinely believe they are not in the wrong, as the dynamics of control and manipulation have been the norm throughout their lives.

Recognising abuse requires a willingness to look beyond the surface and to listen to one's instincts. Trusting your gut feeling when something feels amiss can be crucial, even if it's difficult to articulate why. It is essential to understand that regardless of how someone behaves in public or how charmingly they engage with others, it is their actions behind closed doors, the patterns of behaviour that emerge away from prying eyes that reveal the true character of an abuser. Recognising these signs is vital for anyone seeking to protect themselves or support someone who may be trapped in an abusive situation.

# The Moment You Realise You Are Being Abused

The moment you come to the realization that what you experienced was abuse rarely strikes like a bolt of lightning. Instead, it unfolds gradually, like a shadow stretching across your memories, casting an unfamiliar light on situations you've examined countless times before. Often, this awakening isn't a singular moment but rather a persistent whisper, a flicker of discomfort, a nagging gut feeling that you've brushed aside again and again until it becomes impossible to ignore. You could be engaged in everyday tasks like folding laundry, scrolling through social media, or preparing a meal, when something seemingly innocuous, a faded photograph, a familiar phrase, or a fleeting behaviour you observe in another person lands heavily in your chest. It quietly but emphatically whispers, "That wasn't love. That wasn't okay."

When that realization finally settles in, it can shatter you, leaving you in a state of emotional upheaval.

This process of recognition can unfold over weeks, years, or even decades. For many survivors, the absence of physical bruises can create significant disbelief. Emotional and psychological abuse may not leave visible scars, thereby convincing the first and foremost sceptic of its reality: the survivor themselves. You may find yourself questioning your own recollections, minimizing your pain, and rationalizing what transpired. Thoughts like "They were just under a lot of pressure," "I was difficult," or "It wasn't that bad" seep in and erode your certainty. But this confusion isn't a flaw in your perception; it's a symptom of the trauma you endured.

From a psychological standpoint, this dilemma is termed cognitive dissonance, a state where your lived experiences and deeply held beliefs come into conflict. You believed that this person loved you; you believed you were safe. Yet, the truth looms: they silenced you. They threatened you, manipulated your emotions, withheld affection, controlled your actions, and gradually dismantled your sense of self, piece by piece. The moment you begin to accept this painful reality; your mind can feel like it's fracturing. This is why the realization can inflict as much agony as it does clarity. You don't just lose the relationship; you also lose the version of yourself that believed you were okay.

In therapeutic settings, we refer to this as the collapse of the assumptive world. Trauma psychologist Ronnie Janoff-Bulman explains that everyone carries within them a psychological map that outlines their sense of safety, fairness, and trust in the world. When someone you cared for deeply violates those foundational elements, that map is irrevocably burned. Survivors often experience this as an existential crisis, asking questions like: If what I thought was love was actually control, then who am I? If I stayed, am I at fault? If I didn't scream or run away, did I somehow allow the abuse to happen?

These reflections are not signs of weakness; they are the thoughts of survival. The human brain, especially amid trauma, prioritizes familiarity over freedom. It clings to the known, even if that knowledge is rooted in pain. Your nervous system, finely attuned to detecting threats, can misinterpret a peaceful moment as danger or chaos as comfort. This is why abuse often feels less like outright abuse and more like a tense struggle, like putting in extra effort to keep the peace while labelling it a necessary compromise.

Survivors frequently internalize blame and distort red flags into miscommunications. They hold tightly to memories of good times, apologies, and promises, because those fleeting moments of tenderness were real. This complexity is what makes abuse challenging to define; it exists in shades of grey, a fog that makes it difficult to discern reality. Inside that fog, you not only lose your voice but also your capacity to trust your own perceptions. Thus, the moment of realization can itself be deeply traumatizing. To see the truth clearly requires revisiting every time you ignored your instincts, forgave what didn't belong to you, or contorted yourself to maintain a semblance of harmony.

It also necessitates the painful admission: "I wasn't safe." This admission carries an unbearable weight. If you weren't safe in the past, what does that suggest about the present? If you have experienced abuse, does that label you a victim? This term, 'victim,' is one many survivors resist vehemently, having been conditioned to believe that victims embody weakness, helplessness, or brokenness. You didn't weather all that trauma just to be reduced to a single, limiting label.

This underscores the critical importance of validation. When someone says, "What you experienced was wrong," or "You didn't deserve that," or simply "I believe you," they disrupt the cycle of internalized shame. Such validation gently lifts the oppressive burden of proof from your shoulders. When that affirmation comes from yourself, it holds even greater transformative power. Speaking your truth aloud, even if only in a whisper, marks the beginning of reclaiming your power.

In counselling, our focus extends beyond merely naming the abuse; we delve into making sense of its aftermath. This is where self-compassion serves as a lifeline. You are not defined by the choices you made in survival mode, nor by the silence you maintained for self-preservation. The understanding you carry now is not a form of judgment; it's an open doorway, a new beginning. And like all beginnings, this journey can be messy, emotional, and at times overwhelmingly difficult.

You might fluctuate between anger and uncertainty, grief and numbness, longing to obliterate the past while simultaneously desiring to rewrite it. This is not regression; it's grief. You're mourning not only what transpired but also what should have been, the apologies you never received, the person you wished they could have become, the time lost to the abuse. Most poignantly, you're grieving that version of yourself who believed it was all just love.

Yet, here's the truth amidst the turmoil: this realization is sacred. It marks a turning point in your journey, from mere survival to genuine healing. It is not a sign of weakness to unravel here; rather, it is the genesis of your strength. The part of you that felt small is finally finding its voice. The portion of you that questioned everything is starting to own its truth. This is where your journey toward understanding, growth, and self-empowerment begins.

This awakening can be profoundly heart-breaking. It forces you to confront the fact that what you once believed was love was, in reality, a meticulous form of control. The boundaries that should have been safeguarded weren't just disrespected; they were trampled upon. Your sense of safety was compromised, and your voice, once vibrant, became a faint whisper drowned out by the chaos. Often, this moment of recognition doesn't just elicit sadness for the experiences endured; it triggers a tidal wave of grief for the years lost, for the self that remained silenced, and for the vibrant life that never materialized due to fear and careful repression.

Yet, that moment of clarity is not solely one of loss. It also marks the beginning of a reclamation journey. Yes, there is a rupture, but alongside it, a return, a return to truth, to clarity, and ultimately, to yourself. Even as the healing process unfolds slowly, and as trust feels precarious, and your nervous system remains primed for danger, that initial moment of recognition acts as a crack in the wall you built to shield yourself from pain.

It's through that crack that light begins to pour in, illuminating the path forward. With each step, you start to rebuild not just your external life, but also your internal landscape; you rediscover who you truly are beyond the pain, beyond the fear, and beyond the lie that you were ever to blame. This transformative journey is both challenging and liberating, opening doors to empowerment and growth, as you embrace your newfound strength and reclaim your narrative.

*Toolkit for Clarity and Healing*

This collection of prompts and practices has been thoughtfully crafted to support you as you navigate the transformative moment of realization. Approaching this process with gentleness, courage, and care can help you uncover deeper truths within yourself.

1. Memory Trace

Reflect on this question: "When did I first begin to feel afraid, small, or unsure in that relationship?"
Find a quiet space, close your eyes, and sit in stillness. Allow your body to lead the way with its sensations; pay attention to feelings like tension, heaviness, or lightness that arise, rather than relying solely on your thoughts. Often, our true emotions and memories are stored in the body long before we articulate them in words.

2. Name the Harm

Write down this sentence verbatim: "What I experienced was abuse."
Now, personalize it: "[Their name] abused me."
Take a moment to pause and breathe deeply. Notice how your body reacts to this acknowledgment. Do you feel a tremor, do your muscles tighten, or does a wave of numbness wash over you? Recognize that your body holds onto truths that your mind may seek to bury or protect you from confronting.

3. Validate Your Story

Ask yourself, "If a close friend shared this story with me, how would I respond?"

Now, take that compassionate response and turn it inward, writing affirming words as if you were speaking to yourself. This exercise not only fosters self-compassion but also marks the beginnings of cultivating self-trust, allowing you to honour your feelings and experiences.

4. Challenge the Inner Critic

When feelings of guilt arise, meet them with curiosity:

- "Where did I learn to assign blame to myself?"
- "Who stands to gain by my silence?"
- Understand that guilt is not always a reflection of truth; often, it serves as a survival mechanism. By unravelling the origins of this guilt, you can start to differentiate between what is genuinely your fault and what has been instilled in you by external pressures.

5. Reclaim Power Through Choice

Identify three small but significant aspects of your life in which you now have a say:

- Your voice. Your personal space. Your narrative.
- Write down one specific action you can take this week that affirms your autonomy however minor it may seem. By reclaiming power in these areas, you begin to restore your sense of agency and control over your life.

6. Therapy Language

Share this sentiment with a trusted therapist or confidant:

- "I'm beginning to realize that something wasn't right in my experience. I don't require advice right now; I simply need someone to listen without minimizing what I've faced."

- Allow this statement to stand on its own; there is strength in simply being heard without judgment.
- Journal prompt: 'What fear, hope, or belief kept me in the relationship longer than I expected?'
- Reframing Exercise: Replace 'I should have left sooner' with 'I left when I was ready.'
- Safety network: List 3 people or places that feel emotionally safe.
- Resource: Trauma bonding explainer from The National Domestic Violence Hotline

**Final Words**

If you've engaged with this chapter and felt emotional responses such as tears, anger, fear, or disbelief, know this: you are not alone in your journey. Realization seldom arrives with fanfare; instead, it tends to come quietly, subtly shaking your foundation, not to shatter it, but to clear the space for something more authentic and liberating. This is an invitation to reclaim your voice.

This chapter does not aim to diagnose or label you but rather to illuminate the path toward clarity, which, while sometimes painful, is ultimately a means of rescue.

You did not fail because you chose to stay.
You did not break because you loved deeply.
You have survived, and now you are beginning to see and understand the depth of those experiences.

You have every right to name what occurred.
You are allowed to grieve the reality of what should have been.
And most importantly, you are allowed to heal.

This is not the conclusion of your narrative; rather, it's a pivotal moment that marks an important page turning. The truth may bring discomfort, but the journey toward your freedom? It starts right here.

# The Leaving and the Aftermath

Leaving isn't just a single moment it's a profound journey that requires careful planning and consideration. The hardest part isn't merely stepping out the door; it's understanding how to leave safely and securely. When the time comes to orchestrate your exit, every detail becomes paramount, whether it's knowing the safest routes to take, having a whistle or personal alarm at the ready, or establishing a code word with a trusted ally.

First and foremost, prioritise your safety. Start by turning off location services on your phone or utilizing a device that the abuser cannot access. Use incognito or private browsing settings to ensure your online activity remains confidential and does not raise suspicions. If possible, secure a separate phone one that the abuser cannot monitor through bills or call logs. This phone can be vital for staying connected with your support network.

Establish a code word with someone you can rely on, whether that's a neighbour, trusted friend, or family member. This word serves as an urgent signal that your exit is imminent, prompting them to be ready to assist you in any way needed. Prepare an emergency bag packed with essentials, keeping it hidden in a safe place such as a friend's home or your workplace. This bag should contain critical items like identification, cash, keys, medications, a charger, and copies of important documents, including passports, birth certificates, and legal orders.

Identify a safe location where you can seek refuge this might be a friend's house, a family member's address, or even a local shelter. It's vital to avoid confrontation as you leave; your primary goal should be your safety, not drama or emotional turmoil. Timing is crucial; aim to leave when the abuser is away from home or otherwise distracted. Keep a discreet list of important contacts at hand, including helpline numbers, local solicitors, and domestic violence services. Whenever possible, consult with a domestic violence advocate or support worker ahead of time whether over the phone or in person to ensure you are emotionally and practically prepared for the transition. Research supports the necessity of a well-thought-out plan. Studies indicate that abusive partners frequently escalate their behaviour when they sense their control is threatened, particularly during the leaving process. Therefore, careful planning acts as both a shield and a roadmap for your journey. Within your home, minimize potential triggers for violence; avoid secluded areas like kitchens, bathrooms, or small spaces where weapons could be found or where you could feel cornered. Show your children or housemates your bags are ready; practice routes quietly, teaching them where to go if a situation becomes volatile.

Ensure your car is prepared for a quick escape make sure it's fuelled up, parked strategically with the back end facing the exit, doors unlocked (except for the driver's side), and the keys hidden in a discreet spot. Leave spare keys or duplicates with someone you trust. Familiarise yourself with various escape routes; consider options like the backyard gate, a side door, or even a first-floor window. Identify fire exits in public spaces you frequent as potential safe exits.

Be aware that technology can pose a risk if used carelessly. Avoid logging onto social media platforms that could inadvertently share your location. Consider acquiring a new SIM card or a prepaid phone number for secure communications with friends and support agencies during your transition.

The emotional landscape after leaving can be just as critical as the logistical aspects. Many describe this experience as akin to a roller coaster feelings of relief may be intertwined with moments of intense fear and uncertainty. It's essential to acknowledge these feelings as natural and expected. Ground yourself during this tumultuous time: breathe deeply, maintain a journal of your experiences, and surround yourself with supportive individuals who validate your feelings those who listen without judgment.

The aftermath of leaving encompasses real, legal, and practical considerations. Collect evidence soon after you leave this may include photographs of injuries, screenshots of abusive messages, medical reports, and police records. These documents will be vital if you decide to pursue protective orders, court filings, or custody claims.

Consider informing schools, your workplace, and trusted neighbours about your situation. Provide them with photographs of the abuser and share details about how and when they might appear, along with instructions on how they should respond if approached.

Fortunately, a variety of support networks exist to assist you. Domestic violence professionals can offer personalized risk assessments, secure emergency accommodation for you and your children, and extend emotional support tailored to your specific circumstances. Beyond shelters, self-care remains crucial: seek out therapy, engage in trauma-informed care, move your body through exercise, express yourself creatively, and spend time in nature all of which can help rewire a mind and body accustomed to fear and instability.

Leaving isn't simply an end; it signifies a new beginning. It marks the first chapter in the process of rebuilding your life. It's about embracing freedom not just from violence, but towards reclaiming your autonomy, integrity, and hope. Take one quietly planned, courageous step, and then another until your narrative transforms from one defined by violence to one characterised by the triumph of survival, safety, and renewal.

# Why We Go Back

Leaving an abusive relationship is not a mark of failure; rather, it serves as a profound testament to your resilience and strength, even if that strength doesn't always manifest as a clean and decisive break. Returning to an abuser does not signify weakness; it reflects the complex reality of being human and navigating tumultuous emotional landscapes.

The raw truth that is often left unspoken is that abuse profoundly disorients the nervous system, reshapes the mind, and distorts our fundamental understanding of love. The decision to leave, or even the attempts to do so, typically exists within a whirlwind of conflicting emotions, fear, hope, shattered memories, trauma, and the instinct for survival. This isn't merely about poor judgment or naivety; it's about brain wiring that has been altered through emotional, neurological, and relational upheaval.

*The Trauma Bond: When Survival Masquerades as Love*

Abusive relationships frequently exhibit a relentless pattern known as intermittent reinforcement, a psychological mechanism where cruelty and threats are intermittently punctuated by moments of affection, apologies, or temporary tenderness. Over time, this cycle can foster what psychologists label as a trauma bond. The brain starts associating the abuser not just with fear but also with an unexpected sense of relief, particularly when moments of kindness arise following episodes of emotional or physical violence. This stark contrast amplifies the attachment.

The bond does not form because the abuse is benign; it takes root precisely because the moments of care are genuine. These fleeting reprieves become the lifelines that our brains cling to, creating a complex psychological dependency where we begin to tie our sense of safety, self-worth, and even identity to the very person causing us harm.

This phenomenon is neither irrational nor a simple choice. It's rooted in neurobiological conditioning. When exposed to abuse, the brain is flooded with cortisol, and over time, it becomes addicted to the dopamine hits that arise during moments of kindness from the abuser. Much like addiction, this emotional rollercoaster is compulsive, chemically driven, and extraordinarily challenging to break without significant effort to rewire the brain.

*The Survival Brain Doesn't Care About Logic*

When individuals discuss leaving an abusive situation, it is often framed in terms of sheer willpower or rational choice. However, it is crucial to understand that the amygdala, the part of the brain that governs fear and threat perception, operates primarily on instinct rather than logic. In scenarios of trauma, the brain's circuitry prioritizes immediate survival over long-term planning, a state commonly referred to as survival mode.

In survival mode, the nervous system might respond by freezing to avoid danger or adopting a fawn response, which entails appeasing the perceived threat. For some, returning to the abuser can feel like a safer option compared to the uncertainty of venturing into the unknown. This instinctual behaviour highlights the powerful grip that fear has on decision-making.

Moreover, this same brain may have sustained traumatic injuries, something all too common in the context of domestic abuse. Repeated physical violence, including strikes to the head, strangulation, or suffocation, can severely impair vital functions such as memory, attention, emotional regulation, and impulse control. Survivors may be labelled as "erratic" or "confused" when what they are grappling with is often undiagnosed and untreated brain trauma.

*Childhood Wounds and Attachment Patterns*

For individuals raised in environments where love is conditional and affection is given and taken in unpredictable ways, a deep-seated belief may form: that love must be earned. This attachment pattern can make abusive relationships feel familiar and, paradoxically, comfortable. The emotional dynamics echo the chaos of their childhood, where expectancy and affection coexisted uneasily.
The concept of betrayal trauma theory explains that when a caregiver becomes the source of harm, the mind often shields itself by minimizing or compartmentalizing the abuse. This protective mechanism helps individuals unconsciously preserve their relationships, dulling their awareness of the betrayal to cope with the emotional distress. This is not mere denial; it is a form of psychological survival.

Professional counselling often facilitates the surfacing of these entrenched patterns. Survivors may come to realize they are unconsciously revisiting old wounds, hoping desperately for a different outcome. The objective isn't to shame these patterns but to foster understanding. Healing requires naming and acknowledging these deep-rooted issues.

*Empathy: A Double-Edged Sword*

Survivors of abuse often possess profound empathy, which can be both a source of strength and a vulnerability. When we perceive the wounded child within our abuser and hear their apologies and promises for change, our instinct is to believe them, not only for our own sake but for theirs as well. A glimmer of hope can prompt us to over-function, over-forgive, and over-give, as we hold onto the belief that our patience might bring about healing.

However, empathy devoid of boundaries can lead to self-abandonment. Loving an abuser doesn't indicate that something is broken within you; it illustrates that your incredible capacity to care has been misdirected and turned against yourself.

*The World Isn't Always Safer*

It may seem easy to advise someone to "just leave" an abusive relationship, but the reality is far more complex. What happens when the abuser controls finances, housing, immigration status, or access to children? What if family and friends downplay the situation or fail to provide support? What if legal systems and authorities dismiss their experiences, or cultural stigmas keep them silent?

Leaving an abusive situation transcends the simple act of walking out the door; it requires stepping into a world that can feel exponentially more perilous, isolating, and fraught with uncertainty. The fear surrounding the prospect of leaving is not only real; it is deeply valid.

And yet, even with this understanding, many still find themselves returning to the abuser. This may stem from lingering hopes for change, an ingrained familiarity with chaos, or the weight of shame associated with perceived failure. Such responses are not moral failings; they highlight the intricate and often painful nature of trauma responses.

*What Therapy Can Offer*

This delineates why trauma-informed therapy is imperative for survivors. Instead of questioning, "Why didn't you leave?" it emphasizes exploring, "What happened?" This approach seeks to unravel the complexities of experience and support individuals in their healing journey, helping them to reclaim their narratives and understand the multifaceted dynamics that influenced their decisions. In doing so, therapy lays the groundwork for true healing and empowerment.

*Toolkit: Reclaiming Autonomy*

Trauma-Bond Awareness Exercise:

Begin by reflecting on your past experiences. Write down specific instances where you received kindness and compare them with moments that caused you harm. As you examine these memories, look for patterns that emerge. Circle any recurring themes or behaviours that stand out to you. Then, ask yourself: Was the kindness genuinely nurturing, or was it merely a temporary reprieve from the harm that often overshadowed it? This exercise will help you discern the true nature of your past relationships.

Safety & Return Plan:

To create a comprehensive plan for "returning", whether emotionally, physically, or digitally, first define what returning means to you. What feelings and circumstances would signify a safe return? Next, establish a "reset checklist" to ensure you're fully prepared before re-engaging. This might include reaching out to supportive friends or family, checking in with yourself mentally, or reviewing your goals. Ask yourself important questions: Have I consulted with my support network? What boundaries will I set to protect my well-being?

Self-Compassion Prompts:

Practice self-compassion by taking time to reflect on your experiences. Ask yourself: "What did my return offer me at that moment?" Consider the emotional needs you were trying to fulfil through this return. Then, explore alternative ways to meet those needs that prioritize your safety and well-being. Acknowledge that it's okay to recognize your desire for connection, while seeking healthier avenues for fulfilment.

Therapy Guidance Questions:

When engaging with a therapist, consider asking these crucial questions to ensure you are both on the same path during your healing journey: "Can we explore my attachment history and how it shapes my current relationships?" "Can we work together to elucidate my survival responses, approaching them without judgment?" "Do you utilize trauma-informed practices and client-led models that empower my narrative and experience?" This will guide you in finding a therapist who understands your unique needs.

**Final Words**

Returning to past situations does not signify naivety; rather, it reflects your resilience and hope for a better connection. It reveals a longing for love, especially in scenarios where it may have been weaponized against you. Remember that healing is a journey filled with possibilities. You have the power to unlearn the patterns set by trauma and redefine what love means to you. You can establish safety not only around you but also within yourself.

You are not alone in this process, and perfection is not required. Each time you choose to prioritize your well-being, no matter how small, you are taking meaningful steps along your path toward healing and autonomy.

# The Grief That No-one Talks About

When we think of grief, our minds often conjure images of funerals, flowers, and poignant final farewells. However, an aspect of grief that remains largely unaddressed is that which follows the end of an abusive relationship. This type of grief emerges not from the loss of life but from the profound emotional and psychological turmoil of leaving a relationship marked by harm, manipulation, and control. Survivors face an invisible, complicated mourning that is often dismissed or misunderstood.

In the aftermath of an abusive relationship, survivors may grapple with a mixture of emotions, confusion, relief, guilt, and sorrow. Society often expects them to feel only joy and liberation upon escaping an abusive partner. Instead, they find themselves in a state of mourning, grieving not only for the love they once believed in but also for the dreams that were shattered along the way. They mourn the person they were before the trauma began, now overshadowed by self-doubt and pain.

Research reveals that survivors of intimate partner violence endure a profound sense of loss, not just of the partner they thought they knew, but of their own identity and sense of self. Studies indicate that the emotional fallout is immense and multifaceted, leading to conditions such as depression, post-traumatic stress disorder (PTSD), anxiety, and severe psychosocial distress. This distress often stems from long-term trauma, ongoing economic instability, and an unrelenting concern for their children's welfare. The grief experienced by survivors is twofold: they mourn the relationship that once was, while simultaneously mourning the self they feel has been irrevocably altered.

This particular type of grief is often disenfranchised, meaning that society tends to overlook its legitimacy and complexity. Statements like, "Surely you're happy you left," can invalidate their feelings, leaving them grappling with an aching heart that wishes to be recognised. Mental health professionals note that survivors may find it challenging to distinguish between missing their abuser and longing for the safety they once felt, or even the familiar dysfunction that defined their lives. Terms like "unrecognised grief" have emerged in therapeutic circles, articulating the bittersweet longing for a future that was stolen, the identity that was forcibly reshaped, and the loss of hope that accompanied the abusive relationship.

A 2023 qualitative study targeting survivors more than a year post-separation underscored lingering emotional scars that include shame, self-blame, loneliness, and alienation, even when the direct threat is no longer present. Many survivors report feelings of disorientation, struggling to rebuild trust in themselves and the world around them. They frequently wrestle with conflicting emotions, torn between relief at their escape and sorrow for the love they lost. This grief is distinct; it is shaped not by death but by relinquishing a past self and stepping into an uncertain future.

Furthermore, survivors may experience prolonged grief disorder, even in the absence of death. Much like those grieving violent losses, survivors of abuse suffer from the emotional aftermath of their relationships, mourning the traumatic end that leaves deep psychological imprints. The bonds once shared do not simply vanish; they morph into a haunting mixture of regret, longing, and fragmented memories that persist long after the relationship has ended.

Self-blame is a pervasive issue among survivors. Often subjected to gas lighting, they may internalize the belief that they caused their suffering, that they were "too sensitive," "deserving" of the abuse, or simply "not enough." Such destructive narratives make it increasingly difficult to grieve authentically. If they feel responsible for the pain endured, they question their right to mourn the loss of their relationship or their former self.

Secondary victimisation also plays a critical role, particularly when survivors encounter disbelief or blame while seeking help. Comments from professionals or loved ones questioning why they remained in an abusive situation can exacerbate feelings of shame and invalidation, silencing their grief, where they should find support.

Nevertheless, recognition of this grief is essential for healing to begin. When grief is openly acknowledged and witnessed, it creates space for survivors to start the healing process. Therapeutic models like trauma- and violence-informed care emphasise the importance of providing survivors with safe environments to express their losses, validate their complex feelings, and gradually reclaim their grief in a way that honours their identity, dreams, and pain.

Amidst this complexity, hope is not lost. Features in platforms like Self highlight the significance of recognizing and celebrating small victories, whether that involves opening new doors, tapping back into creativity, or rebuilding trust in oneself. Such narratives illuminate the resilience that emerges from the depths of grief, showing that healing is possible.

Grief following abuse is rarely linear; fear, anger, despair, and relief can coexist, creating an emotional tapestry that is rich but difficult to navigate. Embracing this grief, allowing oneself to mourn the end of the relationship, to cry for the self that once was, and to grieve the lost future possibilities is not a sign of weakness; it is an essential aspect of survival and a testament to our shared humanity.

Your grief deserves to be honoured. It requires space, and it deserves witnesses who affirm, "I see you. I believe you." It needs recognition, especially in a world that struggles to articulate and validate such a profound loss. Only through this acknowledgment can the potential for rebuilding take root, a life not solely defined by loss but one reshaped by the strength to survive, the bravery to feel deeply, and the ability to grow beyond the pain of the past.

# Fear After Freedom: Trauma in the Quiet

A peculiar silence envelops survivors once the abuse has ended one that doesn't always usher in peace and solace. For many, this absence of chaos is not a soothing balm but rather a breeding ground for tension. It breeds a nagging sense of unease, as though something is amiss or that worse is looming just out of sight. You may be physically free from your abuser, yet your mind and body remain intertwined with the remnants of fear.

This phenomenon encapsulates what many refer to as trauma in the quiet. While the mind can rationally acknowledge the end of the relationship and the cessation of danger, the body might continue to react as if it were still trapped in that perilous environment. The nervous system, conditioned over time to anticipate violent outbursts, slamming doors, veiled threats, or seemingly benign control masquerading as concern, remains perpetually on alert. This heightened state, known as hypervigilance, is a hallmark symptom of complex Post-Traumatic Stress Disorder (PTSD) that many survivors grapple with long after the last abusive episode.

Neuroscience studies reveal that prolonged exposure to interpersonal violence, particularly forms of coercive control, can significantly alter brain function. The amygdala, the brain's alarm system responsible for detecting threats, often becomes hyperactive, while the prefrontal cortex, which governs rational thinking and decision-making, may fall into disarray. The outcome of this stark imbalance is a survivor who, despite knowing on an intellectual level that they are safe, still finds themselves susceptible to panic attacks, vivid flashbacks, insomnia, or overwhelming anxiety triggered by mundane occurrences like a text message or an unexpected knock at the door.

In these moments of silence, echoes of the past can resound louder than any verbal confrontation. You might find yourself replaying conversations in your mind, scrutinizing your decisions, and bracing for disbelief or punishment from those around you. The struggle to remain grounded in safe spaces becomes an exhausting battle. This is why the very notion of freedom can feel overwhelmingly terrifying, it illustrates a transition from mere survival to a daunting quest to learn how to truly live.

The impact of trauma doesn't dissipate the moment the relationship concludes; it lingers, woven into the fabric of muscle memory. You may instinctively flinch at the sound of raised voices, habitually scan for exits as you walk into a room, or grapple with self-doubt when your instincts urge you to be cautious. True freedom necessitates a journey of healing, and healing is not merely a flick of a switch; it is a gradual, often arduous process that demands patience, self-compassion, and time.

*The Shame That Was Never Yours*

One of the heaviest burdens that survivors of abuse often carry is not the fear of their past, but a profound sense of shame. This shame can quietly seep in after they've finally gained their freedom, leaving them with questions that echo painfully in their minds: Why didn't I leave sooner? Why did I allow myself to be treated that way? Why did I return to that toxic situation? How could I let this happen to me?

This insidious shame feels like an undeniable truth, but it is neither just nor accurate. Abusers are exceptionally skilled at planting seeds of self-blame, manipulating their victims into believing they are too sensitive, too needy, or fundamentally broken. Over time, these negative messages become internalized, morphing into a relentless inner monologue that perpetuates the cycle of shame. When survivors finally break free from their abusers, they often find that these damaging thoughts did not leave with their captor; instead, they linger, festering in the corners of their minds.

It is crucial to acknowledge, with clarity and conviction, that this shame is not the survivors to carry. In trauma psychology, the shame experienced after abuse is often referred to as "self-stigma" or "internalized blame." It emerges from pervasive societal narratives that too often hold victims responsible for their abuse. Many question the survivor's choices, disbelieve their accounts, or pathologize their responses to trauma, such as staying with an abuser, freezing in the face of danger, or repeatedly returning to a harmful situation.

Survivors frequently hear the question: Why didn't you just leave? What is rarely asked, however, is: What might have happened if you did? Leaving an abusive relationship is not simply a matter of willpower; it can be fraught with danger. Indeed, statistics reveal that the period immediately following separation is often the most perilous for a victim, marked by an alarming spike in homicides, stalking incidents, and escalated violence. Survivors often choose to stay because they are carefully calculating risks, not out of ignorance or naivety.

There is also a unique and complex shame that comes from still loving the person who caused so much pain. This includes missing the good moments, reminiscing about the person they once were the charm, the tenderness, the broken promises. Such feelings are entirely normal; trauma bonds are not severed instantaneously the moment a survivor walks out the door. Instead, they unravel gradually, often accompanied by intense emotional turmoil and reflection.

For those who have endured financial abuse, spiritual manipulation, or years of gas lighting, the layers of shame can run even deeper. Many survivors grapple with feelings of having lost themselves along the way, of having moulded into a different person just to survive. Yet it is vital to understand: you did not lose who you are. You adapted. You coped. You did what you needed to do given the circumstances you faced at that time.

That survival instinct is not shameful; it is a testament to your resilience. True healing begins when we can shift the narrative and return the weight of shame to where it belongs, not on the shoulders of the survivor but rather upon the abuser who inflicted the harm. It is through this process of reclaiming agency and recognizing the truth of one's experience that survivors can begin to heal and move forward.

**Navigating the System: A Survivor's Journey**

For many survivors of domestic abuse, leaving the relationship is just the beginning of a long and arduous journey. What follows is often an exhausting and dehumanising process: navigating a complex system that is meant to offer protection and support. Unfortunately, the very institutions established to safeguard survivors frequently end up inflicting additional pain, a phenomenon known as secondary victimisation.

Survivors often find themselves recounting their traumatic experiences over and over again to strangers who may lack the necessary empathy, understanding, and training. This repeated exposure to their trauma can be profoundly distressing and may lead to feelings of helplessness and re-traumatisation. A troubling statistic from a 2022 UK study highlights this issue, revealing that over 60% of survivors felt that the criminal justice system failed to protect and support them. Many survivors reported encountering law enforcement officers who were inadequately trained to recognise and address coercive control, a form of psychological abuse that doesn't always leave visible scars. Furthermore, some officers failed to take non-physical abuse seriously, while others suggested mediation with abusers, an approach that neglects the critical power imbalances inherent in abusive relationships.

The family court system presents its own set of challenges. Abusers often exploit post-separation dynamics to inflict further harm through legal means, employing tactics such as protracted custody disputes, filing false allegations, or manipulating visitation rights to maintain control over their victims. This insidious form of legal abuse has garnered increasing recognition in domestic abuse literature but remains inadequately addressed in practice. Survivors often find themselves trapped in a cycle of litigation that not only drains their emotional and financial resources but also undermines their capacity to heal and move on.

Access to shelters can also be limited, with many facilities reaching full capacity and waiting lists for counselling services stretching for months. Financial assistance and benefits for survivors may be delayed due to bureaucratic hurdles, leaving them in precarious situations. The barriers can be even more formidable for survivors who belong to marginalised communities, including those who identify as LGBTQ+, disabled individuals, people from Black, Asian, and Minority Ethnic (BAME) backgrounds, or those who are undocumented. These survivors often face compounded challenges that make navigating the system even more daunting.

What survivors truly need is not a system that poses the question, "Why didn't you leave?" but one that asks, "What do you need to be safe now?" This shift in perspective is essential for fostering an environment conducive to healing and recovery.

Trauma-informed services provide a vital framework for addressing the needs of survivors effectively. These services prioritise:

- Safety: Ensuring that emotional, physical, and psychological safety are at the forefront of all interactions.
- Choice: Empowering survivors to reclaim their autonomy and make decisions that best suit their needs.
- Trust: Establishing consistent, transparent, and respectful communication to build rapport and trust.
- Empowerment: Recognising and affirming the survivor's inherent strength and resilience in their journey toward healing.

While advocates, helplines, and domestic violence-specific charities often play a crucial role in bridging the gaps left by formal systems, it is unacceptable that survivors should have to depend on luck or local funding to achieve justice, healing, or stability.

Survivors should not be forced to become warriors in order to obtain the support they need and deserve. Survival itself is a significant battle; the systems in place should facilitate recovery, not impede it.

**Conclusion**

Freedom after experiencing abuse marks a significant turning point, yet it often serves merely as the beginning of a complex journey filled with ongoing fear, shame, and struggle. The impact of trauma doesn't adhere to a neat timeline; it lingers and sometimes resurfaces unexpectedly, casting shadows over moments that might otherwise be joyful. Similarly, shame doesn't simply fade with distance; it can cling to us like a weight, often rooted in societal perceptions and the manipulation of our worth.

It's important to recognize that the fear you experience is not irrational; it is a biological response, hardwired into your very being as a protective mechanism. Your feelings of shame are not intrinsic to you; they have been instilled through external narratives and harmful influences. Navigating the systems meant to offer support should not require a display of strength that you may not possess; it should not feel like a relentless challenge to prove your worthiness for help.

To every survivor reading this: your trauma responses are not signs of weakness or character flaws. They are valid manifestations of a body and mind doing their best to protect you in the face of danger. Your grief, far from being a hindrance, is a profound step toward uncovering your truth and reclaiming your narrative. Your inherent right to support, justice, and healing is unconditional; it does not rely on any external approval or validation.

You deserve systems and spaces that not only honour your unique story but also empower you to share it without fear of scepticism. You deserve safety that requires no lengthy justification and exists not just in the absence of danger, but in the presence of understanding and care. Most importantly, you deserve a sense of peace that transcends the silence that follows conflict. This peace is the kind that gradually infuses your nervous system, enriches your relationships, and encourages the authentic expression of your voice. It is a deep, abiding tranquillity that restores your sense of self and nurtures your journey toward healing.

# Learning to Feel Safe Again (In Your Own Skin)

Freedom from abuse is often mistaken as the conclusion of a harrowing experience. However, for many survivors, the true journey of reckoning commences after the noise subsides. Long after the last argument echoes, when the door has closed for the final time, your body may still instinctively brace for an impact that no longer comes. You may find yourself flinching at the sound of footsteps, tensing up at raised voices, or being startled by your own reflection in the mirror. This is not merely a psychological battle; it embodies the unseen residue of trauma, where your nervous system remains entrapped in a past your conscious mind is striving to escape.

Research in trauma psychology reveals that prolonged exposure to domestic violence fundamentally alters brain function. The amygdala the brain's fear centre becomes hyperactive, perpetually poised in a state of alarm. Simultaneously, the prefrontal cortex responsible for rational thought and calming emotional responses becomes less responsive. This neurological rewiring means that even the most innocuous stimuli, a creaking floorboard, a gentle touch on your shoulder, or a specific tone of voice, can elicit a fight, flight, or freeze reaction. This response is not an overreaction or dramatization but rather a learned reaction from a body conditioned to perceive these signals as precursors to danger.

This phenomenon is grounded in reality: it reflects the biology of survival. Experts at My Thrive Psychology emphasise how the body of a trauma survivor continuously scans for threats, even in environments devoid of actual harm. Given that this response is somatic, deeply rooted in muscle memory, breath patterns, and heart rate, genuine healing requires addressing the body as well as the mind. But how does one start to feel secure in the very skin that once housed betrayal?

The reality is that the process unfolds slowly, often requiring gentleness and patience, and sometimes feels agonizingly protracted.

Trauma-informed therapeutic approaches such as Trauma-Focused Cognitive Behavioural Therapy (TF-CBT) and Eye Movement Desensitisation and Reprocessing (EMDR) are invaluable in helping survivors reframe traumatic memories, mitigate emotional flashbacks, and soothe an over reactive nervous system. These therapies don't erase the past; rather, they assist your brain in reorganizing these memories, so you no longer find yourself reliving the trauma repeatedly. Yet, access to therapy can be limited, and the journey of healing doesn't pause for ideal conditions.

This is where body-based healing practices become vital. Organizations like SafeAustin.org and other trauma-informed groups underscore the efficacy of holistic approaches such as yoga, mindful walking, deep breathing exercises, progressive muscle relaxation, and even intuitive movement. These practices help survivors reconnect with their physical selves without the accompanying fear, conveying a powerful message: you are present in this moment. You are not back in the kitchen where you felt cornered; you are not in the car where screaming rang out; you are not in the room where silence was forced upon you.

You are here. You are now. You are safe.

Healing begins with small, almost imperceptible victories. It could be sitting in a room alone without the relentless urge to check all exits. It might be learning to rest without keeping one ear alert for every sound. It could be allowing your shoulders to relax from their tense perch near your ears or enjoying a shower without panic or fear. Standing by a window during a storm and feeling the thunder without flinching can be a significant triumph.

Every instance of stillness is an act of resistance against the chaos of the past. Each calm moment serves as a counter-spell to the turbulence you once endured.

Many survivors note that the toughest challenge isn't solely about feeling safe in the outside world; it's also about cultivating a sense of safety within oneself. After experiencing abuse, your body can feel like a traitor: it froze when you desperately needed to fight, it trembled when you longed to flee, and it remained quiet when you wanted to scream. A crucial aspect of healing involves reconciling with your body offering forgiveness, expressing gratitude, and recognising that it did what was necessary to survive.

In this chapter of your healing journey, you begin to reclaim your skin not as a battleground, but as a sanctuary.

You are not broken. You are not weak. You are not overly dramatic. You are healing.

Healing can be messy, slow, and devoid of glamour, yet it stands as an act of radical defiance. You are constructing a sense of safety not only around you but also within you—discovering that peace is achievable and, more importantly, something you truly deserve.

One breath. One grounding moment. One quiet room at a time.

*Loving Yourself Without Permission*

When someone systematically breaks you down, consistently telling you that you're too much or not enough, belittling your dreams, monitoring your happiness, and distorting your perception of reality, it leaves lasting scars far beyond what is visible. Abuse doesn't merely mark the skin; it rewires the very foundation of how you see yourself.

Many survivors of abuse emerge from these toxic relationships bearing invisible scars: persistent self-doubt, guilt for having left, a profound shame for having stayed, and an internal critic whose voice eerily echoes that of the person who caused them harm. Over time, that voice becomes a relentless companion, whispering messages of unworthiness: "You're unlovable. You're weak. You're nothing without me." When this negative reinforcement has echoed in your mind long enough, it becomes indistinguishable from your own thoughts.

This is why healing transcends the need for physical safety. True recovery involves rekindling your sense of self-worth. Learning to love yourself again, especially after having been conditioned to believe you did not deserve love, becomes one of the most radical, defiant, and crucial steps in the healing process.

One of the most challenging aspects of this journey is the inner belief that you don't deserve to love yourself. Ironically, these feelings are precisely when you need self-love the most.

Cultivating genuine self-compassion is essential, but it's important to clarify what that means. This isn't about the superficial, inspirational quotes often found on social media, but rather a deep, empathetic understanding of yourself as you navigate your struggles. It's the gentle voice within that reassures you: "You don't need to earn rest, softness, or kindness; you are inherently worthy of these things."

Survivors are often encouraged to start this journey by speaking to themselves as they would to someone they love dearly, a cherished friend, a child, or even a beloved pet. This means approaching yourself not with blame, but with care; not with shame, but with a softness that acknowledges your humanity.

Embracing this shift can feel uncomfortable at first, especially for those who have been conditioned to suppress their own needs, prioritise others, or bear the guilt of simply existing. It's a natural response; healing often begins at the point of resistance.

Begin with small steps. Daily affirmations might feel overly simplistic or even cheesy, yet asserting that "I am enough" or "I am allowed to take up space" can gradually rewire your brain's neural pathways. This process illustrates neuroplasticity at work; according to trauma specialists, replacing self-criticism with self-affirmation literally "fires and wires" new pathways in the brain, diminishing the stronghold of shame while bolstering your sense of dignity and self-trust.

Engaging in creative expression can be another transformative avenue. Many survivors have faced discouragement or outright prohibition from pursuing creative outlets. Yet, art, music, photography, dance, or even simply arranging a space to reflect your personality are not just superficial hobbies, they are vital avenues for reclaiming your voice, choices, and joy. Every moment spent creating something meaningful reinforces your sense of autonomy and empowerment.

Journaling serves as a powerful daily practice that allows for self-exploration. It's an opportunity to disentangle the thoughts and beliefs that have been imposed on you by your abuser and to recognize your authentic desires and truths. Questions like "Is this my truth, or was it theirs?" or "What do I want?" become pivotal as you sift through the remnants of external criticism. Eventually, journaling transforms into a mirror reflecting not the brokenness projected onto you, but the resilience that has always resided within.

Reclaiming your hobbies or setting personal goals, no matter how small, signals to your brain that you matter. Whether it's learning a new language, enrolling in a course, committing to a morning walk, or nurturing a plant, these actions aren't indulgences; they are reparative efforts. They affirm your right to belong, emphasizing that you are not simply surviving, but actively choosing to thrive.

Above all, remember that none of this requires permission. You do not need applause or external validation to begin treating yourself kindly. You don't have to wait for someone else to say "you're allowed" before you embrace your own life and its inherent value.

The truth is, your worth isn't up for debate. It has always existed; it was merely obscured by layers of fear, criticism, and manipulation. Your healing journey is the process of unearthing that worth.

So whether it involves standing in front of the mirror and making eye contact with yourself, surrounding yourself with individuals who speak kindly to you, taking guilt-free breaks, or daring to desire more from life, each act of self-love becomes an act of rebellion against the conditioning that sought to diminish you.

You were never the problem. You have always been worthy. And now, you no longer need permission to embrace that truth.

# Dating After Domestic Violence

The prospect of dating after experiencing domestic violence can elicit a complex mix of emotions, simultaneously terrifying and enticing. For many survivors, the thought of re-entering the dating scene might feel like a distant, almost unreachable goal, as they grapple with their healing journey. For others, it could serve as a powerful symbol of reclaiming their joy, restoring connections, and rediscovering aspects of themselves that were buried under the weight of control and manipulation. Regardless of where you find yourself on this spectrum, one undeniable truth prevails: re-entering the realm of intimacy after trauma is not merely a simple transition; it is a sacred process that demands gentleness and patience.

Survivors don't walk into new relationships with blank slates; instead, they carry a tapestry woven with both the beauty of their resilience and the scars of their past betrayals. Research from trauma specialists, including insights from DrTaji.com, underscores that post-traumatic stress symptoms can often manifest in romantic dynamics. These symptoms may include hypervigilance, constantly scanning for potential threats, difficulty in trusting others, a fear of abandonment, emotional numbing, or sudden shutdowns in response to emotional stimuli. Triggers are unpredictable and can arise from a variety of sources, a familiar scent, a particular tone of voice, or even the sensation of being held, prompting a survivor to be thrust back into a memory associated with their trauma, a memory from which their body has never truly recovered.

This experience is not indicative of brokenness; rather, it reflects a body that learned to survive in the face of adversity and still struggles to fully embrace the notion of safety and softness. Thus, experts advocate for a trauma-informed approach to dating, starting with deep self-reflection and inquiry: Am I genuinely ready to engage with someone new?

What does safety feel like to me now, post-trauma? Am I seeking love, or am I trying to escape the loneliness that accompanies healing? Do I trust myself to recognize when something feels off and to walk away if necessary?

This process isn't about crafting an impossible checklist of criteria or striving for perfection; instead, it's about allowing yourself the grace to move at your own pace. It's crucial to honour your nervous system and acknowledge that taking breaks without guilt or hesitation is not only acceptable but essential. Opening up to someone should only happen when you feel adequately safe and ready to let them in.

Establishing boundaries is vital; they are not markers of unpreparedness. In fact, they form the very foundation for readiness. Thus, it's imperative to communicate your needs and limits early on. Be clear about what you are comfortable with and what you aren't, without feeling the need to over-explain your rationale. If physical touch, emotional intimacy, or certain types of conversation evoke discomfort, it's perfectly okay to express those feelings. A supportive partner will not merely tolerate these boundaries, they will respect and honour them.

Additionally, the environments in which you choose to meet or spend time with potential partners can significantly impact your comfort level and sense of safety. Safe spaces can be as straightforward as:

Meeting for coffee during daylight hours in public venues,

- Informing a trusted friend of your plans and sharing your location before a date,
- Using your own transportation to maintain independence,
- Having a clear "exit plan" in place if you sense that things are becoming uncomfortable,
- Regularly communicating with your support system after each date to process your experiences.

You should never feel compelled to apologise for prioritising what helps you maintain your sense of grounding and stability.

If someone disregards your boundaries, pressures you to move faster than you're comfortable with, or questions the validity of your trauma, heed that warning. Believe them the first time they demonstrate a lack of respect. You owe no one a relationship that compromises your healing process.

Resources like Teen Vogue and Talk space emphasize the importance of supportive partners engaging in gentle grounding techniques with trauma survivors. These techniques may include the 5-4-3-2-1 method, identifying five things you can see, four things you can touch, etc., offering choices instead of imposing demands, and always prioritizing consent before moving into emotional or physical closeness. Sometimes, a healing partner's most profound act is not one of overt affection but rather the practice of patience.

Even within supportive conditions, it's normal for fear to sit alongside you at the table. You may find yourself questioning whether you are being too guarded or too open, or you may flinch at expressions of kindness, unsure if they are genuine or merely a facade. This ambivalence is part of the healing process; trauma doesn't solely in still a fear of pain, it can also breed a deep-seated suspicion of peace and happiness.

Yet, with time, trust, and consistent positive experiences, your nervous system can learn that love does not equate to suffering. Importantly, you don't need to rush this journey.

Society often propagates the notion that you must "move on" and that healing inherently means dating again, leading many to believe that finding a new partner is a reward for having survived an abusive relationship. However, the truth is that emotional safety is far more critical than adhering to societal timelines. Whether it takes six months or six years, you possess the autonomy to decide when, if, and how you wish to step back into intimacy.

This time, it's not about merely filling a void; it's about making a conscious choice from a place of fullness and self-worth. You deserve a love that does not feel like a continual struggle for survival but rather a gentle and nurturing experience. Remember, you have every right to take all the time you need to discover that love.

*When Triggers Disguise Themselves as People*

One of the most bewildering aspects of navigating life after experiencing abuse is the unsettling realization that danger often doesn't present itself in the way we expect. Sometimes, it appears as a friend exhibiting a sharp, biting tone during a seemingly trivial conversation. Other times, it manifests in a partner who walks with an unnerving silence, or a stranger who wears the same cologne as someone from our past. It can even arise when someone unexpectedly touches your arm, their intention benign, but your body reacts with an alarm that feels uncontrollable.

Triggers are frequently subtle and insidious, disguising themselves in the behaviours and traits of ordinary people. They don't come with warning labels, and most importantly, they don't announce themselves with the ferocity we might expect from real danger. Instead, they show up during routine interactions, and due to our past experiences, our nervous system struggles to recognize normalcy. Instead of perceiving the moment as safe, it regresses to a state of alertness, interpreting every cue through the lens of past trauma.

This is the painful irony of trauma: it teaches our bodies to scan the environment not for the present reality but for echoes of what has already transpired. When trauma embeds itself within our nervous system, it alters the wiring of our brain, leading to reactions that occur before our rational mind even has a chance to assess what's actually happening. This phenomenon, known as a neuroceptive response, is an unconscious, automatic judgment generated by the brainstem. It reacts to perceived threats based solely on sensory information: the cadence of a voice that strays too close to the sound of past aggression, the creak of a door closing that mimics a familiar pattern of fear, or the way someone's shoulders slump, triggering memories of vulnerability.

These reactions are not deliberate. In those moments, you may not consciously believe you're in danger. Your body, however, has made an instinctive decision to defend itself, reacting in a way that feels necessary, even if it seems irrational to others.

As a result, survivors of trauma may find themselves instinctively recoiling from people they genuinely like or mistrusting partners who have not demonstrated any wrongdoing. Their hearts may race, and their breathing may quicken, even when those around them remain calm and collected. This isn't indicative of a broken spirit; rather, it reflects the persistent nature of trauma memory, which can become an unwelcome remnant of survival, replaying endlessly in the background of our physiological responses.

The shame that accompanies these reactions can be overwhelmingly heavy, especially when those triggers are linked to individuals who are otherwise kind and well-meaning. You might find yourself questioning: Why can't I simply relax around them? What if I risk pushing away someone who genuinely cares for me?

But it's crucial to understand this: trauma does not dictate who you should or should not trust. Instead, it serves as a barometer for what your body has endured. Acknowledging this truth is the first step towards healing, not through shame, but through understanding.

Awareness is essential. When you notice yourself experiencing a shutdown, snapping in irritation, withdrawing into yourself, or feeling an inexplicable sense of anxiety in someone's presence, take a moment to pause. Ask yourself: What about this moment feels eerily familiar? Is it their posture? Did they say something that mirrors the language of your abuser? Or perhaps it's their silence—a void that stirs up fears your nervous system has come to dread most.

By naming the trigger, even if just to yourself, such as recognising that a certain tone evoked feelings of fear, or that a sudden movement felt invasive, you begin the process of reclaiming the moment. This act of awareness transforms your automatic response, enabling you to engage thoughtfully rather than simply drifting into autopilot.

Incorporating grounding techniques can further assist in reconnecting your body with the present. Press your feet into the ground, feeling the stability beneath you. Take a moment to observe your surroundings, count five things you can see, four you can touch, three you can hear. Breathe deeply three times, allowing this simple act to communicate to your body: We are not back there. We are here. We are safe.

Over time, especially with the guidance of therapy, journaling, or a supportive network, you can revisit those trauma memories with conscious awareness. This allows your brain to reprocess them. You can learn to tell yourself: It's not happening again. That was not them. That was a different time.

It's important to recognize that this process doesn't erase the past; it reshapes your associations, gradually disentangling the remnants of trauma from your current reality. Eventually, individuals who once evoked feelings of danger may begin to lose that power over you. Their words will transform into mere words, and their actions will remain firmly rooted in the present, no longer tainted by the shadows of past experiences. Within this newfound space, you can cultivate fresh associations with trust, calm, and the sense of autonomy that comes from healing.

Sometimes, the individuals who trigger us are also the ones who play a crucial role in our healing journey. Their consistency, kindness, and patience allow us the time and support we need as we work through the process of untangling our complex history from our present.

There may also be moments when walking away is the healthiest choice, not because the other person is "bad," but because your nervous system still isn't equipped to handle the interaction. Recognising this is perfectly valid; honouring your body's response is essential. Healing doesn’t mean forcing yourself to endure situations that feel unsafe. Instead, it involves acknowledging and validating your feelings, reassuring your body that safety is attainable once more.

So, when you encounter triggers that manifest as people, resist the urge to withdraw in fear. Instead, approach those feelings with curiosity. Listen to your body’s signals, soothe the anxious parts within you, and remember: this journey isn't about determining whether someone else is trustworthy. It’s about validating your own right to feel safe before deciding who is deserving of your trust.

*Rebuilding Boundaries & Trust from the Ground Up*

The aftermath of abuse leaves a profound imprint on one’s psyche, often manifesting as a slow and insidious erosion of personal boundaries. This deterioration doesn’t always stem from overt violence; it can be rooted in the subtle art of manipulation, where guilt, gas lighting, and control stealthily replace autonomy. Initially, it may seem innocuous, a careless comment brushed aside, a decision made in the guise of concern, or an intimate moment intruded upon. These small transgressions accumulate, layering over time a pervasive message: your limits are inconsequential. Eventually, you might find yourself ceasing to draw lines entirely.

Abuse conditions individuals to suppress their needs as a means of survival, gradually compressing their sense of self to accommodate another's unpredictability. Voices once strong become hesitant, self-doubt takes root, and apologies spring forth for wrongs that aren't your burden to bear. With each instance of self-denial, the ability to trust oneself diminishes.

Yet, this narrative doesn't have to be your conclusion. Healing begins at the core of self-identity: your boundaries.

Boundaries are not impenetrable walls; instead, they serve as doorways equipped with locks and keys, yours to control. They define who enters your life, when they may enter, how they engage with you, and the terms of these interactions. Establishing boundaries is not about excluding others; rather, it's about inviting in those who genuinely respect and honour the sacred spaces you've bravely reclaimed.

Rebuilding these boundaries calls for a series of deliberate, consistent choices rather than a single grand announcement. Start with small, manageable steps. Decide the moments when you will respond to messages, allowing yourself the grace of solitude. Offer "no" without lengthy explanations, cherishing your right to prioritize your own needs. Close your door to invite silence when overwhelmed. Before saying "yes" to a favour, ask yourself: Am I committing out of genuine desire or out of obligation?

Every one of these intentional acts sends a compelling signal to your nervous system: I am making decisions; I am in control; I choose my path. After the chaos of abuse, reclaiming this sense of agency isn't merely empowering; it represents a profound revolution within.

However, boundaries are inherently intertwined with trust. While learning to assert "no" to others is crucial, the journey of saying “yes” to yourself, affirming your own worth and instinct, is where the deeper healing truly begins.

Trauma doesn’t only damage connections with others; it fractures the vital relationship you have with yourself. You may find yourself questioning your own judgment and fearing you are “too much” or “too broken.” Trust in your own intuition may wane, leading to a paralyzing fear of cyclic patterns resurfacing.

The "shattered assumptions" theory within trauma psychology posits that abuse fundamentally disrupts our core beliefs regarding the world: that people are inherently good, that life unfolds fairly, and that we are deserving of love and security. Yet, this theory also assures us that such beliefs can be reconstructed, stronger, wiser, and more resilient than before.

This rebuilding process is neither swift nor easy, but it is transformative. You start by softly whispering affirmations to yourself: “I deserve to be treated with kindness.” Gradually, these words gain weight until they are a part of your truth. You reaffirm, “I can trust my instincts,” and take action grounded in this new assurance. You acknowledge, “Some people truly are safe,” and you cautiously allow one into your life, inching forward with hope.

Trust doesn’t have to extend to everyone; it begins with you, trusting your own voice, honouring your needs, and recognizing your right to withdraw when something feels amiss, even if your knees tremble as you take that stand.

There will be moments of stumbling along the way. This is entirely acceptable. Boundaries aren’t static; they are living entities that bend, shift, and adapt as you grow. What matters most is that these boundaries are yours, crafted by you for your protection and peace.

Peer support plays an indispensable role in this journey of rebuilding. Whether through group therapy, survivor networks, or trusted friendships, the simple act of hearing someone express, "Me too," serves to shatter the isolation that trauma thrives in. Research consistently validates that survivors engaging in peer support report elevated levels of empowerment, self-worth, and sustainable healing.

There's a profound kind of healing that occurs when your story is witnessed without the pressure to fix it. It's in having a fellow survivor hold space for your experiences, honouring them without analysis, that true connection is forged. When others entrust you with their truths and you reciprocate in kind, a new foundation begins to solidify, built not on fear, but on mutual recognition and shared understanding.

And this is how trust returns, slowly, steadily. Not in a rush or a deluge, but drop by drop, boundary by boundary, moment by moment. Until one day, you awaken to the realisation: I no longer flinch at the warmth of kindness. I no longer apologize for existing in this world. I no longer seek permission to embrace my wholeness.

This is the essence of healing: a return to the self you were always meant to be.

*Conclusion: Healing Is a Journey, Not a Destination*

The chapters of this journey, learning the nuances of safety, reclaiming self-love, navigating relationships, managing triggers, and rebuilding trust, do not signify final destinations. They serve as milestones on a much longer path, one that meanders, loops back, and at times, fades into the fog, only to re-emerge stronger and more vibrant.

Domestic violence may be a thread in your story, but it does not define your essence. It is not your identity, nor does it determine your legacy. It should not overshadow the myriad truths that make you who you are.

Just as a seed breaks through concrete to find the light, so too does your healing symbolize the indomitable life force still residing within you. It represents the dignity you've never lost, the voice you are bravely reclaiming, and the boundaries you are resolutely redefining with bold, bright strokes.

With each step you take, whether whispered or shouted, you are reclaiming your authorship over your life. This reclamation reflects the most courageous narrative of all.

# The Freedom Programme: Understanding Abuse Through Education and Empowerment

The Freedom Programme, established by Pat Craven in 1996, stands as a nationally recognised initiative in the UK, tailored to equip individuals with a comprehensive understanding of domestic abuse, its manifestations, operational dynamics, and its profound impact on survivors and their children. Initially crafted to support women who have endured abuse, the programme has since expanded to encompass tailored offerings for men, students, professionals, and even educational institutions, thus broadening its outreach and relevance in today's society.

At its essence, the Freedom Programme seeks to dismantle prevalent myths surrounding abuse, utilising clear and accessible language to delve into the complexities of controlling behaviours. Central to the programme are two pivotal psychological constructs: The Dominator, which embodies the mind-set and tactics of abusive individuals, and The Survivor, representing the resilience and responses of those who navigate the tumultuous landscape of abuse. By employing these archetypes, participants gain insights into various forms of abuse, including physical violence, coercive control, emotional manipulation, financial restriction, and intimidation tactics that often go unnoticed.

What distinctly sets the Freedom Programme apart is its non-judgmental, psychoeducational methodology. Instead of shaming survivors or solely focusing on crises, the programme empowers individuals through knowledge and awareness. It encourages participants to articulate their experiences, affirming that they are not to blame for the abuse they endured. Through this process, individuals begin to rebuild their confidence, reclaim their identity, and restore self-trust foundational elements crucial for healing.

Over the years, Pat Craven has continuously adapted the programme to resonate with a wider audience, ensuring accessibility for men, LGBTQ+ individuals, and professionals across various spheres. Notably, she has reframed the language around male participants, opting to refer to them as "students" rather than "perpetrators." This intentional choice creates a learning environment that fosters reflection and insight without the weight of judgment. The men's courses are often delivered through intensive weekend workshops, designed to create a focused atmosphere conducive to growth. During these sessions, participants refrained from sharing personal stories to minimize defensiveness and prevent victim-blaming, cultivating a space for genuine self-awareness and introspection. This framework has made the programme equally beneficial for both individuals who have perpetrated abuse and those who have fallen victim to it.

Moreover, the Freedom Programme welcomes various professionals, such as probation officers, social workers, and educators, who attend sessions to enhance their training and awareness regarding domestic violence. Partnerships, such as the collaboration with Certain Curtain Theatre Company, further enrich the programme by utilising theatrical performances like 'Lady in Red' to powerfully illustrate the stark realities of domestic abuse, making the subject matter not only relatable but profoundly resonant.

While the Freedom Programme is not a therapeutic intervention, it often serves as a critical first step toward healing for many survivors. It provides the language for the unspoken, clarity amidst confusion, and validation for experiences that have long been dismissed or ignored. Numerous women who participate in the programme describe their experience as "life-changing," often because it reframes their perception of love from a misguided notion of affection to an understanding of control and transforms what they once viewed as weakness into a recognition of their strength and survival.

The programme's insights are deeply rooted in decades of direct engagement with both men and women affected by abuse. It is constructed not merely on theoretical foundations but is enriched by lived experiences, thoughtful reflection, and careful listening to those whose lives have been impacted by domestic violence.

In essence, the Freedom Programme refrains from dictating paths for survivors; instead, it facilitates an understanding of the actions that have been perpetrated against them. In this profound understanding, many participants discover their initial steps toward reclaiming their freedom and autonomy.

In the next section, you'll meet the characters used within the Freedom Programme to help explain the dynamics of abuse and survival.

(Please note the next pages are taken from the freedom programme)

# The Dominator

In Britain, 112 women a year are killed by a male partner or former partner. (Home Office 2007)

In Britain, 22 men a year are killed by a female partner or former partner. (Home Office 2007)

The majority of women who kill their partners have been subjected to prolonged and severe violence.

From the available statistics, it is clear that, in the majority of cases the perpetrators of domestic abuse are men and the majority of victims are women. The next question to ask is, why do they do this? When we women are on the receiving end of violence and abuse we often ask ourselves this question. We also try to answer it.

Perpetrators tell us, and we believe, that the violence was caused by drink, stress, unemployment, overwork, low self-esteem or insecurity.

Many of the professionals we meet also accept these explanations. The reality is that these are all excuses. They may have been drunk when they hit us but they didn't usually hit anyone else. Being insecure doesn't make people violent. Why should it?

The real reason for their violence and abuse is the desire to keep women under control. They do not need to use violence every day.

Some abusive men never need to use it at all, because they can control us by using other tactics. They will usually use violence when they believe the other tactics are failing.

Some women can also use many of the controlling and abusive tactics of the Dominator. The difference is that, in the case of abusive men, they are more likely to use violence when they believe the tactics of control are failing. As a result, a woman is murdered every three days.

Some of the tactics used to achieve power and control are depicted now in the analysis of the Dominator. In this chapter we will have a brief look at some of these tactics and will return later to examine them all in greater detail.

The Dominator was inspired by the Duluth Domestic Violence Intervention Project in Minnesota. He is one man, but I describe him as changing into the other characters to use different kinds of controlling behaviour. He can change from one character to another with lightning speed. Often, when I show him to women on the programme, they say: "You must have met my husband!" I joke that I believe that all abusive men are abducted when they are six months old and taken to a school in the mountains where they all learn to do and say exactly the same thing! One of the first people I trained to run the Freedom Programme was a specialist domestic violence police officer. When she started her programme her group was comprised of women whose abusers had been arrested and charged by her. She had also accompanied the women to court and knew their histories.

One of the women looked at her picture of the Dominator and then compared it to everyone else's Dominator. She said that it was so like her partner that she initially believed each one had been done for an individual man from their police records and case histories. the Bully

He uses intimidation to control his partner by: shouting, glaring, sulking, driving too fast and firing questions at her without giving her a chance to answer. As a result, she believes he is angry and tries to placate him. The men on my programme have told me that the Bully is not angry. He is cool, calm and collected and completely in control of his emotions. What does he have to be angry about? the Headworker He uses emotional abuse to control his partner by telling her she is stupid, ugly, and incompetent. He is unfaithful and he puts her down in front of others, usually using humour. As a result, she loses all self-confidence.

The Jailer, he isolates his partner by sulking when her friends visit. He refuses to look after the children when she has arranged to go out or go to work. He charms friends and family so they do not believe her. He moves her to remote places. As a result, women are completely isolated.

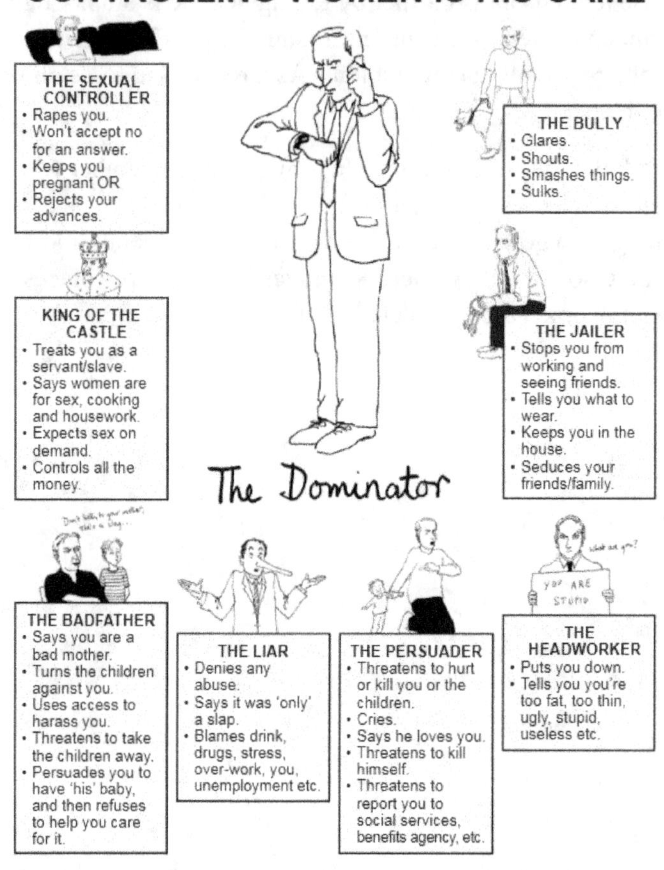

THE DOMINATOR IS HIS NAME
CONTROLLING WOMEN IS HIS GAME
THE SEXUAL CONTROLLER
• Rapes you.
• Won't accept no for an answer.
• Keeps you pregnant OR
• Rejects your advances.
THE BULLY
• Glares.
• Shouts.
• Smashes things.
• Sulks.
KING OF THE CASTLE
• Treats you as a servant/slave.
• Says women are for sex, cooking and housework.
• Expects sex on demand.
• Controls all the money.
THE JAILER
• Stops you from working and seeing friends.
• Tells you what to wear.
• Keeps you in the house.
• Seduces your friends/family.
The Dominator
YOU ARE STUPID
THE BADFATHER
• Says you are a bad mother.
• Turns the children against you.
• Uses access to harass you.
• Threatens to take the children away.
• Persuades you to have 'his' baby, and then refuses to help you care for it.
THE LIAR
• Denies any abuse.
• Says it was 'only' a slap.
• Blames drink, drugs, stress, over-work, you, unemployment etc.
THE PERSUADER
• Threatens to hurt or kill you or the children.
• Cries.
• Says he loves you.
• Threatens to kill himself.
• Threatens to report you to social services, benefits agency, etc.
THE HEADWORKER
• Puts you down.
• Tells you you're too fat, too thin, ugly, stupid, useless etc.


*The Liar*

This persona is adept at minimizing harm and manipulating reality through the careful use of language. He often employs the term "only" to trivialize acts of violence, a comment like "It was only a slap" or "I only lost my temper once" serves to diminish the severity of his actions. This single word acts as a powerful eraser, softening the impact of his behaviour, deflecting personal accountability, and leading others to underestimate the seriousness of the situation.

In many cases, he outright denies any form of abuse or shifts the blame entirely onto his partner. Notably, men who attend the Freedom Programme often arrive not with a desire to take responsibility for their actions, but rather seeking help to "manage" a woman they claim has provoked their aggressive behaviour. This narrative allows them to evade responsibility, framing their violent actions as reactions to the perceived shortcomings of their partner.

The Liar also presents a flood of justifications for his behaviour: citing alcohol, stress, drugs, overwork, unemployment, or mental health issues as reasons for his outbursts. These rationalizations can be so compelling that even survivors and professionals start to doubt the severity, or in extreme cases, even the existence, of the abuse. However, it's crucial to understand that these are not legitimate reasons; they are strategic moves designed to sidestep accountability and maintain control over the narrative.

*The Bad Father*

This persona weaponised the couple's children, using them as tools to manipulate and exert control long after the romantic relationship has ended. He undermines the mother's authority, turning the children against her, and uses his parental rights as a means to perpetuate harassment. As she attempts to leave, he might exploit the legal system to push for ongoing access to the children, not out of concern for their well-being, but to maintain his grip on her life.

Moreover, he may deny paternity or cast doubt on her competency as a mother, planting seeds of uncertainty in both her mind and the minds of professionals. The effects of this behaviour can be devastating. Many women find themselves losing custody of their children, not due to any inadequacy of their own, but because the abusive narrative crafted by the father is unjustly believed. Even in cases where they retain custody, the psychological impact stemming from such manipulative tactics can significantly erode their confidence and sense of self as a capable and nurturing parent.

*The King of the Castle*

This character perceives the relationship as a strict hierarchy, with himself at the apex. He expects unwavering obedience rather than mutual partnership, relegating his partner to a role akin to that of domestic staff. In this dynamic, she becomes responsible for all household chores, childcare, and her availability for sexual intimacy, while he controls the finances and decision-making processes. He reduces her identity to a series of roles that serve his needs.

Men participating in earlier versions of the Freedom Programme have been known to joke about their views on women, using flippant acronyms like "CFCs", Cooking, Fucking, and Cleaning, while others have referred to "WIFE" as an acronym for "Washing, Ironing, Fucking, Etc." Although such comments may appear humorous on the surface, they reveal deeply entrenched beliefs surrounding entitlement, power dynamics, and traditional gender roles.

Over time, this form of oppression can lead many women to internalize their perceived inferiority. They begin to view themselves as less important, less capable, and ultimately unworthy of equality or mutual respect in relationships. This damaging perception can have far-reaching consequences, affecting their self-esteem and their interactions with others long after the relationship has ended.

*The Sexual Controller*

This persona utilizes sex as a strategic weapon for exerting power and control over others. Such individuals may withhold affection as a form of punishment, coerced sexual activity without regard for consent, or, in extreme cases, resort to outright rape. These actions are not driven by a desire for intimacy or connection; rather, they are fundamentally about establishing dominance and subjugation. The emotional aftermath for survivors can be devastating, leaving them feeling utterly violated, degraded, and disempowered. Many find themselves trapped in a cycle of fear and trauma, often feeling too overwhelmed or scared to resist or to speak out against their abuser.

*The Persuader*

This character typically emerges when the survivor attempts to exit the abusive relationship or seeks external help, such as involving law enforcement. The Persuader resorts to emotional blackmail and manipulation tactics to reassert control over the situation. He may resort to pleading, crying, or begging for another chance, portraying himself as utterly helpless or lost without the relationship. In more sinister manifestations, he might threaten self-harm or suicide, or manipulate the situation by threatening harm to pets or loved ones if the survivor does not comply with his demands. These tactics can be chillingly effective, often coercing survivors into withdrawing charges or returning to the relationship despite the ongoing risk to their safety.

It's crucial to understand that these harmful behaviours are not limited to heterosexual relationships. Domestic abuse can manifest in various forms across the LGBTQ+ spectrum, with The Dominator potentially being an abusive woman in a lesbian relationship or an abusive man in a gay partnership.

*Understanding the Motivations of the Dominator*

At the heart of the Dominator's behaviour lies a deeply ingrained belief system. Human actions are largely driven by our beliefs, often situated in our subconscious, even when we may not fully recognize them. Abusive individuals, including The Dominator, frequently harbour a complex and contradictory mind-set that justifies and facilitates their abusive behaviours. This internal conflict within their belief system, known in psychology as cognitive dissonance, produces actions that defy their own moral compass while simultaneously reinforcing their abusive tendencies.

These toxic beliefs are not developed in isolation. The Dominator is shaped by the societal context in which he exists. Although specific justifications for abusive behaviour may vary across different cultures, the underlying impulse to exert control remains a consistent theme.
Abusive behaviours are learned, normalized, and pervasively reinforced by cultural narratives and social expectations.

In this program and within the pages of this book, we will primarily examine how British cultural values and entrenched gender roles contribute to sustaining the Dominator's belief system. However, readers from diverse cultural backgrounds can apply this framework to analyse how their own social conditioning has influenced their understanding of abuse and the tolerance of harmful behaviours.

*The Impact of Shared Conditioning*

It is imperative to recognize that women are raised in the same societal atmosphere as the Dominator. Both genders are exposed to similar cultural messages and societal expectations, leading some women to inadvertently internalize beliefs that excuse or normalize abusive actions. Such beliefs can profoundly affect their self-perception, their views of their partners, and the boundaries they establish within relationships.

Throughout this book, each archetype of the Dominator will be accompanied by detailed explanations of his tactics, the underlying beliefs that fuel these actions, and the social conditioning that enables their proliferation. Additionally, we will explore how survivors may, often unknowingly, share or accept certain beliefs, sometimes as a survival mechanism, because adhering to them can feel like the only viable option in a difficult situation.

*A Vital Clarification*

It is essential to underscore that not all men are abusive. Many women also seek and deserve healthy, respectful relationships founded on mutual understanding and consent. By adopting the belief that all men are inherently bad, we risk resigning ourselves to a relationship with a known abuser or overlooking opportunities to cultivate healthier connections.

As many of us navigate parenthood, particularly in raising sons, we are hopeful for the emergence of non-abusive, emotionally intelligent men. This desire for healthier future relationships underscores the necessity of first acknowledging and embracing the concept of Mr. Right, a model of healthy, non-violent masculinity, before delving into the full spectrum of The Dominator's behaviours. By countering the narrative of abuse with examples of respect and equity, we can foster stronger, more positive relationships for generations to come.

# NOT A SAINT THAT WE ARE SEEING
# JUST A DECENT HUMAN BEING

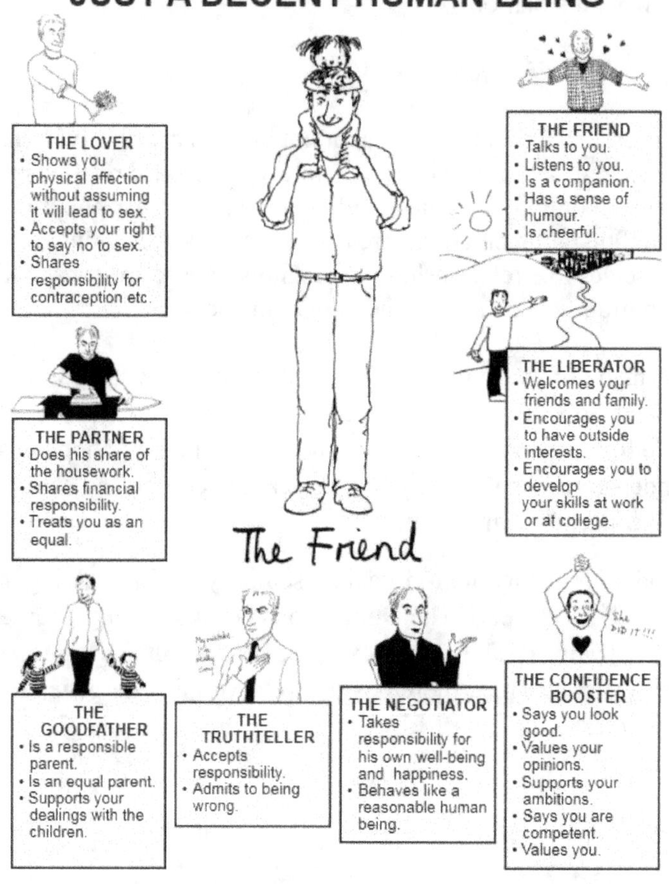

THE LOVER
• Shows you physical affection without assuming it will lead to sex.
• Accepts your right to say no to sex.
• Shares responsibility for contraception etc.
THE FRIEND
• Talks to you.
• Listens to you.
• Is a companion.
• Has a sense of humour.
• Is cheerful.
THE PARTNER
• Does his share of the housework.
• Shares financial responsibility.
• Treats you as an equal.
THE LIBERATOR
• Welcomes your friends and family.
• Encourages you to have outside interests.
• Encourages you to develop your skills at work or at college.
The Friend
THE GOODFATHER
• Is a responsible parent.
• Is an equal parent.
• Supports your dealings with the children.
THE TRUTHTELLER
• Accepts responsibility.
• Admits to being wrong.
THE NEGOTIATOR
• Takes responsibility for his own well-being and happiness.
• Behaves like a reasonable human being.
THE CONFIDENCE BOOSTER
• Says you look good.
• Values your opinions.
• Supports your ambitions.
• Says you are competent.
• Values you.


Mr Right represents the qualities of a non-abusive individual, someone grounded in respect, empathy, and equality. While the name implies a male figure, the characteristics of Mr Right are not limited by gender; they reflect the blueprint for any healthy friend, partner, or parent.

Throughout this book, each chapter explores a specific aspect of the Dominator's behaviour. At the end of each section, I introduce the healthy counterpart—an aspect of Mr Right—to offer contrast, clarity, and hope. For instance, in a chapter about the Bully, I'll conclude with the Friend, who embodies non-threatening, respectful communication and emotional maturity.

This structure helps us not only understand the patterns of abuse, but also envision what safe, respectful relationships look and feel like.

# The Bully

In the UK, a woman loses her life to a violent partner every three days (London Home Office, 2007). According to Amnesty International (2007), the Russian Government reported that in 1999 alone, 14,000 women were killed by partners or family members.

*How the Bully Intimidates*

The Bully is a master manipulator of physical presence, using his body to impose fear. From top to toe, every movement is deliberate. He glares, fixes his stare, reddens his face, grinds his teeth, and may even foam at the mouth. His chilling grin never reaches his eyes, his eyes glare while his mouth forms a deceptive smile. He sneers and smirks.

His breathing becomes exaggerated, deep sighs, huffs, puffs. His voice either drops into a cold monotone or rises in explosive rage. At times, he'll retreat into eerie silence, sulking and leaving his partner in a state of fear and confusion. Whistling and humming become unsettling behaviours that signal tension rather than calm.

He intrudes on his partner's space, looming over her, creeping up from behind, leaning in to shout or glare. He crosses his arms, taps his foot, drums his fingers, clenches his fists. He interrogates her rapidly, not allowing space to respond. He lashes out at walls and furniture, often smashing items she treasures. His sitting posture may exude hostility, including thrusting his pelvis and puffing up to exaggerate size. He often sends coded threats through subtle gestures or familiar facial expressions only she would interpret as danger.

He might send the children to bed, an ominous warning. He paces, slams doors, points aggressively, and makes sudden gestures as if to strike, stopping just before contact.

He weaponises the car, driving recklessly with family inside. He may clean weapons, obstruct doorways, and injure pets. He leaves without notice and offers no idea of when or if he'll return, leaving the household paralysed in fear.

These manipulations can, of course, happen in same-sex relationships as well. Abuse doesn't discriminate by gender or sexuality. A Dominator can be an abusive lesbian or gay man.

It's important to understand that the Bully's methods are deliberate. He isn't out of control, he's cold, calculated, and strategic. He is not angry. He is abusive by design.

*The Bully's Beliefs*

The Bully doesn't see these behaviours as abusive; he sees them as justifiable. To him, they are not only acceptable, they are correct, masculine, and effective. He believes it's right to bully to get what he wants. To him, not doing so makes a man weak or effeminate. He holds that women are property, submissive beings who must be trained, controlled, and protected, like dogs. He believes women are inferior, while men are inherently superior, because of physical strength.

This reasoning is flawed. If superiority were defined by strength alone, then the world would be ruled by elephants or whales. Clearly, strength does not equate to value or leadership. Yet the Bully conflates the two, convinced his dominance is not only valid but necessary.

He believes violence is acceptable when provoked. In his worldview, hitting a partner who has, say, cheated, is not only excusable, it's expected. When challenged, many men have stated they'd find it "understandable" to kill a cheating partner. But infidelity is not illegal. Murder is.

*Where These Beliefs Begin—and How Society Reinforces Them*

The Bully's beliefs may stem from early experiences. He may have watched his father dominate his mother, or his brothers intimidate their sisters. He may have learned as a child that tantrums earn results. If he copied his father's rage and saw his mother give in, it reinforced the belief that aggression leads to control.

However, abuse isn't always generational. Some abusers had peaceful homes; some peaceful men were raised in violence. Beliefs can be shaped elsewhere, peer groups, schools, sports culture, media.

He may have been bullied himself, and internalised that domination equals power. A football fan might witness a player lash out, only to see commentators question what the other player "did to deserve it." This blame culture solidifies the idea that the victim is responsible for provoking violence.

Society still holds toxic relics: phrases like "rule of thumb," which originally referred to a law allowing a man to beat his wife with a stick no wider than his thumb. A BBC programme once quoted a saying:

*"A wife, a dog and a walnut tree—the more you beat them, the better they be."*

These ideas have real consequences. The UK still sees a woman killed by a partner every three days. The statistics haven't changed since the Freedom Programme began in 1999. Courts often convict abusers of manslaughter, not murder, issuing short sentences. The message is loud and clear: kill your wife, and you might keep the house.

Marriage vows once instructed women to "obey." Fathers still "give away" their daughters. The armed forces train soldiers through intimidation, shouting, throwing possessions, instilling fear. These rituals mirror how Bullies break down their partners.

Media glorifies male aggression. Films portray violent men as heroes. Soap operas model abuse as dominance. Sports like boxing make violence seem noble. Children are still physically punished, teaching early that harm is how you correct behaviour.

Songs promote violence against women, like the notorious "Slap the Bitch." Even love songs like "Delilah" glorify killing a woman for cheating, sung passionately by crowds at rugby games. Video games encourage shooting prostitutes. Religious institutions deny women leadership. Gender pay gaps persist. Parliament debates resemble playground brawls. News anchors berate guests. Reality TV celebrates humiliation and bullying.

*Internalised Beliefs in Women*

Many women share the Bully's beliefs without realising. Before joining the programme, some women admitted they preferred controlling men and found respectful partners "too nice." They were conditioned to see submission as normal and strength as masculinity.

Some even believed bullying was a sign of love and power. This mind-set stems from centuries where women exchanged sex and servitude for food and safety. Though some women now enjoy independence, old narratives persist. Many still view single life as failure. The line between protection and control is easily crossed.

*A Fairy Tale Reimagined*

Once, there was an unmarried princess who ruled her land with wisdom and fairness. One day, a frog approached her, claiming to be a cursed prince. If she kissed him, he promised to become human, marry her, and let her bear his children, cook his meals, clean the palace, while he ruled and collected taxes.

That night, while enjoying sautéed frogs' legs in tarragon and cream, the princess muttered, "I don't fucking think so."

The point is clear: why do so many of us still accept the frog's offer?

*The Emotional Toll on Women*

Living with a Bully is like walking on eggshells. There is no safety, only anticipation of the next storm. Every action is scrutinised. Disagreement is dangerous. Expression becomes a risk.

Confidence evaporates. The woman becomes a shadow, timid, apologetic, afraid to sleep, afraid to speak. She might replicate the behaviour, bullying others or choosing worse partners to shield herself from the last. She may seek courage in alcohol or drugs. She may avoid her own children out of fear he'll retaliate.

She believes he's angry, something she can soothe. But this isn't anger. This is strategy. It is not emotional loss of control. It is control itself.

# The Non-Abusive Counterpart to The Bully is The Friend. He Can be an Example to us all. The Friend

*This Is How the Friend Conducts Himself*

The Friend greets the world with a genuine smile that lights up his entire face, radiating warmth not just from his lips but also from his expressive eyes. This authenticity in his gaze reflects the kind and friendly thoughts he cultivates about those around him, fostering an environment where everyone feels valued. His upbeat demeanour and approachable nature are complemented by a delightful sense of humour that makes interactions enjoyable. His body language conveys relaxation; he stands or sits with an open posture, inviting conversation while ensuring that his presence is comforting rather than intimidating. Additionally, his tone of voice remains steady, soft, and pleasant, creating a safe space for dialogue.

When engaging in conversation, the Friend ensures that he connects not only with adults but also pays special attention to children. He listens intently, showing that he values their thoughts and feelings just as much as anyone else's. This willingness to engage leads to meaningful conversations and balanced discussions. In the face of disagreement, he demonstrates remarkable respect for differing opinions, he never seeks to dominate the conversation or "win" any debate; instead, he values the exchange of ideas and strives for mutual understanding.

As a partner, the Friend delights in sharing life's experiences. He thrives on going places together, whether it's an outing to a favourite café or a spontaneous adventure, and finds joy in simple pleasures, like enjoying a dessert together. He also embodies emotional consistency; the version of him who leaves for work in the morning is the same caring individual who returns home in the evening. When he enters the house, he does so with enthusiasm, warmly announcing, "Hello, I'm home! How are you?", a vivid contrast to the Bully, who often storms in, neglects greetings, and immediately retreats into his own world, consumed by distractions like the TV remote.

Moreover, the Friend holds a deep respect for women, appreciating their company and acknowledging their contributions as equal partners deserving of dignity. He is self-aware enough to recognize and admit his faults, showing the emotional maturity that is essential in healthy relationships. Importantly, he stands firmly against any form of bullying, maintaining the belief that no adult has the right to dominate or control another person. His character brings a sense of safety and empowerment to all those around him, enriching their lives through genuine kindness and respect.

# The Bad Father

*Pregnancy and Risk of Harm*

Women are statistically three times more likely to suffer injury during pregnancy (Refuge, 2007).
The abusive men I've worked with often admitted that they only became physically violent once they felt secure in the relationship, what they described as having their "feet under the table." In their view, pregnancy makes a woman more vulnerable and dependent, increasing their confidence that they can act with impunity. Disturbingly, some disclosed that when they look at a pregnant woman, they no longer see her as a person carrying life, but as an unattractive, overweight "object."

*The Badfather's Use of Children for Control and Abuse*

Importantly, the individual known as the "Badfather" doesn't need to be the biological parent of the children he manipulates to exert power.

*How He Turns the Children Against Us*

He uses numerous strategies to erode our relationship with our children. He constantly contradicts our parenting, such as encouraging them to stay up late after we've sent them to bed, or dismissing our meals with offensive remarks like, "You don't have to eat that shit!"

He ridicules us in front of them, making jokes at our expense and calling us degrading names. Over time, the children begin to mimic his verbal abuse, often believing that derogatory names like "slag" or "filth" are actually our real names, as those are the only terms they've ever heard him use.

To buy their affection, he gifts them with expensive presents, purchases we could never afford, especially once he stops contributing to their financial support after separation.

*How He Uses Children to Trap Us in the Relationship*

He threatens violence against the children if we attempt to leave. These threats must be taken seriously, there are tragic cases where men have killed children in retaliation against a partner's decision to separate.

He might refuse to allow the children to leave with us or retain one child as leverage. When the relationship is ending, he emotionally manipulates the children by crying and painting himself as the victim, claiming we are forcing him out or depriving them of their father.

In more disturbing cases, he coerces the children to witness sexual acts, then threatens to report us for it if we attempt to leave. As he's conditioned them to see him as the preferable parent, they resist leaving and blame us.

He strategically favours one child while mistreating the other. If we leave, the favoured child won't want to come with us; if we stay, the mistreated child continues to suffer. It's an unbearable and unfair situation.

*How He Uses Children to Emotionally Abuse Us*

Once the baby is born, he restricts our ability to bond. He forbids us from comforting, feeding, or caring for the baby. Some women have even been locked out of rooms where their infants cried. He rationalises this as "not spoiling" the child.

Out of fear for the baby's safety, we comply. This leads to child welfare professionals accusing us of not forming proper attachments with our baby. In our confused and fearful state, we internalise the blame. He reinforces this by insisting we're "bad mothers."

Following separation, he uses access rights to manipulate us further, failing to show up for visitation, leaving the children waiting in distress with coats on. He challenges paternity or falsely claims fatherhood to disrupt our lives, demanding DNA tests in both scenarios.

He pressures or coerces us into pregnancies, and then into abortions.

*How He Uses the System Against Us*

Many women have shared this devastating experience: after violence from him puts the children on the Child Protection Register, we are told they may be adopted if we reconcile with him. He then relentlessly pressures us to take him back, even convincing us that authorities prefer him as an in-house father figure. We give in, only to find our children are adopted anyway. Without even breaking a law or laying a hand on us, he has destroyed our world.

*How He Uses Children to Isolate Us*

He persuades us to have children but refuses to share any responsibilities. Without support, we can't work or socialise. When he does "help," he does so inadequately, forcing us to remain housebound due to fear for our children's safety. He treats parenting as "babysitting," further minimising his role.

He often manipulates the children into monitoring our movements. He keeps us in a continuous cycle of pregnancy; just as one child begins school, he either coerces sex or forces another pregnancy.

Missed access visits disrupt our routines, making employment or social interaction nearly impossible.

*How He Uses Children to Intimidate Us*

After separation, he continues abuse under the guise of visitation, shouting, physically intimidating, and even damaging property while claiming he only wants to "see my fucking kids!" Drunk and aggressive, he breaks windows and doors to reinforce control.

He uses the children as messengers, sending threats or personal remarks through them. Notes are slipped into nappies. He manipulates the children into asking about our relationships or pressuring us into joining family outings that are conditional on our presence.

He shouts at the children to scare us and mistreats them as a way of punishing us. He targets stepchildren as scapegoats and controls our ability to show love by making us afraid that affection will provoke his anger.

*Beliefs That Drive the Badfather's Behaviour*

He believes only he has rights, and that the rights of women and children are irrelevant. He views us and the children as his property, accessories to his life. Regardless of past violence, he believes he's entitled to see the children whenever he wants, and that his abuse has no impact on them.

To him, the home belongs to him, whether or not his name is on the tenancy agreement. He doesn't view his behaviour as abusive; to him, it's normal.

He sees childcare as exclusively women's work. "Real men," he believes, don't change nappies or look after children. Women should stay at home.

Paradoxically, he also believes we are incapable of raising children, therefore justifying his presence in the home, even if he's violent. He holds the delusion that he's a good father despite abusing their mother. This contradiction is an example of *cognitive dissonance*.

*Where These Beliefs Come from and How They're Reinforced*

These attitudes often take root in childhood, modelled by both parents and are reinforced by systems that favour them. Courts often grant child access to even the most violent men, and political systems promote the idea that two-parent households are preferable, regardless of safety.

Society praises lone fathers while vilifying single mothers. "He gave up work for the children, what a hero!" But when was the last time a single mother received that same praise?

Fathers' rights groups claim they're unfairly denied access. With support from influential figures, they protest and lobby publicly, reinforcing his sense of injustice.

Even public officials support outdated ideas. When Tony Blair took paternity leave, John Prescott, the former Deputy Prime Minister, said on air: "You wouldn't catch me changing nappies!"

*How These Tactics Impact Women?*

**When he turns children against us:**
We can't assert authority or discipline. He's trained the children to ignore us and destroyed our confidence. We're labelled unfit mothers. Some of us are forced to flee and leave children behind. The children abuse us, verbally or physically.

**When he uses them to make us stay:**
We feel trapped, unsafe, and afraid. He always keeps one child, making escape feel impossible. The children beg us to stay or return. Reunification results in child protection concerns, sometimes leading to adoption.

**When he emotionally abuses through them:**
We lose all decision-making confidence. We're painted as mentally unwell. We feel useless, only valued for childcare. With no self-worth or financial freedom, we may commit benefit fraud out of desperation. We return to abusive partners or enter new abusive relationships.

**When he isolates us through parenthood:**
Constant pregnancy and sole parenting prevent work or education. Even if confidence were regained, lack of childcare keeps us housebound.

# The Goodfather

*What Are the Behaviours of the Goodfather?*

The Goodfather is deeply familiar with his children. He not only remembers their names but also knows their birthdays, their favourite foods, and the names of their closest friends.

He takes an equal role in the responsibilities of parenting. He changes nappies, wakes during the night to attend to them, and feeds them when needed. He contributes fully to watching over the children and does it competently. When we leave the children in his care, whether to go to work or spend time with friends, we return to find them well-fed, well-cared-for, and safe. This allows us to confidently trust him to look after them again, without concern. He never refers to this care as “babysitting” his own children. If we plan a night out together, he takes his fair turn in arranging childcare.

He treats both daughters and sons with the same level of respect and warmth. When problems arise, he addresses them with reason. He actively plays with the children and talks with them openly. He encourages them to explore toys beyond gender stereotypes and supports them in developing friendships and social confidence by welcoming their friends into the home.

The Goodfather celebrates their successes at school and in other areas of their lives. He gets involved with homework and remains aware of their preferences and interests.

He shows us respect, affection, and genuine appreciation in front of the children and expects them to reflect the same. He reinforces our decisions. For instance, if we say it’s bedtime, he supports that decision without question.

He contributes financially and openly acknowledges his role as a parent. He is cheerful, pleasant, and emotionally stable. He takes ownership of his actions and admits when he is wrong. He values honesty and is someone the children can look up to.

The Goodfather holds the belief that both women and children are entitled to rights and respect. He recognises that women are entirely capable of raising children and acknowledges that he, too, should take equal responsibility. He firmly believes that violence and abuse have no place in a relationship. He upholds the view that children deserve to grow up in an environment filled with peace and happiness. He genuinely enjoys the company of women and delights in being around children.

# The Effects of Domestic Violence and Abuse on Children

At least 750,000 children a year witness domestic violence. Nearly three quarters of children live in households where domestic violence occurs. (Department of Health 2003)

I originally wrote the sessions on the effects of abuse on children in conjunction with two workers from the NSPCC. They had a lot of experience in helping children who had been traumatised by being exposed to domestic violence, and their expertise was invaluable. I no longer use much of the rest of the original probation programme as my material has evolved and changed following the input of so many men and women who have completed the programme. However, this session remains virtually unchanged and is powerful and effective when used with both perpetrators and survivors of abuse. For the purposes of this book I have combined two sessions of the programme into one chapter.

To discuss the effects on children in a focussed way, I have created three metaphorical groups. The first group is comprised of an unborn child, a pregnant woman and a new-born child. The second focuses on a six-year-old. The third considers a teenager.

*Group 1: What does an unborn child, a pregnant woman and a new-born baby need to survive and thrive?*

Shall we start with the pregnant mother? When we are pregnant we need good nutritious food and a calm atmosphere. We need plenty of rest. We need to attend regular medical checks. At this stage, the needs of our unborn child are inextricably involved with our needs.

When we are giving birth, there is a consensus that natural childbirth is the safest and that breast milk provides the best nutritional start to the baby's life.

When our baby is born it needs cuddling and to be told it is loved. Our baby will feel loved and safe right from the start. It also needs to be fed and kept clean and warm.

*How are we and our unborn child affected by violence and abuse?*

As we are living with a Bully, who also uses physical violence, we are unlikely to experience a calm atmosphere at any time. Instead, we will be physically and emotionally stressed. We will probably be short on sleep and constantly subjected to intimidation. There is evidence that unborn babies can hear and that our stress is communicated to them. They may be born with colic as a result.

As we have identified, statistically we are at greater risk of violence when we are pregnant. If we are being assaulted, we may miscarry. Our baby could be born dead or premature. If the Dominator has kicked us his kick may have damaged the baby. The baby could then be born with brain damage and suffer for example, from epilepsy or cerebral palsy.

As we are living with a Jailer, he may prevent us from keeping our medical appointments. Our general health and that of the unborn child can be compromised. He has alienated our friends and family so we have no emotional or practical support. He will refuse to look after the other children when we need to rest. There is no one else to help, so we do not rest. He may also refuse to let us have money for decent nutritious food. Again, our health and that of the baby may suffer. Our baby may be born premature and, or underweight.

The tactics of the Headworker can result in us abusing drugs and alcohol. Our baby's kidneys may be damaged. If he has told us we are fat and disgusting every time we eat anything we may become anorexic and our baby will not be properly nourished. When the time comes to give birth, the tactics of the Sexual Controller may affect us. He may insist upon us having a caesarean and may force us to demand one. The medical staff will probably be told this is our choice.

The Sexual Controller will probably also forbid us to breastfeed. Both these tactics will impede our ability to bond with our baby and may hinder its development. Sexual controllers cut or break stitches so they can have sex after we have given birth. This can slow the recovery

process. Every time we pick up our new baby to cuddle it he shouts at us that we will 'spoil the baby. We are locked out of the room and forbidden to change or feed it. We are forced to listen to the baby crying. If we cannot cuddle our new baby, it will not have that early message that it is loved and will not begin to develop the self-confidence it needs in later life.

*Group 2: What does a six-year-old need to survive or to thrive?*

Our six-year-old needs love. It needs to be cuddled and kissed and to be told it is loved. It needs this to help it grow into an adult with some sense of its own worth. It needs this love from significant powerful adults in its life.

Extended family members provide an essential balance for our children. They can be a sympathetic ear or an umpire who has influence within the family. 38

The next thing our child needs is safety. It needs to be in a physically safe environment, and it needs to be taught self-protective strategies. Security is also an emotional requirement. Our child needs to know that its world is a safe, predictable place. We give it this security with routine. Our child needs to know when it is time for school or bed and to know where it lives.

To provide this kind of security, our child needs the powerful adults in its life to be consistent. This will ensure that the rules are consistent. If something they do is acceptable today it must be acceptable tomorrow. If one of their actions is wrong today it must also be wrong tomorrow.

Our child learns how to behave from a very early age from role models. It is watching us from its pram and absorbing essential lessons with its rusks.

We need to spend time communicating with our children. This gives them the stimulus to develop. That is how they learn to speak and read and to sing and draw. This is how they learn to have fun. They need fun. They need a house where people laugh and smile and play. They also need toys both for fun and to learn. Studies show that if a child receives this stimulus in pre-school years they do better than children who have been left in front of the television.

Our children need friends. We all need friends to learn social skills and also to make us feel liked. If we have friends, they tell us they like us. We will be starting our lives believing that our parents love us and our friends like us. This will help us to like ourselves.

Our children need to be kept clean and tidy and physically warm. They need appropriate clothing. Our children need education. To achieve this, they need to go to school. While at school, they need to be comfortable and accepted to learn. In order to do well at school, they need to sleep at night. Sleep also provides them with the rest they need to grow and develop.

Children also need food. They need nutrition to grow and develop. They need to know when that food will come. In other words, they need regular meals. They also use food to learn how to eat socially. They will spend much of their adult life eating in the company of others, so this skill is important.

To maintain good health, our children need medical check-ups. They need to make regular visits to the dentist and the school nurse. Finally, if they are to make any sense of the world they live in, they need to be told the truth. They need honesty. How else are they to grow into honest human beings?

*How is a six-year-old child affected by violence and abuse?*

Many women on the programme have told me that they dare not show their children affection as to do so will attract the attention of the Dominator. So, to protect their children, they have to virtually ignore them. This will deprive the child of the affection it needs to learn to like itself.

We are not allowed to communicate with our children, any more than we are allowed to show them any affection. We cannot play with them, talk to them or sing to them. They are often left in front of the television, so they do not get the stimulus they need. They may have a slow start, academically and intellectually, for this reason also.

The Jailer has alienated all extended family members and close friends. There is now no one for the child to turn to for help. Children in households where there is violence are not safe. They are killed or injured either deliberately or caught up in the cross fire whilst trying to protect their mother.

The next need we discuss is security. The Dominator will make sure there is no routine and no predictability. The family may be forced to move around. This may be a tactic of the Jailer or because we flee with the children to refuges. School and other routines are disrupted.

The next need is consistency. In this house there is a Dominator who will change into a Badfather and a Headworker. He changes the rules and his behaviour all the time. No one knows what is going to happen next. Our children are confused, and their behaviour can become bizarre.

When there is a Dominator in the house, the children have him as a role model. For example, the Bully is a giant baby who gets his own way by having tantrums. Our children will observe that tantrums work. They may then go off to nursery school or school and have tantrums. They then may be labelled as disruptive. Their education will begin to suffer. They may be diagnosed as suffering with ADHD. They may be prescribed medication.

Similarly, children do not have much fun in the house of the Dominator. No one does. Their toys get broken too. This often happens at Christmas before they get a chance to play with them.

Although our children need friends, they will not be able to bring friends home. They may be too embarrassed, or simply not allowed. Other parents may not want their children to go into a house where there is known to be violence. As a result, they will not be asked back to other children's houses and they will not have friends. This can cause loneliness and a failure to acquire social skills. It will be another reason why our child will not feel liked and feel unable to like itself. This could be another reason why our child is not doing well at school.

Sleep is very important to a child's development. However, if they are lying awake in bed listening to the sounds of battle below, they are not going to sleep well, if at all. Whilst lying terrified in the dark, they may wet the bed. They may then be smacked for this. Sometimes we are so busy trying to stay out of the way of the Dominator that we may not be able to clean them and dress them properly. They may go to school smelling of urine. This will further increase their isolation. If they have no friends, they may be bullied.

Sometimes lack of sleep will destroy our child's ability to concentrate in school. They may also be worried about what is going on at home. Sometimes we are too bruised to take them, so they miss days. So, at six years old, the rest of our child's life will start to be affected.

We mentioned regular nutritious meals. Most violence occurs either in the bedroom or when food is served. He shouts and screams and throws plates around. Interestingly, many of the men on the programme have told me that they don't throw the food high up the wall. They throw it 'woman height'. This is so we can clean it off quickly without having to stand on a chair or a ladder. Our children may come to associate food with tension and fear and develop eating disorders. They may be so tense that they cannot swallow, or they may hoard food or overeat when they have it in case there is no more for a while. Women have identified that their toddlers also throw plates of food at the wall.

Often, the Jailer does not allow his partner to visit the dentist or the school nurse, so our children do not get their medical check-ups. Illnesses can be missed, often to the detriment of the child's health. Their dental health can suffer markedly.

Finally, we are often unable to tell them the truth. If they ask "why is Daddy hitting you?" we are often forced to lie. We deny it completely or we give them the excuses he uses. "Mummy deserved it. Daddy didn't mean it." They may hear him saying: "Why are you making me do this to you?" or "I'm only doing this because I love you!"

*Examples of the beliefs children may develop*

At six-years-old, they may start to develop the beliefs, that will shape the rest of their lives. They may believe that women are stupid and should be subservient. Men are the bosses and women have no rights. They could be starting to believe that violence is normal and that violence means love. They have learned that bullying works

They will also have heard the excuses used by the Bully. They will hear that we could not tell them how much we love them. They had no friends or extended family to do this. This may have diminished their self-confidence.

They may also have had a poor start at school at the age of six. They could have been underachieving since then. As a result, they may continue to truant. They are still afraid to leave their mother alone and they also may be truanting because they are unpopular or bullied.

When the Dominator is terrorising us we encourage our children to get out of the house for their own protection. They may go to their rooms or out on the street. On the streets, they will probably meet all the other children who have been similarly tipped out. A gang may form which could soon start to abuse drugs or alcohol and break the law.

These teenagers could have absorbed many of the beliefs of the Dominator. They may believe that violence is acceptable. Both boys and girls may be using violence in all sorts of situations. News reports tell of violent 'laddettes' - girls who are using violence often when drunk. They may assault the father to protect the mother. This can lead to criminal convictions or imprisonment. They are hearing that violence is acceptable if you have a good excuse.

They will also have heard their mother being called a slag. That will destroy their respect for her even if they don't know what it means. They will, therefore, learn early that to be a woman is to be something unpleasant. Children of both sexes can absorb these beliefs.

*One in five young men and one in 10 young women think that abuse or violence is acceptable. (Zero Tolerance Charitable Trust 1998)*

*Group 3: the needs of the teenager*

Their needs should have been met when they were six and continued to be met in the intervening years. This did not happen and the effects of domestic abuse on the teenager are now cumulative. Teenage years are always difficult even when there is no abuse in the home. Life for a teenager with a Dominator is even harder.

*The effects of domestic abuse on a teenager*

We have identified many ways in which our new-born babies and six- year-olds have been affected by being exposed to domestic violence and abuse. Ten years later, everything will probably be much worse.

Children of both sexes can abuse their mother emotionally and physically. They could have eating disorders due to poor self-image or too many mealtimes marred by violence. They could also be self-harming especially if they have been sexually abused. Many women on my programme have been sexually abused as children.

Girls could be unable to refuse sex with boys because their self-image is too poor for them to believe they have the right to say no. They may not have the confidence to insist on protection from disease or pregnancy.

Girls may underachieve because they believe they are stupid, worthless and only good for CFCs (Cooking Fucking and Cleaning). Boys may have learned to abuse their girlfriends. In the programme for women and the programme for men, we finish the session by making a list of the ways in which a child's life has improved when the Dominator is no longer in the home. This means either the woman has left him, had him removed by injunction or that he has done the Freedom Programme and changed from (as one women put it) ‘horrible’ to ‘lovely’.

These are the improvements that the men and women in the programme have listed in the last nine years. Women will tell each other that these things take time, as often the children are initially more difficult to deal with as a result of the tactics of the Badfather.

# Home Improvements

Improvements for the pregnant mother, foetus, and new-born baby when the Dominator is removed at six months into the pregnancy.

These improvements, as reported by women on the Freedom Programme, reflect access to support and, in some cases, participation by their partners in the programme.

Without the threat of physical violence, the baby has a significantly better chance of being born unharmed. Mothers can now attend vital medical appointments and receive proper antenatal care. This increases the likelihood of a healthy birth and allows for early detection and treatment of any health issues.

Nutritional needs are met, contributing to the baby's development. Without constant verbal abuse about their appearance, women feel freer to eat healthily. Restful sleep is possible, extended family can return to assist with other children and household responsibilities, and

the home environment becomes calm, reducing stress levels, which also benefits the baby by decreasing the risk of colic.

Women are also more likely to stop using harmful substances such as alcohol, nicotine, or drugs, reducing the risk of kidney damage or other complications in the baby.

With the freedom to choose natural childbirth, both maternal health and maternal-infant bonding are enhanced. Women can also choose to breastfeed, giving their baby a nutritional start that supports long-term well-being.

Once the baby is born, mothers can express love and affection, fostering the child's self-confidence. They now have the freedom and time to meet the baby's practical needs, feeding, changing, and comforting at night.

If the father has completed the Freedom Programme, he is more likely to participate equally in childcare, including night-time responsibilities.

*Improvements for a six-year-old when the Dominator leaves when the child is five.*

The removal of the Dominator allows us to show our children affection, tell them they are loved, and help them believe they are lovable. They can finally sleep through the night, becoming more energetic and open to new experiences. This new emotional stability lays the groundwork for future academic success. Bed-wetting may cease, but until it does, we can now comfort and clean them without fear.

In the year leading up to school, we can provide stimulating activities like reading, singing, and playing, better preparing them for academic engagement.

With extended family and friends welcomed back into the home, children benefit from broader emotional support and social interaction.

Children can now attend school consistently and with improved concentration, which encourages achievement and boosts motivation.

They can invite friends over, improving social skills and helping them to feel liked, thereby liking themselves. This social reinforcement enhances school life and learning.

Meals become safe and pleasant, helping improve children's relationship with food and potentially preventing future eating disorders. We are free to answer their questions truthfully, helping them make sense of their world. Regular medical appointments ensure their general health is supported.

Communication opens up. When they ask, "Why did Daddy hit you?" we can respond honestly: “Daddy hit me because I did something he didn’t like and he was wrong to do that.” This helps undo the belief that violence is a valid response to disagreement. If their father has completed the Freedom Programme, his acknowledgement of wrongdoing reinforces this lesson.

*Improvements for teenagers when the Dominator is removed at age thirteen.*

Many of the benefits seen in younger children apply here, although progress may be slower. Nevertheless, we can now support our teens in processing past trauma. We can listen to them, informed by insights from the Freedom Programme, and help them seek external support like counselling. With no one to silence us, we can finally speak the truth about our situation.

Living independently and finding personal happiness sends a powerful message to our teenagers. If their father has also participated in the Freedom Programme, he is likely to engage more openly with them, explain his past behaviour, and serve as a far better role model moving forward.

# The Head Worker

It's estimated that one in four women will face domestic abuse at some point in their lives (Home Office 2007). From my own observations, I believe the actual number is much higher. If you directly ask a woman if she's experienced domestic abuse, she may say no, even if she's being physically assaulted. Often, women don't recognise certain behaviours as abuse. Personally, three different men have physically assaulted me. I only came to understand that I had experienced domestic violence when I began developing and facilitating the Freedom Programme.

*The Headworker and His Emotional Abuse*

The Headworker uses emotional tactics to break us down. He manipulates us into feeling unintelligent, incapable, and without worth.

Often, he wraps his insults in humour. He makes degrading jokes about us in public, criticising our driving, technical skills, or intelligence. When we speak, he responds with a dismissive "what?" and mimics our words in a mocking tone. He corrects our grammar or invalidates our ideas. Even when we push back, he accuses us of being overly sensitive: "Can't you take a joke?"

He rarely uses our name, instead choosing generic or belittling terms like "babe," "princess," "she," or "the wife." He may also opt for cruel names such as "slag," "bitch," "cow," or "whore," or offer degrading nicknames like "little pig" under the guise of affection. While not all men who avoid using our name are abusive, every abusive man I've encountered does this.

He attacks our appearance. Whether we're fat, thin, tall, short, old, or pregnant, he insists we're unattractive. He makes frequent, hurtful comments about our looks, especially during pregnancy. One common tactic involves telling us our vaginas are too large for him to feel pleasure, allegedly due to childbirth. Women without children hear the same claim, which midwives confirm is a harmful myth.

He compares us constantly to women on TV, favouring celebrities and singers. Since TV is a daily activity in most homes, these comparisons become routine. He may cheat with our friends or family members, reinforcing the belief that we're not good enough.

He also gaslights us. He moves or hides things and denies ever doing so. He'll say something, then later insist he didn't. He changes expectations and rules constantly to confuse us. The kettle must be full; unless this week it must be empty. He tells us we must be hormonal or mentally ill. He plants seeds of doubt so effectively that we begin questioning our own sanity.

Some women shared how he staged situations to make them appear mentally unstable. For example, he might say, "Quick! Call the police, there's a burglar in the attic!" When officers arrive, he calmly explains, "Sorry, she always does this." Soon, agencies see us as unreliable, making it easier for him to gain custody and push us out of the home.

He may encourage substance use, suggesting tranquilisers or alcohol, knowing that the more clouded our minds, the easier it is for him to manipulate us. Later, he uses this to justify physical violence: "I had to hit you because you're mad, drunk, or on drugs."

*The Beliefs That Justify His Actions*

The Headworker genuinely believes we're so unintelligent that if he repeats lies long enough, we'll accept them. He sees his actions not as abusive, but normal. He views control as his right and assumes women should be submissive. In his eyes, we're too weak and incompetent to survive alone. If a woman finds success in her career, he attributes it to sleeping her way up or claims she's not a "real" woman.

He holds deep-rooted misogyny. He sees women as filthy, as objects, as things men are entitled to own and use. He uses vulgar metaphors like "snakes with tits" or "snails with tits." These beliefs aren't isolated. One six-year-old boy once shouted at a female driver, "That car's too good for a woman!" A man at a pub bragged, "If you tell a woman she's stupid enough times, she'll believe it." Even a group of taxi drivers changed their GPS voices from female to male because they didn't like being told where to go by a woman.

He despises femininity so deeply that even the colour pink disgusts him. When a UK concrete company adopted pink branding, profits plummeted because British builders reportedly refused to use it.

*How Society Supports These Beliefs*

Let's examine where he learns these views. He may have watched his father disrespect his mother, and possibly joined in the mockery. Sexist jokes, subtle and overt, reinforce these views. Women drivers are ridiculed, despite insurance companies offering them cheaper premiums. If challenged, abusers claim women cause accidents by driving too slowly.

Even language reflects this. "Woman" or "girl" becomes an insult. Phrases like "Bimbo," "Airhead," and "Essex girl" imply we're unintelligent. When 100 new women MPs were elected to correct gender imbalance, the media called them "Blair's Babes"—belittling their accomplishments and implying they were merely decorative.

Economic inequality reinforces this too. Women are still paid less than men for equal work. Advertisements perpetuate harmful ideas, such as a woman offering sex in exchange for a car in a radio commercial.

*The View That Women Are Objects*

Abusive men often joke, "How can you trust something that bleeds for a week and doesn't die?" Women are commonly referred to using meat metaphors, "mutton dressed as lamb," "done up like a dog's dinner," or said to be attending "meat markets." Sex is described in grotesque terms: "porking," "beef bayonet," "beef curtains," "spit roast." Regional slang insults our anatomy, comparing us to tunnels or wide roads.

At one group session, every woman shared that their abuser made cruel comments about their vaginas. When someone joked, "Maybe it's because he has a small prick," we all burst into laughter. It was healing. For once, we realised there was nothing wrong with us. The idea of a "Designer Vagina" became absurd, we imagined catalogues with names like "The Litchfield" or "The Balmoral," even bringing mirrors on sticks to the supermarket for "show and tell."

*Media and Internalised Misogyny*

Look at magazines. Boys have publications on hobbies, motorbikes, football, computers. Girls' magazines are entirely about becoming an attractive sex object, offering diet tips and sex advice, rarely mentioning careers or personal development.

Even we, as women, internalise these harmful beliefs. Some think powerful women must be gay. A woman once called our facilitators "a bunch of hairy-legged lesbians." We call each other names, "slag," "cow," "bitch." We sometimes defer to men's intelligence, losing confidence in ourselves.

*The Impact on Women*

Headworkers are often highly successful, leaving us feeling unattractive and hateful toward ourselves. Many slim women on the programme believed they were obese. Pregnant women felt disgustingly fat. These beliefs lead to eating disorders and surgeries, from breast enlargements to anal bleaching.

Many women admitted envying those their partners cheated with. Some overcame this by forcing themselves to watch videos of the other women until the jealousy faded.

We lose respect for other women and ourselves. Some of us turn to substances. If the Headworker convinces others we're mad, we're diagnosed and medicated. Postnatal depression is often the result of his tactics.

Eventually, we can't trust our own judgement or decisions. We stay in abusive relationships. We struggle to parent effectively. We become more dependent, lose employment, and fear retraining.

*Living in a Society That Mirrors the Headworker's Views*

We become chronically unhappy with ourselves. Constant dieting, body hatred, and competition with other women replace mutual support. We're bombarded with messages telling us we're inferior. And how can we ever thrive in such a world?

*The Nelson Mandala Story*

When a person or an entire group is repeatedly told that they are inferior, they may eventually begin to accept this idea, often without being aware of it. There is a clear comparison between sexism and racism. In pre-independence South Africa, white supremacists benefited from demeaning and exploiting black people. Similarly, male supremacists gain from oppressing women. In both scenarios, a form of systematic 'brainwashing' has been applied.

Some years ago, I heard Nelson Mandela speak in a radio interview. He was deeply aware of the cultural conditioning that had shaped the thinking of black South Africans throughout their struggle for independence. He understood that his people had been told over and over that they were unintelligent, inferior, and unfit to govern. They were repeatedly taught that they didn't belong in the same spaces as white people and were certainly not worthy of equal pay.

Mandela recognised that, on some level, many black South Africans had internalised these beliefs. He admitted that even he had been affected by this widespread sense of collective inferiority.

To demonstrate this, he shared a story from shortly after his release from Robben Island. As he walked towards the plane that was to take him to freedom, he noticed that the pilot was black. For a split second, he found himself questioning whether a black man could fly a plane. This moment served as a powerful example of how deeply and unconsciously our self-beliefs can be shaped by what we've been taught.

This story invites us to reflect on how we might respond in a similar situation. For instance, how would we react if we boarded a plane and discovered that the pilot was a woman? Some of us might respond with excitement or support, but that very reaction exposes how uncommon it still is to see a woman in such a role. Others might perhaps jokingly say something like, "I hope she isn't dealing with PMT!" This too reveals how ingrained these societal assumptions and gender biases really are.

# The Confidence Booster

*This is the way the Confidence Booster acts:*

The Confidence Booster embodies an uplifting presence in our lives, acting as a source of positive reinforcement and genuine support. He consistently compliments our appearance, not merely out of obligation but from a place of sincere appreciation, making us feel valued. When we spend time together, it's clear that he enjoys our company; he engages in meaningful conversations that celebrate our ideas and perspectives.

He takes the time to appreciate our opinions, recognizing the strengths and talents we bring to the table, and he listens with intent, ensuring that our voices are heard and respected. In every interaction, he fosters an open line of communication, creating a safe space where we can express our thoughts and feelings without fear of judgment.

Importantly, he refrains from making or laughing at derogatory jokes about women, standing firmly against any form of disrespect. Instead, he actively encourages us to pursue our goals and dreams, no matter how ambitious they may be. His unwavering support motivates us to step outside our comfort zones, explore new opportunities, and develop new skills that enhance our personal and professional lives.

He holds a deep-seated belief in our intelligence and capability, affirming that women are deserving of the same respect and recognition afforded to men. His conviction reinforces our own self-image, empowering us to embrace our potential fully. He reminds us that we are perfectly fine just as we are unique individuals with our own strengths and qualities, worthy of love and respect in all its forms.

# The Jailer

*Every minute in the UK, the police receive a call from the public for assistance to deal with domestic violence. This leads to police receiving an estimated 1,300 calls each day, more than 570,000 each year. (Professor Stanko, E. 'The Day to Count: A Snapshot of the Impact of Domestic Violence in the UK'. Criminal Justice 1:2, 2000.)*

The Jailer employs a range of isolating tactics to exercise control over his partner, making it difficult for her to pursue employment or education. He neglects or entirely fails to care for their children, ignoring basic needs such as putting them to bed, providing adequate supervision, or ensuring they are fed. During this neglect, he may call, creating an added layer of distress as the sounds of crying children serve as a backdrop to his demands. This behaviour closely mirrors traits seen in the archetype of the Badfather.

The Jailer manipulates his partner into believing that she should not leave him alone. He might suggest that they should stay in bed together, leading her to frequently call in sick to work, which ultimately jeopardizes her job stability. He professes a desire to have her home, cloaking his jealousy of her interactions with other men as a form of love. Even in his unemployment, he makes grand claims of financial security, with an implied promise to take care of her.

At times, the Jailer takes his control a step further by showing up at her workplace, often inebriated and confrontational. His behaviour toward her co-workers and supervisors is increasingly hostile; he calls her incessantly, instigates arguments before she leaves for work, and even manipulates time by altering clocks to ensure she is late, a tactic designed to undermine her professionalism. In more brazen acts of sabotage, he might delete important assignments from her computer or create scenarios that force her to stay late or skip work altogether, further entrenching his control.

In a more severe manifestation of control, the Jailer may confine his partner physically to their home. This confinement can be so extreme that some women experience it for years. He may black out windows to obscure the outside world, leaving her unsure of the time of day. At times, he might remove her keys, making it impossible for her to leave without waiting for his return, or he could hide or destroy her clothing and shoes as a further means of restriction. Some women are even kept perpetually pregnant, with unrealistic expectations for household tasks imposed upon them while he retains the car, thus limiting their mobility.

The Jailer keeps a tight grip on his partner's whereabouts and social interactions. He might meticulously monitor car mileage or demand receipts for any travel, regularly calling her to verify her location. In some cases, he installs videophones under the pretext of ensuring her safety, coercing her to prove where she is at all times. He could impose strict time limits on grocery trips or deny her access to medical appointments, either for herself or her children. Additionally, he may place surveillance cameras throughout the house, further surveilling her every move.

In terms of relationships, the Jailer systematically prevents her from maintaining connections with friends and family. When visitors drop by, he might sit inappropriately dressed and engage in crude behaviour, dominating the atmosphere with distractions like loud television or uninvited outbursts. His presence becomes a source of embarrassment, causing her friends to question his well-being or distancing them from future visits. When she prepares to leave, he often criticizes her appearance, employing derogatory language to diminish her self-esteem.

To further establish control, the Jailer will often accompany his partner everywhere, preventing her from having one-on-one interactions with her friends. He masquerades this behaviour as devotion, insisting that it is unsafe for her to venture out alone, reinforcing a narrative that positions him as her protector. In some extreme cases, he may suggest relocating to a more isolated area or even another country in the guise of romantic adventure or in pursuit of career opportunities, thus severing her from her support network.

The underlying beliefs that justify this isolation are troublingly entrenched. The Jailer operates under the misguided conviction that a "real man" must confine his partner to the home, viewing isolation not as a form of abuse but as normal behaviour. He considers women akin to possessions, believing they should be controlled to prevent infidelity. His worldview reduces women's value to that of child bearers, rendering them untrustworthy and incapable of serious work. He might dismiss any income she earns as mere “pin money,” positioning himself as the sole provider, even if he is unemployed and reliant on her earnings.

These distorted beliefs often originate from childhood environments where traditional gender roles were reinforced. Whether through observing women being discouraged from employment or noting the lack of media representation for women's achievements, this mind-set is deeply ingrained and often perpetuated by societal norms. Historically, women faced exclusion from various aspects of public life, including sports and social institutions. Legislation and cultural practices have further marginalized women's roles, historically limiting their freedoms and reinforcing the idea that their primary duty lies within the domestic sphere.

Women internalize these beliefs over time. Initially, they may interpret possessiveness as romantic affection, gradually relinquishing social ties without question. Statements like, "He lets me go out with my friends," highlight a troubling acceptance of his controlling behaviour as a granted privilege, with some women even going so far as to criticize peers who engage in independent social interactions. A sense of autonomy diminishes as they mistakenly believe they need protection, developing a sense of gratitude for being kept at home.

Living under the conditions imposed by a Jailer has profound effects on women's mental and emotional well-being. Denied opportunities to work or study, many face significant financial deprivation and loss of independence, leading to a pervasive sense of entrapment that can diminish their self-worth and overall quality of life. The psychological toll of such isolation manifests in various ways, making it essential to recognize these patterns of control as valid forms of abuse that must be addressed with urgency and compassion.

# The Liberator

The Liberator embodies a welcoming spirit, always eager to embrace our friends and family, making their visits feel special and memorable. Upon their arrival, he attentively ensures that everyone feels at ease, fostering an atmosphere of warmth and inclusion. His support for our social lives is palpable; he actively encourages us to spend quality time with our loved ones and enthusiastically motivates us to enjoy outings, whether it be a casual dinner with friends or a celebratory gathering.

When the occasion calls for us to dress up and head out, he is quick to shower us with compliments, making sure we know just how amazing we look. His reassuring words, coupled with his thoughtful gesture of leaving the lights on as a beacon of warmth, creates a sense of welcome that comforts us as we return home at night.

Beyond his nurturing support for our social engagements, the Liberator also plays a vital role in uplifting our confidence in professional and educational pursuits. He actively encourages us to chase our ambitions, whether that means advancing our careers or furthering our studies. His involvement goes beyond mere encouragement; he engages in hands-on support, taking the initiative to prepare meals, share household responsibilities, and fully participate in childcare.

By fostering our independence, he encourages us to seek out and explore our own interests and hobbies, celebrating our individuality. His unwavering trust in our capabilities shines through in his belief that women deserve the freedom to determine their paths. He has a profound faith in our potential to achieve success based on our own hard work and merits, rather than relying on external validation.

Moreover, he deeply values our financial independence, recognizing and appreciating the meaningful contributions we make to the overall wellbeing and quality of life within our shared home. Through his actions and beliefs, the Liberator stands as a pillar of support, empowering us to dream big and pursue our goals with confidence and determination.

# The Sexual Controller

*One in 20 women in England and Wales has been the victim of rape. Only one in five attacks is reported to the police. 'Current partners' (at the time of the attack) were responsible for 45% of rapes reported to the British Crime Survey. 'Strangers' were only responsible for 8% of rapes. (Amnesty International 2007)*

For many women, the moment they begin to reclaim a sense of self building friendships, entering the workforce, or pursuing education, they find the abuse intensifies. Confidence becomes a threat to control. Survivors have repeatedly described how, at the point where they started to challenge the abusive dynamics, their partners became more sexually violent. It was not about desire; it was about dominance.

It is within this context that the true intentions of the Sexual Controller emerge. Much like invading armies throughout history who raped not from lust but from the urge to humiliate, to degrade, to destroy, the Sexual Controller weaponises sex in the most brutal and systematic of ways. This is not about passion. It is conquest. It is about reducing a person to nothing.

Over the years, these harrowing patterns have been disclosed by thousands of women across the UK to the Freedom Programme. They have come not just from survivors but also from healthcare professionals and, chillingly, from the perpetrators themselves often with unnerving honesty. The tactics shared paint a picture that many women will sadly recognise, and in doing so, may come to understand that what happened to them was abuse, not consent. And that they were never responsible for it.

The Sexual Controller degrades through coercion and force. Survivors have spoken about being made to engage in rape and anal intercourse, or even being coerced into sexual acts with his friends or animals. Practices like 'dogging' have been sensationalised in the media, framed as consensual or even desired by women. But the stories from refuges across the country tell a very different tale, women forced into public sex acts, their humiliation disguised as participation.

The term 'dogging' is said to originate either from the excuse perpetrators give ("I'm walking the dog") or from the deeply misogynistic belief that women are dogs. Others report the use of 'scarfing', where a plastic bag or scarf is used to cut off a woman's oxygen during sex, bringing her to the brink of unconsciousness, all for the perpetrator's gratification. If she dies, he tells police it was a sex game gone wrong.

Devices marketed as sex toys are regularly used for sexual torture. Survivors speak of ball gags, scarf-bound rubber balls that silence them while being used like objects. The silence, the objectification, the lack of consent, this is precisely the dynamic the Sexual Controller craves.

Sex is used to exhaust, demean, and destabilise. He demands it constantly, in every room of the house, at all hours. He interrupts daily life to assert control. He dismisses protests by claiming a strong libido or sex addiction. Even some men who seek help admit this, eventually conceding that their behaviour was never about intimacy, but about control.

Pornography becomes another weapon. Women are forced to watch and replicate violent sex scenes. Some are told to wash with bleach before sex. Many were sexually abused as children and recognise these tactics all too well. Others recount postnatal abuse, with stitches being cut or wounds used for sex, leading to repeated infections.

Infidelity, too, is used strategically. By cheating, the Sexual Controller aims to break the spirit of his partner. It reinforces her supposed worthlessness and keeps her dependent on his emotional crumbs.

Behind these acts are deeply rooted beliefs. Survivors and even perpetrators on the Freedom Programme share that the Sexual Controller believes women exist solely to serve men sexually. Once women age past their mid-twenties, they are seen as disposable. Their worth is reduced to their sexual utility. Companionship, intellect, contribution to society, none of this holds meaning to him.

He believes women are foolish, helpless, incapable of surviving without male authority. To him, men own women. Our bodies are not ours. He believes women are slags, cannon fodder, property. He refers to them as toilets, as receptacles. When asked whether they truly like women, many abusers have paused before admitting: "I thought I did, but now I realise I hate them."

These beliefs have been handed down through centuries and embedded in culture. Ancient Greek philosophy, with Aristotle famously referring to women as "a bag of manure," set the foundation. Figures like Henry VIII reinforced these norms, treating women as property. Cultural messaging, phrases like "conjugal rights" or "lie back and think of England", further eroded women's autonomy.

Religious doctrine often echoes these ideas. Some churches promote the idea that sex is a wife's obligation, regardless of her wishes. Even in modern Britain, clergy have publicly opposed condom use, putting women at risk. Women are taught from pulpits to obey, not to choose.

Art, advertising, and media join in. Paintings show naked women as objects; men are shown powerful, clothed, significant. Adverts use women's bodies to sell spark plugs or beer. Pornography is a daily norm. Music videos glorify male power and surround men with semi-naked, submissive women. Even young girls are sexualised by the fashion industry.

Even within healthcare, women have been degraded. Surgeons have reportedly joked about their genitals while they were unconscious. Some offered to "stitch them up tight" after childbirth to please their husbands.

These messages are absorbed by women, too. We start believing that our value is sexual, that we are only worthy if desired. That we must compete with other women for men's attention. That our only route to success is through sexual attraction.

We stop saying "no" to sex and instead make excuses. We define our worth by who we're with. We equate personal value with the job, status, or wealth of our partner. Some women seek doctors or footballers not because of love but because society tells us our value is measured by the calibre of man we attract.

These beliefs have a cost.

Women subjected to this form of abuse feel owned, dehumanised, and emotionally stripped. They feel their only purpose is sex. They lose confidence, struggle to find work, suffer sexual health consequences, and often experience the same effects as survivors of childhood abuse.

Sex becomes a source of degradation. Women self-harm, develop eating disorders, or turn to addiction. Some are driven to sex work just to feel seen. Others are so devalued they will exchange sex for a drink or a cigarette. The damage is profound. Trust evaporates. Isolation deepens.

And when our genuine love and desire for a partner is weaponised against us, it becomes even more confusing. If the same man who abuses us suddenly offers tenderness, it creates cognitive dissonance. If he tells us we're so attractive that he loses control, it makes us believe we have power. But we don't. Not in those moments. The control is always his.

Society validates his beliefs. Teen girls who are academically gifted may still face bullying until they have a boyfriend. Their status rises with male approval. When sex is demanded, they fear saying no. If they ask for condom use, they are mocked. If they get pregnant, they are shamed. This cycle stops them from pursuing education or building a life on their own terms.

When women are pitted against one another, we enable infidelity. When we believe we aren't attractive enough, we change our bodies, we punish ourselves. We become competitors, not allies.

And at the heart of all this is a lie: that our only worth is sexual. That our no doesn't matter. That we are bodies, not beings.

This is the legacy of the Sexual Controller. But as we will explore next, there is an alternative. A man who values, uplifts, respects, and loves without domination. A man I call The Lover.

# The Lover

*How Does the Lover Behave?*

The Lover is characterized by his ability to express physical affection in a way that is free from the expectation that it must lead to sex. This approach is frequently highlighted by women who participate in the Freedom Programme, who consistently identify this trait as one of the most cherished aspects of the Lover's demeanour. They appreciate not only his affectionate gestures but also his willingness to receive their affection without any implicit demands for a sexual exchange.

Central to the Lover's behaviour is his recognition of women's agency in sexual relationships. He actively encourages them to feel empowered to initiate intimacy and creates an atmosphere where they can do so comfortably. Importantly, should a woman choose to decline an invitation for sex, he respects her decision completely, understanding that "no" is simply a definitive answer that requires no justification or excuses.

When it comes to the act of lovemaking, the Lover brings a profound emotional presence and open communication into the experience. He sees and treats his partner as a whole person, someone with thoughts, feelings, and desires rather than reducing her to a mere object of desire. This thoughtful blending of intimacy, tenderness, and affection fosters a deeper connection that enhances the overall experience for both partners.

Moreover, the Lover believes in the principle of shared decision-making concerning contraception, ensuring that both partners have an equal say in matters that affect their bodies and lives. He is unwaveringly loyal to the relationship, respects personal boundaries, and upholds trust by refraining from sharing intimate experiences with anyone outside that bond.

At the core of the Lover's identity is a strong belief that sex should be a mutual and voluntary act, with both partners fully informed and engaged. He embodies the notion of equal power dynamics within the relationship, understanding the importance of maintaining balance and respect.

The Lover holds steadfast to the truth that women are autonomous individuals who are free, equal, and deserving of independence. His genuine fondness and appreciation for his partner stem from this respect. This deep-rooted admiration motivates him to avoid places, like lap dancing clubs, which may objectify women, showcasing his commitment to standing up against societal pressures and the expectations of other men. He exemplifies the courage to challenge norms when necessary, reinforcing his values and the respect he holds for women in all aspects of life.

# The King of the Castle

*A woman is assaulted on average of 35 times before she seeks help. (Amnesty UK 2006)*

*The King of the Castle and the Use of Male Privilege to Control Women*

The King of the Castle does not enter our lives as a tyrant barking orders from the beginning. Instead, he employs subtle manipulation, gradually turning us into unpaid housekeepers. He initiates this by involving us in individual household tasks until we assume responsibility for all of them.

It might begin with laundry. He arrives with a small bundle of washing, perhaps clothing he left behind. When we suggest he use our machine, he insists he doesn't understand the controls. If we press, he repeatedly calls on us for assistance. Eventually, we may give in, opting to do it ourselves. If we resist, he escalates adding a red sock to whites or washing everything on the hottest cycle, ruining the load. It's a tactic to ensure we surrender the task.

With cleaning, his strategy involves living in squalor, creating a mound of dirty dishes, ashtrays, newspapers. When asked to clean, he might say, "Just relax, I'll do it later," or "Stop nagging." We tire of the constant battle and tidy up ourselves. Early in the relationship, he might plug in the vacuum, missing most of the dirt, failing to empty the bag. He might ineffectively dust or avoid cleaning the toilet. Again, we take over out of frustration.

In the kitchen, he may cook once, burning everything and dirtying every utensil. He leaves the mess for us. The pattern repeats across chores: he performs poorly, we take over. He complains loudly when tasked with anything, claiming, "I've brought the washing in for you," or "I've helped with your housework."

He subtly coerces us into menu planning and grocery shopping by asking what's for breakfast, lunch, dinner. Soon, we answer instinctively. He avoids responsibility by constantly asking, "Where's my shirt?" "Where are my socks?" and expects us to know.

Eventually, he assumes all the entitlements that come with male privilege. He leaves dirty clothes on the floor, demands ironed shirts, and expects meals. He runs his fingers along dusty ledges and orders us to serve him and his friends. Daughters may be ordered to wait on him and his sons. He claims a special chair, expects the remote, and controls the TV. He leaves us with impossible to-do lists.

Financial control is another lever. He may keep all the money, forcing us to ask for everything, even though we don't know his earnings. He may keep "pocket money" and expect us to manage household expenses from what's left. Alternatively, he may use reverse tactics insisting we're too incompetent to manage household duties.

**Beliefs that Justify His Behaviour**

Many perpetrators believe women exist for CFCs: cooking, fucking, and cleaning. They see women as unintelligent, easily manipulated into servitude. He views domestic work as inferior meant for second-class citizens. In his eyes, women are beneath men, thus should serve. Real men, he believes, do not clean; they are served.

To him, only gay men or failures do their own housework. He sees his entitlement as normal, not abusive. Even if unemployed, he considers himself the breadwinner simply because he's a man.

**Origins and Societal Reinforcement of These Beliefs**

These ideas often originate in childhood. He may have watched his father being served by his mother. As a boy, he was likely catered to by his mother and sisters. The media also reinforces these views, showing women as housekeepers in adverts, soap operas, and films. Women's magazines teach us to clean and cook.

Words like "housewife" reinforce these roles. Childhood books like "Janet and John" depicted mothers and daughters doing domestic chores. Even toys enforce these roles, with miniature cleaning sets for girls.

During WWII, women ran the country. We worked, flew planes, built bombs, and earned wages. When men returned, the government dismissed women and used propaganda to convince us that our true destiny was in unpaid domestic work. One propaganda example, the 'Latch Key Kids Study,' claimed delinquency was caused by working mothers.

After experiencing freedom and equality, women were brainwashed into thinking our true purpose was to serve men. We were told we were too stupid for anything else. The 1950s 'Good Wives Guide' illustrates this manipulation perfectly:

- Plan meals the night before to welcome your husband home.
- Rest before he arrives, touch up your makeup, put a ribbon in your hair.
- Make the house clean and peaceful for his arrival.
- Light a fire in cold months, just for him.

- Prepare the children, wash them, dress them, and keep them quiet.
- Be cheerful and silent; let him speak first.
- Never complain if he stays out. His needs are more important.

These instructions remind women to focus all activity on his return, catering solely to his needs, even if he doesn't come home.

**Shared Beliefs and Consequences**

We often believe we are naturally responsible for all domestic tasks. We thank partners for "helping" or refer to chores as "ours" when they are done for the whole household. We may even dismiss this behaviour as non-abusive.

When we internalise these ideas, we struggle to see the abuse. We undervalue ourselves, lack confidence, avoid careers, and settle for menial roles. We let partners control money, defer to men socially and at work, and believe we are second-class.

If the King of the Castle prevents us from doing anything at all, we may become emotionally paralysed. We lose confidence in our abilities entirely. The conditioning is so deep that when he asks, "What's for supper?" we reply automatically. And by then, he has succeeded in taking control of our lives.

# The Partner

*How does the Partner behave?*

The Partner takes an active and equitable role in our shared household responsibilities. He consistently participates in housework, dividing tasks fairly and ensuring that everything is managed smoothly. From vacuuming the floors to ironing our clothes, he approaches each chore with a sense of duty and care, never viewing them as merely her responsibilities.

When it comes to meal preparation, he excels in cooking, crafting delicious dishes that everyone can savour. After dinner, he takes the initiative to wash and clean the dishes, pots, and pans, leaving the kitchen tidy for the next meal. He skilfully operates the washing machine, ensuring that our clothes maintain their colours and fit properly, reflecting his attention to detail. He remembers to empty the vacuum cleaner bag regularly, ensuring our home remains clean and dust-free.

We also engage in meaningful discussions about our meals, where he takes an interest in planning together what we will have for dinner, reflecting his desire to collaborate rather than dictate. He is fully aware of where everything is kept in the house, this familiarity means he never has to ask for directions or assistance, which adds to the flow of our daily routines.

He keeps the remote control on the table after use, promoting a shared space rather than clutter, and is open and transparent about his income, fostering an atmosphere of trust and mutual respect between us.

Importantly, he never frames his contributions in a way that diminishes our partnership; he avoids saying phrases like:

- "I help her with the housework."
- "I have brought the washing in for you."
- "I have washed the dishes for you."
- "I have cleaned your windows for you."
- "I have cooked the dinner for you."

The Partner firmly believes in the principle of equality between women and men, advocating for mutual respect and dignity in our relationship. He understands that we are not here to act as unpaid servants and values the partnership we've built. He represents a modern man who embraces responsibility, confident in his abilities and self-sufficient in daily life. His self-assurance allows him to stand apart from traditional, outdated ideals often propagated by those who subscribe to the notion of being the "King of the Castle," demonstrating that a truly supportive partner nurtures equality and inclusivity in the relationship.

# The Liar

*Most women are killed or injured when leaving the relationship (Lees, S. 'Marital rape and marital murder', In Hanmer, J. et al. Home Truths about Domestic Violence: Feminist Influences on Policy and Practice: A Reader. London: Routledge, 2000.)*

Up until now in this book, we have explored a range of tactics that the Dominator uses to maintain control over us. I've also explained that when the Dominator senses these methods are no longer effective, he will escalate to using violence.

In this chapter, we will examine how an assault unfolds in detail.

On the following page, you will find the **'Rules of the Game'**, which we'll explore next.

RULES OF THE GAME
Women are possessions.
She should obey.

ATTEMPTS TO RE-ESTABLISH THE RULES
Threats, promises.
ABUSIVE BEHAVIOUR
The tactics of the Dominator keep the rules in place.

VIOLENCE
OK because of the excuses.
SHE REFUSES TO COMPLY
Says 'no', leaves.

EXCUSES
She is a slut, a bad mother.
BELIEFS ABOUT WOMEN COME UNDER THREAT
Feelings of panic, powerlessness, outrage.

Throughout this book, we've explored many of the control tactics the Dominator uses. Now, let's examine what happens when he feels those tactics are no longer effective: he resorts to violence.

This chapter walks you through **how an assault unfolds**. On the next page, you'll find a diagram labelled *Rules of the Game*, which outlines the mechanics of an assault. Let's now break down this diagram together.

At the top is the box titled *Rules of the Game*. These represent the Dominator's core beliefs. They reflect how he expects women to behave and what rights he feels entitled to himself. Though he likely holds hundreds of these so-called "rules," we'll focus on eight:

- Men have ownership over women and we must obey them entirely.
- Women must lack self-confidence, never answering back, offering opinions, or making decisions.
- Women should remain at home and not pursue lives of their own.
- Women must believe every excuse he offers to justify his violence.
- Women are solely responsible for childcare, while he claims the role of disciplinarian.
- Women must serve, fulfilling unpaid domestic roles.
- Women must provide sex whenever demanded.
- Women should never be allowed to leave the relationship, no matter how abusive it becomes.

Moving clockwise on the diagram, the next box is *Abusive Behaviour*. Here lie the tactics he employs to enforce each of these rules. These are broken down in order:

- To enforce the idea that men own women, the **Bully** uses shouting, glaring, sulking, and smashing things.
- To crush a woman's confidence, the **Headworker** humiliates her, constantly criticising her intelligence, appearance, and worth.
- To confine women to the home, the **Jailer** isolates them, preventing social contact or education.

- To get women to believe his excuses, the **Liar** minimises and blames others, drugs, alcohol, stress, but never himself.
- To dominate parenting while avoiding responsibility, the **Badfather** manipulates children or threatens to take them away.
- To force women into servitude, the **King of the Castle** treats them like slaves.
- To demand sex, the **Sexual Controller** ignores refusal, using coercion or force.
- To prevent women from leaving, the **Persuader** manipulates with guilt, threats of violence or suicide, and love-bombing.

As we follow the cycle, we come to the next box: *She Refuses to Comply*. This explores what happens when women break these unspoken rules.

But first, it's essential to recognise that most women don't even realise what the rules are. They're constantly changing. One rule might be that we're supposed to *know* the rules without ever being told and to instinctively know when they've changed. It's a no-win situation.

Here are examples of how women "break the rules": we talk back, delay compliance, look directly at him, ignore him, or simply say "no." We start building lives, making friends, working, joining a gym, or studying. We reach out for help seeing a health visitor, staying too long at the supermarket, going to a Freedom Programme session, or attending assertiveness classes.

We might gain or lose weight, and even say we don't care about our weight. We might challenge him refuse medication, call out lies, or insist on boundaries. We may tell him to leave or report him to the police. We could refuse sex or say yes but show no pleasure. We might have affairs, identify as lesbians, or lock the bedroom door.

Each of these "rule-breaking" acts threatens the Dominator's core beliefs about women. This is the next stage: *Beliefs About Women Come Under Threat.*

When this happens, his entire worldview becomes destabilised. He's overwhelmed with panic and a need to regain control if not, he no longer feels like a "real man." That's why many assaults occur when a woman is leaving. She's violated the unspoken rules.

To regain control, he believes violence is necessary. However, even before he hits us, he must convince himself that we deserve it. This internal "wind-up" phase begins. He stops listening or engaging. Women often describe it as if "no one is home." He's having a conversation in his head, justifying the assault with internal excuses.

Let's move to the next box: *Excuses for Violence*.

Many abusive men claim they were drunk or provoked. They might say, "She's asking for it," or blame our appearance, friends, mood, or tone. They may claim we're cheating or "pushing their buttons." Some common justifications include:

- She knows I hate that."
- "She knows I need sex."
- "She's mentally ill."
- "I'm stressed."
- "She made me feel small."
- "She deserves it."
- "I had a terrible childhood."
- "I have PTSD, autism, Tourette's, or ADHD."
- "My team lost."
- "She's a slag."

They dehumanise us, using slurs like "bitch," "whore," or "slag" to justify hitting us. Once he's "wound up," he hits. The assault occurs. This is the box: *Violence Takes Place*.

Afterward, the Dominator needs us to comply again. He switches roles to the **Liar** and minimises or justifies the violence.

He might say, "It was just a slap," "We were play-fighting," or "She's just as bad." He denies wrongdoing or claims he was defending himself. He blames drink, drugs, medical conditions, or us. The real reason? We challenged his power.

He may even say: "She made me do it because she was having an affair" or "I love her too much." He presents himself as the victim, seeking sympathy from courts, police, or services.

How does the Liar affect women? We become confused, trying to rationalise the abuse using his excuses. We blame ourselves, feel depressed, and lose our sense of reality. Some of us start to believe that violence is excusable if justified. We learn to lie to ourselves and others, thinking this is normal. We might even believe the abuse isn't impacting our children when in reality, it does.

We must understand: his anger isn't real, it's constructed. He remains in control throughout. The only way he can truly change is to unlearn these beliefs and reject the *Rules of the Game*.

# The Truth Teller

*How Does the Truth Teller Behave?*

The Truth teller possesses a unique integrity that sets him apart. When he is mistaken or misjudges a situation, he openly acknowledges his errors. Phrases like, "I was in the wrong," or, "That was my fault," are not just words to him; they reflect a deep commitment to personal accountability. He doesn't shy away from admitting his mistakes, thereby setting a standard for humility and openness.

This individual consistently embodies honesty, both in his dealings with others and in his introspection. He does not just tell the truth, he lives it daily, fostering an environment of trust around him. His reliability comes from the fact that he holds himself to the same rigorous standards he expects of others. This forthrightness earns him respect and builds strong, authentic relationships.

As a role model, he stands as a beacon for children and peers alike, demonstrating the importance of integrity in all aspects of life. His actions are guided by principles of honesty and accountability, which he showcases not only in his personal interactions but also in his civic duties. As a responsible citizen, he earns his income through hard work and pays his taxes dutifully.

He believes in the value of contributing to society and does not engage in fraudulent behaviour, such as claiming state benefits unless he is legitimately entitled to them. Furthermore, he does not feign illness to evade responsibility at work, understanding that integrity in his professional life reinforces his moral standing. In essence, the Truth teller exemplifies the qualities of sincerity, accountability, and civic responsibility, teaching others through his actions and lifestyle.

# The Persuader

*There are 275 refuges for women in England.*
*(Women's Aid 2004)*

**How Does the Persuader Use Coercion and Threats to Control Us?**

*The Persuader's Use of Threats*

The Persuader possesses a vast collection of threats, all aimed at coercing us into taking him back, returning to him if we've left, or dropping any legal charges. He might threaten to kill us, our family members, our friends or even our children. The latter is a particularly terrifying threat, given that we watch the news and are painfully aware that abusive men sometimes kill children in retaliation against women who leave them. He might also threaten to abduct the children.

In some cases, he'll threaten to kill himself. He may even attempt suicide or self-harm, sometimes doing so in front of the children. Following this, medical professionals or police officers may contact us, pleading that he needs our support.

Sadly, some Persuaders do go through with suicide, leaving us burdened with long-lasting guilt. Everyone, our children included, may blame us. Unaware that these were strategic manipulations, we may also blame ourselves and carry that guilt for years. These types of abusers can continue to exert control even after death.

He may also threaten to disgrace us. He might say he'll share private photos online, a tactic especially cruel when aimed at women in the public eye. He could plaster those images on public noticeboards near our workplace or local area.

Courts can be weaponised, too. He may threaten to seek full custody of the children or report us to social services. He might say: "If they think I'm violent, they'll take the kids." If he's previously coerced us into sexual acts in front of the children, he may now twist the narrative and claim we instigated it. Since the children can confirm the incident occurred, the truth of who initiated it may become blurred.

The Persuader could also threaten to report us to the Department for Work and Pensions for alleged benefit fraud. He may say he'll take the home from us, render us homeless, or quit his job so he won't have to pay child maintenance. If unemployed, he can also exploit the legal system to pursue us, accessing legal aid while dragging us through court proceedings.

He will threaten to pursue us relentlessly, showing up unannounced or bombarding us with phone calls at all hours. A classic tactic involves turning up drunk in the early hours, kicking down the door or smashing windows, demanding to see "his" children.

*How the Persuader Uses Coercion to Exploit Our Sympathy?*

The Persuader knows how to manipulate our emotions by making us feel pity. He'll appear at our doorstep in tears, wringing his hands, asking: "What will I do without you?" or "Where will I go?" He will say, "I thought you loved me," or guilt-trip us around the holidays: "It's Christmas! I can't do this without you." Sometimes, he'll feign illness, claiming he has cancer.

He'll go to great lengths to demonstrate he's not coping. He might adopt the infamous "Persuader Diet" and rapidly lose weight to prove he's not eating. Men on the Freedom Programme even joke that wearing oversized clothing enhances this effect. He'll skip shaving, look dishevelled, and appear generally unwell.

The Persuader often recruits others to back him up. Our families or mutual friends may come knocking, saying things like: “He’s devastated!” or “He’s never loved anyone like he loves you.” They’ll tell us he’s sorry, that he’s heartbroken, that he’s sleeping on someone’s sofa.

*How He Uses the Children*

He tells the children we’re forcing him to leave and that we want to replace him with a new father. He moves into unsuitable accommodation, a rundown flat, a garden shed, or even his car and then brings the children to see it, presenting himself as the victim. He reminds us, “The children need a father.”

He might tempt the children with exciting trips, but only if we come too. He paints a picture of a perfect family Christmas that will only happen if we agree to reunite.

*The Persuader’s Promises*

He often bases his promises on the very excuses he’s used before. If he blamed insecurity or low self-esteem, he’ll now say he’s getting counselling. If he blamed alcohol, he’ll start attending Alcoholics Anonymous and may suggest we join Al-Anon.

If he cited gambling as a problem, he’ll pledge to go to Gamblers Anonymous. If he previously attributed his behaviour to medication, he’ll now provide new prescriptions to prove he’s getting treatment. He might even show documentation for anxiety, stress, or adverse reactions.

If he claimed psychiatric conditions or “the red mist,” he’ll now promise to seek referrals or join an anger management course. Yet, as noted earlier, this promise is hollow, his problem isn’t anger.

*The Persuader Tries to Spark Jealousy*

If none of his previous strategies work, he'll try to make us jealous. He'll get a job, maybe a better one. He'll move into a nicer place, buy a new car and begin dating someone new. This tactic can be more effective than any other.

*He Suggests That We Help Him Change*

If we've begun to waver or already taken him back, he'll now offer suggestions for improving the relationship, by changing ourselves. If he blamed his insecurity, he may request that we avoid arguing or disagreeing. If we're unmarried, he might say marriage will fix things, only to later claim he's still insecure and suggest having a baby.

He may say our job makes him jealous, and urge us to quit. If diagnosed with "morbid jealousy syndrome," this manipulation becomes even more intense.

He could claim our job damages his self-worth and that our success emasculates him. He'll tell us we should leave our job to protect his fragile self-esteem. If he's blamed physical or mental health conditions, he'll claim he needs our help recovering and insist we avoid saying or doing anything that could "set him off."

He might even claim we made him hit us and insist that everything would be fine if we just showed him more love or complied more often. He'll suggest we cut ties with our "toxic" friends or family. If we have a child from a previous relationship, he may suggest they go live with their father. He might even want us to relocate, perhaps somewhere remote.

*The Persuader's Beliefs*

He believes women have no right to challenge violence and that, once in a relationship, a woman becomes his property. He thinks a "real man" doesn't let a woman leave and certainly doesn't allow her to move on. He believes men should be nurtured like children and that women are responsible for male behaviour. He sees no fault in himself and assumes women are gullible enough to believe anything he says.

*How Society Reinforces These Beliefs*

Society echoes his beliefs every time a man is given a lenient sentence after killing a woman who left him. In his peer groups, men affirm that a "real man" wouldn't tolerate betrayal. Jokes like, "Did she burn the dinner again, mate?" and systemic leniency by police and courts embolden him. Professionals, including social workers, doctors, and counsellors, may reinforce his narrative by questioning the woman's choices or suggesting she provoked the abuse.

Even pop culture, like the song "Stand by Your Man," perpetuates the message that women should tolerate anything.

*Beliefs Shared by Women*

Many women internalise these beliefs, feeling responsible for their partner's wellbeing. We feel guilty for ending things and may even blame ourselves for the abuse. We are conditioned to believe that we're supposed to take care of men, and that somehow we "caused" the violence.

# The Negotiator

*How does the negotiator behave?*

The Negotiator is proactive in taking responsibility for his own well-being, recognizing that personal health and mental clarity are essential for effective communication and negotiation. He understands that self-awareness and emotional intelligence play critical roles in navigating interpersonal dynamics.

Additionally, he acknowledges his own behaviours and their impact on others, fostering a sense of accountability. This self-reflection allows him to engage in discussions with an open mind and heart, ready to accept constructive feedback.

Importantly, the Negotiator respects the autonomy of others, recognizing that each individual has the inherent right to end a relationship if they choose to do so. By adopting this mind-set, he positions himself to facilitate conversations about relationship dissolution in a way that minimizes emotional distress and damage for all parties involved.

He is particularly mindful of the children affected by such separations, prioritizing their well-being and striving to negotiate a separation process that safeguards their emotional and psychological health. This approach helps to create a more stable environment for them during what can be a tumultuous time.

The Negotiator views women as free, independent individuals who are equal in all respects. He firmly believes that no one can truly own another person; rather, he champions the idea that every individual has the right to make choices about their own lives, including the decision to leave a relationship if they find it necessary.

Moreover, he demonstrates a genuine interest in the well-being of others, which is reflected in his willingness to admit when he is wrong. This humility fosters trust and encourages open dialogue, setting a collaborative tone for negotiations that allows both sides to feel heard, respected, and valued.

# Resources

*In the UK, a woman is assaulted in her home every six seconds. (Professor Stanko, E. 'The Day to Count: A Snapshot of the Impact of Domestic Violence in the UK'. Criminal Justice 1:2, 2000.*

**What Support Exists for Women Experiencing Abuse?**

*Specialist Domestic Violence Police*

Across Britain, dedicated domestic violence police units are now widely established. Generally, when a 999 emergency call is made, uniformed officers are the first to attend the scene. Regardless of whether the perpetrator is arrested or charged, details of the incident are forwarded to these specialist teams. Officers within these units typically follow up with the woman involved to provide support.

Although some participants in the programme have reported negative encounters with police in the past, many agree that things have significantly improved in recent years, largely due to the introduction of these specialist domestic violence units. Still, as with any large-scale service, there remain certain regions or departments where further progress is needed.

*Women's Aid Services*

Women's Aid offers refuge accommodation, which can be a crucial lifeline for women and their children fleeing abuse. While some women express concerns about the stigma attached to seeking refuge, many others in the group have spoken highly of the experience. Numerous women credit the refuge with saving their lives.

Beyond shelter, many Women's Aid refuges provide outreach programmes for women who choose to remain in their own homes. Across the UK, many Women's Aid branches also deliver the Freedom Programme as part of their support services. Contact details for these services can be found in the Freedom Programme directory available on my website: www.freedomprogramme.co.uk.

Information about where to get support is now commonly available in public spaces such as libraries, GP clinics, and hospitals. Domestic abuse helpline numbers are often advertised on public transport, including on bus panels. National domestic violence helplines are operational across England and Wales. Additionally, online search engines make it easier than ever to locate local and national support resources.

# Warning Signs

**How to Recognise Early Signs of a Dominator**

This chapter draws upon earlier work with male perpetrators during the original probation programme in 1996. In one session, I asked them to compose letters to a real or imagined daughter, warning her of behaviours to watch out for in a potential boyfriend.

Later, during Freedom Programme sessions, the women began sharing their experiences. Many had left abusive partners only to find themselves with another one. Because the new partner behaved differently from the last, they assumed he wasn't abusive. They were wrong. He was just as harmful, only in a different way.

So in our sessions, we examine how a Dominator might reveal himself in the first two weeks of a relationship. The following insights come from hundreds of Freedom Programme participants over the past nine years.

**Early Signs of the Bully**

In the early days, the Bully may suddenly withdraw into silence, what we might call a "mini sulk", offering no explanation. He may stare intensely or smile with his mouth while glaring with his eyes. His aggression might surface with others, perhaps berating bar staff or waiters. His body language gives him away: tapping fingers, crossed arms, or swinging feet.

If we express a differing opinion, he won't drop it. He'll persist until we concede. He may adopt a dominant stance, like thrusting his crotch forward. He may also go out of his way to say he would never hit a woman, raising the question of why he feels the need to declare this at all.

**Early Signs of the Jailer**

These tactics can be difficult to spot unless one has participated in the programme or read this book. We may mistake them for signs of devotion or romance, just as many films and fairy tales suggest.

If we want to visit a friend, he insists on taking and picking us up claiming it's for our safety, but possibly to monitor our whereabouts. He pushes for daily contact, buys us a phone "for our safety," and constantly calls or texts to ask where we are and who we're with.

He drops by uninvited late at night and avoids spending time with our friends. He may subtly sow doubt, asking things like, "How well do you really know Sharon?" followed by vague replies, leaving us unsettled.

He says we don't need to work and encourages us to take time off to be with him. He uses phrases like "forever" or "soulmate," making big plans that centre around him. If we tell him we usually meet friends on Thursdays, he might "forget" and surprise us with tickets to a show, so we cancel our plans to avoid letting him down.

**Early Signs of the Headworker**

He might start by making inappropriate jokes, racist, sexist, or homophobic. Instead of using our name, he'll use terms like "babe," "princess," or "my bird." In front of others, he'll mock or belittle us, disguising the insult with humour. He'll generalise about women, criticise them, or compliment their bodies to us in comparison.

He may stand us up or show up late, acting patronising. Mind games may begin early on, leaving us feeling unsettled, though we brush it off.

His backhanded compliments are especially telling. He might say, “You’d be really attractive if you lost a bit of weight,” masking criticism as praise.

**Early Signs of the Persuader**

He’ll try to make us feel sorry for him, sometimes mixing this with the Jailer’s controlling gestures, like surprise tickets to an event. He may push us to do things we’re uncomfortable with, such as eating or drinking something we don’t want.

**Early Signs of the Liar**

He may begin with a sob story about a past partner who mistreated him, took his money, and now denies him access to his children. He won’t refer to her by name only “the ex.” He takes no responsibility and blames her entirely.

He might say he’s insecure, has low self-esteem, or was a victim of domestic abuse himself.

**Early Signs of the Badfather**

As noted previously, the Badfather might not be involved with his own children, but he’ll begin to manipulate ours. He may quickly make himself indispensable, offering financial support or treats for the kids.

If we’ve been juggling things alone, this may feel like a welcome relief. Over time, he may start disciplining them subtly: "Do they always stay up this late?" or "You shouldn't let them talk to you like that."

### Early Signs of the King of the Castle

He may influence our clothing choices, casually suggesting: "You look lovely in that dress, but blue would suit you better." He moves in prematurely, often by leaving personal belongings at our place.

Eventually, he takes over all household tasks. While initially helpful, he begins to dominate. If we clean or shop, he'll redo it, saying we didn't do it right.

The DIY enthusiast also shows up early. He turns up with tools saying, "I'll fix those shelves tomorrow," and before long, the house is filled with dado rails, rails he might remove if we try to break up.

### Early Signs of the Sexual Controller

He may rush intimacy or pressure us into things that feel wrong. During sex, there is no real communication, just acts done *to* us, not *with* us.

He avoids using contraception, may be married or in another relationship, and behaves inappropriately in public groping us without consent.

These warning signs usually come in clusters, not in isolation. We often notice more than we think but may ignore the discomfort. Women who've studied these patterns in the Freedom Programme say they now take those gut feelings seriously.

So if our new partner starts exhibiting a cluster of these behaviours, it may be time to trust our instincts and, in no uncertain terms, think: “Absolutely not.”

# Creating a Safety Plan: Preparing for Potential Danger

For survivors of domestic abuse, leaving an abusive relationship represents a moment fraught with peril. Abusers often escalate their violence when they sense they are losing control, increasing the risk of severe harm or homicide during and after separation. Thus, safety planning serves as an essential, life-preserving strategy.

A safety plan is a structured, proactive guide meant to help individuals navigate perilous situations. It encompasses various strategies, physical, digital, emotional, and legal, designed to minimize risk and improve responses when violence escalates. It is vital to engage in safety planning whether one is still living with the abuser, preparing to leave, or has already left the relationship.

*Key Components of a Safety Plan*

1. Identifying Safe Spaces: Determine areas within your home that are free of weapons and allow for easier escape. It's advisable to avoid kitchens and bathrooms during confrontations. Identify trustworthy friends, family members, or neighbours who can assist you, and establish a pre-arranged signal for emergency situations.

2. Emergency Escape Plan: Develop a quick exit strategy. Prepare a bag with crucial items: copies of important documents (IDs, birth certificates, bank cards), spare keys, vital medications, clothing, emergency contacts, and some cash. Keep this bag in a secure yet accessible location or with a trusted individual.

3. Communication and Tech Safety: Exercise caution with communication devices. Consider using secure phones or regularly clearing call and browsing histories. Change passwords frequently and disable GPS and location-sharing features. Be particularly mindful of shared devices, including smart home systems.

4. Children and Pets: Involve children in age-appropriate discussions about safety planning. Teach them how to contact emergency services and where to seek refuge during a crisis. If pets are part of your family, ensure that they have a safety plan as well; many shelters can accommodate pets or work with fostering services.

5. Legal Protection: Familiarize yourself with your legal rights. Protective measures such as non-molestation orders, occupation orders, and prohibited steps orders can create legal barriers between you and your abuser. Consult a solicitor or support worker to understand your options.

6. Financial Safety: Open a new bank account in your name to help you save independently. Gather information about joint debts and shared financial obligations, and if possible, collect proof of income and any incidents of financial abuse to support legal claims.

7. Support Networks: Identify your support system, people such as friends, family, IDVAs, therapists, and support groups. Memorize important contact numbers in case you lose access to your phone, and share your plan with someone you trust, if it is safe to do.

8. After Leaving: Once you have left, consider changing locks, installing security systems, and informing your workplace, your children's school, and local law enforcement about your situation. Be ready to change routines and update your address to a PO Box if necessary. Seeking counselling can promote recovery and emotional safety.

*Emotional Safety Planning*

Safety planning also encompasses emotional well-being. Consider strategies that help you manage trauma, cope with triggers, and preserve self-worth, which may include:

- Daily affirmations and grounding techniques
- Emergency support contacts (hotlines, therapists)
- Reminders of your reasons for leaving (like journal entries or letters to yourself)
- Safe spaces where you feel calm and in control

*Customizing the Plan*

Every safety plan should be personalized to reflect individual risks, resources, and needs. Whether you are still in the relationship, have left, or are dealing with post-separation abuse, a well-crafted plan is an assertion of resilience.

*Conclusion*

Breaking free from an abusive relationship is both complex and courageous. A comprehensive safety plan can be crucial in ensuring personal safety. Remember, you deserve to feel secure, receive support, and know that you are not alone in this journey.

For assistance in developing a personalized safety plan, consider reaching out to domestic violence support services.

**24/7 Resources**

- National Domestic Abuse Helpline (UK): 0808 2000 247
- Refuge: www.refuge.org.uk
- Women's Aid: www.womensaid.org.uk
- Men's Advice Line: 0808 801 0327
- Galop (LGBTQ+ support): 0800 999 5428

- The Mix (Under 25s): 0808 808 4994
- Respect Phoneline (For those concerned about their own behaviour): 0808 802 4040

Dear Reader,

If you're holding this book in your hands, then something within these pages called to you and I want to honour that.

Whether you are a survivor, someone still trying to find the words for what happened, or someone supporting a loved one through their darkest hours, please know this: you are not alone. You are not invisible. And you are not to blame.

This book was written to give voice to what too often goes unspoken. Domestic violence isn't just bruises or broken bones, it's the silence after a cruel word, the hypervigilance you live in, the confusion when love and fear exist in the same room. It's being controlled, gaslit, isolated, and then doubting yourself for even noticing.

Maybe you've been told to "just leave." Maybe you've been made to feel weak for staying. Maybe you've survived, but the aftermath still echoes in your nervous system. Here, we won't shame you. We'll sit beside you.

You'll find truth here, raw, sometimes uncomfortable, but always compassionate. You'll find clinical insight, but also deep humanity. You'll read stories of systems that failed, but also of women who rose. Of men who broke cycles. Of children who grew into safety. Of the strength it takes not just to survive, but to *live* again.

Healing isn't a straight line. Some days you'll feel like you've conquered the world. Other days, a single sound will take you back. Both are valid. This book will walk with you through both.

You are not your trauma.
You are not too much.
You are not too late.

I wrote this for the version of you that still wonders, *"Was it really that bad?"*
Yes. It was.
And you deserve to heal.

With all my heart,
Josiah Cornell
Author of *What Is Domestic Violence?*

# What to Do Next – From Surviving to Thriving

Leaving an abusive relationship or even recognizing that you're in one is an incredibly complex journey. It is a moment filled with emotions such as grief, clarity, doubt, and the first sparks of hope. For many, the end of the abusive circumstances does not automatically mean the end of pain or struggle; however, it can signify the start of a transformative healing process.

This chapter serves as a comprehensive guide tailored for survivors, their friends and family, as well as professionals in various fields. It strives to provide practical next steps, emotional reassurance, and a renewed sense of purpose. Remember, abuse thrives in silence and shame, whereas healing flourishes in connection, courage, and the support of others.

**For Survivors: You Did Not Deserve This**

If you find yourself reading this as a survivor of domestic abuse, it is vital to internalize one fundamental truth: what you experienced is not your fault. You are not weak, nor are you to blame for the abuse. The essence of abuse lies in control, not love and it can affect individuals from all walks of life, regardless of gender, age, or background.

Now is the time for you to reclaim your life. This could mean taking various steps based on your unique situation. Some may seek legal protection through mechanisms such as non-molestation orders, while others might engage in safety planning alongside a domestic violence advocate. For some, the path to healing might begin through therapy, whether that means initiating individual sessions, joining a support group, or exploring various therapeutic modalities.

Evidence-based interventions like trauma-focused Cognitive Behavioural Therapy (CBT), Eye Movement Desensitization and Reprocessing (EMDR), or group therapy sessions have proven effective in assisting survivors to rewire trauma responses, process complex grief, and rebuild their self-esteem. Beyond traditional therapy, many find solace and healing in creative forms of expression such as art, journaling, physical movement, or spiritual practices. Remember, there is no universal "right" way to heal what matters most is finding your own path.

As you navigate this journey, be sure to practice self-compassion. Whether you left the abusive situation years ago or are just beginning to acknowledge the patterns of abuse, every small step you take forward represents an act of both resistance and resilience.

**For Friends and Family: Support Without Pressure**

If you are seeking to support a loved one in an abusive relationship, it can be a profoundly challenging and heart-breaking experience. You may feel a sense of helplessness or the instinct to intervene directly, but the most powerful and constructive approach involves creating a safe, non-judgmental space where your loved one feels believed, valued, and not alone.

Avoid issuing ultimatums; instead, gently offer resources or assistance. Phrases like, "I'm here whenever you're ready to talk," or "You don't have to go through this alone," can convey your support without imposing pressure. It's essential to recognize that many survivors may return to their abuser multiple times before making a permanent decision to leave; what they need most during these times is consistent, patient love and understanding, not blame or judgment.

Educate yourself on the intricacies of trauma and learn to recognize the signs of coercive control. Be aware of the emotional and psychological labyrinth that survivors navigate. Equally important is to ensure you are caring for your own mental health as you provide support to others.

**For Professionals: The System Must Evolve**

Professionals across various fields, whether healthcare providers, educators, law enforcement officers, housing advocates, or social service workers, play a pivotal role in either empowering survivors or unintentionally re-traumatizing them.

Utilizing trauma-informed approaches is crucial. This means acknowledging that behaviours such as delayed disclosures, dissociation, avoidance, or what may appear as "non-compliance" should not be misinterpreted as resistance; rather, they are often survival strategies. Encourage survivors to share their stories by asking open-ended questions, demonstrating genuine belief in their disclosures, and providing consistent support. It's also essential to recognize the layered challenges faced by diverse groups including LGBTQ+ individuals, disabled survivors, migrants, and those from marginalized communities.

Stay informed about relevant legal frameworks, safeguarding policies, and the latest research surrounding trauma. Actively participate in training sessions to enhance your understanding. Advocate for systemic changes within your institution to better serve survivors. It is essential to remember that the way a system responds to allegations of abuse can either empower survivors or contribute to their silence and suffering.

Safeguarding is not merely a professional obligation; it is a societal responsibility. The concept that "safeguarding is everyone's responsibility" has been emphasized in guidelines such as the UK government's *Working Together to Safeguard

Children* and is widely adopted across various public and voluntary sectors. Abuse can occur not just behind closed doors, but in plain sight, highlighting the need for communities to be vigilant and proactive in addressing this issue. Whether you are a neighbour, teacher, colleague, or friend, you are part of a broader safeguarding network capable of preventing harm.

**A Note of Inclusion**

While the majority of domestic violence victims are women, this message extends to all survivors. Abuse impacts men, non-binary individuals, trans people, and LGBTQ+ couples as well; it transcends boundaries of gender, class, sexuality, and culture.

If you don't see your experiences reflected in the media or available support services, it does not diminish the validity of your story. Your experiences matter. You deserve a voice, and your journey toward safety, justice, and healing is equally important.

**You're Not Alone**

This text has aimed to unravel the patterns of abuse, examine its psychological impacts, highlight systemic obstacles, and illuminate the paths to recovery. But perhaps the most vital takeaway is this:

You are not alone.

Support is available. Hope exists. And there is a life waiting for you beyond mere survival, one filled with agency, joy, and a renewed sense of freedom.

*You have already endured more than many could comprehend.*
*Now is the time for you to thrive.*

# Supporting Survivors: A Guide for Professionals

Domestic violence is a significant public health crisis and a pressing social issue that extends into professional duty. Professionals across various fields, such as education, law enforcement, healthcare, housing, social work, therapy, and crisis hotline services often find themselves as the first, or even the only, source of support for survivors. The way you respond in these pivotal moments can profoundly impact a survivor's journey toward safety and healing.

*Understanding the Dynamics of Abuse*

Abuse often remains hidden in everyday life, masked by appearances of normalcy and stability. Survivors might present with vague physical symptoms, mental health struggles, frequent injuries with ambiguous explanations, or children displaying emotional and behavioural difficulties. Many survivors may hesitate to disclose abuse unless they feel fully safe and understood.

The complexities of coercive control lead survivors to:

- Minimize or normalize their plight
- Fear repercussions for speaking out
- Worry about being judged or not believed
- Experience feelings of shame, confusion, or self-blame

In contrast, abusers frequently come across as charismatic, poised, and credible often holding positions of authority or respect. Therefore, it is essential for professionals to be able to discern underlying issues and maintain awareness of personal biases.

*Trauma-Informed Communication: Best Practices*

The way you communicate with survivors is crucial. When a person takes the courageous step of disclosing abuse, consider saying:

- "You don't deserve this."
- "I believe you."
- "You are not alone; there is support available."
- "This is not your fault."

Conversely, avoid statements such as:

- "Why didn't you leave sooner?"
- "Are you sure it's that serious?"
- "He/She seemed so nice."
- "You must stay strong for your children."

These comments, while often well-intentioned, can intensify feelings of shame and further traumatize the survivor. A trauma-informed approach emphasizes validation, avoids assumptions, and empowers the survivor.

*Safeguarding: A Collective Responsibility*

Safeguarding is not solely the duty of designated professionals; it is a collective responsibility. Whether you are a receptionist noticing signs of injury or a teacher receiving troubling disclosures from students, your actions could be crucial in preventing additional harm.

Be familiar with your organization's safeguarding protocols and understand when to escalate concerns. Listening attentively and knowing when to act are essential, particularly when children are involved, as these situations are never simply private matters.

While confidentiality is critical, it is not absolute. Always clarify the limits of confidentiality at the outset of any disclosure and, whenever possible, involve the survivor in safeguarding decisions.

*Actions Professionals Can Take*

1. Create visible, safe environments: Display posters, helpline information, and domestic abuse resources prominently in communal areas.

2. Build trust through consistency: Small gestures of empathy can establish trust over time; consistency in interactions is crucial, even if perfection is not required.

3. Ask the right questions: Open-ended, private, and non-judgmental questions, such as "Are you safe at home?" can be very impactful.

4. Document thoroughly: Record disclosures exactly as stated, including dates and observations, while refraining from adding personal opinions.

5. Know local resources: Familiarize yourself with available local services including Multi-Agency Risk Assessment Conferences (MARACs), Independent Domestic Violence Advisors (IDVAs), refuges, and counselling options to effectively guide survivors.

6. Assess risk: Utilize validated risk assessment tools (e.g., DASH) to evaluate immediate threats or patterns of escalation.

*Responding Without Re-traumatizing*

Professionals may be unprepared for the emotional weight of disclosures. When survivors share deeply personal and traumatic experiences, a trauma-informed approach involves:

- Maintaining calmness and composure, even amid distressing disclosures.
- Being aware of body language, triggers, and emotional responses.
- Understanding how trauma can affect memory, behaviour, and trust.
- Avoiding actions that could lead to re-traumatization, including disbelief, judgment, or invasive questions.

*Collaborating Across Sectors*

Inter-agency cooperation is vital, as no professional operates in isolation. Collaborative efforts among schools, healthcare providers, law enforcement, and social services enhance the protection of survivors. Working together effectively through multi-agency support frameworks is essential for safeguarding.

*Professional Self-Care and Reflection*

Dealing with cases of domestic abuse can be emotionally taxing. Professionals may experience secondary traumatic stress, burnout, or compassion fatigue. It is vital to:

- Seek clinical or peer supervision regularly.
- Debrief after challenging or emotionally intense situations.
- Prioritize self-care and emotional regulation.
- Advocate for workplace policies that are trauma-informed.

Empathy and resilience can coexist, but support for professionals is key.

*Conclusion for Professionals*

While you may not be able to alter someone's past, your actions can significantly influence their future. By being a safe person, asking thoughtful questions, and providing a non-judgmental space, you may be a pivotal factor in a survivor's healing journey. Remember, you don't need all the answers or a complete solution; your presence and support can make a meaningful difference.

# About the Author

Josiah Cornell is a trauma-informed writer, mental health advocate, and survivor dedicated to illuminating the intricate web of human experience through his compelling storytelling. His work seamlessly intertwines raw honesty, clinical insight, and a deep compassion for those grappling with life's challenges. With a career spanning over a decade in justice services, including prisons, probation, and frontline domestic violence support. Josiah has consistently engaged with some of society's most vulnerable and often misunderstood individuals.

His academic journey in psychology and counselling began at South Essex College, where he laid the foundational knowledge essential for understanding mental health. This foundation was further expanded at East London University, where he delved deeper into psychological theories and therapeutic practices. However, it is the rich tapestry of real-life experiences, sitting with survivors, listening to their unheard stories, and navigating the complexities of mental health battles, both personally and professionally that has truly shaped his perspective. His writing does not shy away from confronting the darkness; rather, it walks alongside the reader through it, offering both solace and understanding.

Josiah's bestselling healing guide, Who Am I Without the Trauma? and his empowering exposé, What Is Domestic Violence? have emerged as vital resources for those grappling with complex trauma, emotional burnout, and profound identity loss. These books transcend mere informational guides; they serve as conversations, companions, and lifelines that resonate deeply with readers seeking to navigate their own struggles.

In addition to his non-fiction work, Josiah is the author of The Emerald Guardians, a fantasy novel crafted as a heartfelt tribute to his partner. In this imaginative narrative, he intricately weaves together elements of magic and meaning, leading readers on a gripping journey that mirrors the emotional resonance of healing. Through this work, Josiah underscores the idea that even in the wildest of worlds, healing can be pursued and found.

At the core of all of Josiah's work lies a powerful mission: to help individuals feel seen, validated, and empowered to reclaim their narratives, whether through factual exploration, imaginative fiction, or the delicate spaces in between. Through his advocacy and writing, he aspires to foster a sense of belonging and understanding for those traveling their own paths of recovery.

# Bibliography / References


- Briere, J., & Scott, C. (2014). *Principles of Trauma Therapy: A Guide to Symptoms, Evaluation, and Treatment* (2nd ed.). SAGE Publications.
- Domestic Abuse Act 2021. UK Government. Retrieved from: https://www.legislation.gov.uk
- Women's Aid (UK). (2023). *Survivors' Handbook: Practical support and information for women experiencing domestic abuse*. Retrieved from: https://www.womensaid.org.uk
- NSPCC (2023). *Child abuse and neglect: Domestic abuse*. Retrieved from: https://www.nspcc.org.uk
- SafeLives. (2023). *Insights national dataset: Understanding domestic abuse*. Retrieved from: https://safelives.org.uk
- Refuge UK. (2022). *Supporting survivors of tech abuse*. Retrieved from: https://www.refuge.org.uk
- Coercive Control: Research Overview (Evan Stark, 2007). *Coercive Control: How Men Entrap Women in Personal Life*. Oxford University Press.
- Kelly, L. (1999). *Violence Against Women: A European Perspective*. Council of Europe.
- TEDI BEAR Children's Advocacy Center. (2023). *Child development and trauma resources*. Retrieved from: https://www.ecu.edu/cs-dhs/tedibear
- VeryWell Mind. (2022). *The psychological effects of domestic abuse on children*. Retrieved from: https://www.verywellmind.com
- Centers for Disease Control and Prevention (CDC). (2022). *Preventing Intimate Partner Violence*. Retrieved from: https://www.cdc.gov
- Freedom Programme. (2023). *Understanding the beliefs of abusers*. Retrieved from: https://www.freedomprogramme.co.uk

- Healthline. (2023). *Post-separation abuse and what to watch for*. Retrieved from: https://www.healthline.com
- Get Court Ready. (2023). *Legal guidance for survivors*. Retrieved from: https://www.getcourtready.co.uk
- CAFCASS. (2023). *Children and Family Court Advisory and Support Service*. Retrieved from: https://www.cafcass.gov.uk
- Femicide Census. (2022). *Deaths of women killed by men*. Retrieved from: https://www.femicidecensus.org
- Frontiers in Psychology. (2023). *Neurological impact of trauma in children*. Retrieved from: https://www.frontiersin.org
- ScienceDirect. (2023). *Trauma-Focused CBT research and application*. Retrieved from: https://www.sciencedirect.com
- EMDR International Association. (2023). *Eye Movement Desensitization and Reprocessing Therapy*. Retrieved from: https://www.emdria.org
- World Health Organization (WHO). (2022). *Violence Against Women: Prevalence and Health Impact*. Retrieved from: https://www.who.int
- Amnesty International. (2023). *Women's Rights Around the World*. Retrieved from: https://www.amnesty.org
- UN Women. (2023). *Global data on gender-based violence*. Retrieved from: https://www.unwomen.org
- United Nations (2021). *Declaration on the Elimination of Violence Against Women*.

www.ingramcontent.com/pod-product-compliance
Lightning Source LLC
Chambersburg PA
CBHW060124130626
46556CB00006B/2228

*9798899659874*